D1461906

Fisher: The Admiral Who Reinvented the Royal Navy

Fisher: The Admiral Who Reinvented the Royal Navy

David Wragg

The History Press

First published 2009

The History Press
The Mill, Brimscombe Port
Stroud, Gloucestershire, GL5 2QG
www.thehistorypress.co.uk

British Library Cataloguing in Publication Data.
A catalogue record for this book is available from the British Library.

ISBN 978 0 7524 4847 3

Typesetting and origination by The History Press
Printed in Great Britain

Contents

Acknowledgements

One problem with writing the biography of a person long dead is that not only can one not interview one's subject, one cannot even interview anyone who knew him, at least as an adult, still less anybody who knew him at the height of his powers. Inevitably, I am grateful for those who did and for their published works, for the newspaper coverage his life engendered, for his own *Memoirs* and *Records*, and for the existence in archives, such as that at the Admiralty, of documents relating to or signed by the great man. An invaluable help is *Fear God and Dread Nought: The Correspondence of Admiral of the Fleet Lord Fisher of Kilverstone*, edited by the American historian Arthur J. Marder, and so too are *The Papers of Admiral Fisher*, edited by Lieutenant-Commander P.K. Kemp.

Introduction

This is the biography of a great man who did his best to ensure that his country was ready for war. From 1899 onwards, he became increasingly convinced that that war would be with Germany, and that the big threat to the freedom of the British people and the freedom of the seas would be German maritime power. More extraordinary than that, he accurately forecast when war was likely to break out, and even his first estimate, later amended, was only a couple of months astray. He was a martinet, ruthless in his quest for efficiency and discipline. He placed fighting ability above all other matters in a service that had not fought a major naval battle since the early nineteenth century, yet had seen technological change dramatically transform both the ships and their armament, and introduce new factors into the balance of power such as the threat from under the water, by mines and torpedoes, and from the submarine, the torpedo boat and the minelayer, as well as the threat from the air.

Yet, there were those who resented change. Those who hated the end of sail, or who thought that submarines were 'ungentlemanly', or felt that the airship and the aeroplane were irrelevant. Indeed, some years after his death, one warship commanding officer could only conceive of the aeroplane being useful for travel to and from the shore if the ship was anchored some distance off a port. Another commander had envisaged, had war broken out between Russia and Great Britain in late 1904, simply sending four of his battleships to attack the Russians, sending the rest only if they encountered difficulty.

Many enjoyed the spit and polish above all, so much so that on some ships the watertight doors had been polished so thin that they were useless, and gunnery practice was discouraged because it blackened the paintwork and the holystoned decks. It was not these people alone who held the service back, for many colonial governors and consuls felt that their status was enhanced by the presence of warships, overlooking the fact that many of these ships were old and, in Fisher's words 'unable to fight or run away'.

Always a controversial figure, while Fisher liked to think of himself as another Nelson, this was something he was not. He lacked the mild manners of his hero, who described his captains as 'a band of brothers', while Fisher was invective personified. He reduced the normal courtesies between a flag officer or commander-in-chief and his commanding officers to extreme brevity, and took pride in doing so. Nelson had three famous victories, at the Nile (or Aboukir Bay), at Copenhagen and at Trafalgar. Fisher had no major battle at sea and his two pieces of genuine action were along the coasts and estuaries of China and then later in shelling forts in Egypt, followed by his leading a shore party. This may be one reason why his plans for operations once war came were somewhat extreme, and when they involved the Army, as they so often did, overlooked many of the realities of land warfare. Indeed, he was violently opposed to sending large numbers of troops into a European land war, and that included the dispatch of the British Expeditionary Force to France in August 1914. It would have been difficult to see what else could have been done. True, the Germans dreaded an attack through the Baltic at the start of hostilities, and no doubt at the time such an attack, or landings in Schleswig-Holstein, would have changed the war completely, but in 1914 the Royal Navy did not have the means of making an opposed landing on an enemy shore. Even in 1940 and 1941, in Norway and at Crete, the Germans themselves lacked this in sufficient measure.

It is also fair to remind ourselves that Fisher lived through a period during the late nineteenth and early twentieth centuries when there were three great 'naval scares', each prompted by concerns over the standards and standing of the Royal Navy. It was British government policy that the fleet should be equal to the fleets of any two nations with which the country was likely to go to war. This was the famous 'Two Power Standard'. It might seem overblown in the straitened circumstances of our armed forces today, when membership of the North Atlantic Treaty Organisation and the collapse of the Soviet Bloc have combined to bring about a less than robust defence posture. This followed the post-First World War Washington Naval Treaty that committed the Royal Navy to being no more than the size of the United States Navy, and then the post-Second World War withdrawal from east of Suez.

Even in the Victorian and Edwardian periods, however, the 'Two Power Standard' was less imposing than it sounds; the Royal Navy was widely scattered around the world, and in many places it maintained a thin presence. One piece of outstanding foresight on Fisher's part was to create a strong fleet in home waters against the emerging threat of Germany. In fact, the target became 'two power plus ten per cent'.

Where Fisher was strongest was in the technological aspects of maritime warfare. Nelson had lived in an age where the pace of technological change was much slower, but in Fisher's lifetime warships changed completely; steam took over from sail, iron from wood, and then the turbine from the reciprocating steam engine, oil from coal, and steel from iron. Breech-loading guns, torpedoes and mines became the weapons of choice, and increasingly the main armament was ranged on the centre line, with 'super-firing', that is the raising of 'B' turret to be able to fire ahead over 'A' turret. New types of warship appeared, notably the torpedo boat, the torpedo-boat destroyer, the minelayer, the submarine and, before his death, the aircraft carrier, although known at first as an 'aerodrome ship'. It was Fisher who inspired and drove the design of the first modern battleship, HMS *Dreadnought*, but it was also Fisher who predicted the demise of the big gun battleship, more than twenty years before Taranto or Midway. It needed a technologically-inspired enthusiast to see these developments, place them in context and look ahead.

It is worth remembering that when Fisher joined the Royal Navy, he met men who could remember Nelson. Before he died, he had come across men who would hold high command in the Second World War, such as the submariner Max Horton.

Fisher was a great administrator and shared with his illustrious predecessor a concern for the welfare of his men. He improved the work of the Royal dockyards. He improved training of officers and men, broke down the barriers between the engineers and the executive, and did much to develop the Britannia Royal Naval College, as well as creating a pre-Britannia establishment at Osborne, and improving the specialist schools at HMS *Vernon* and *Excellent*. He saw that men of ability should, and could, be commissioned from the ranks. He was an enthusiast for the submarine, and for the Royal Navy having its own aircraft.

Yet, there were weaknesses. He wanted ships built in small numbers, which was costly, rather than standardising and bulk building. He shortened specialist training, and made life hell for the commanding officers of the specialist schools when they objected. His enthusiasm for technology raced ahead of what was available and possible in his day. He wanted diesel-powered battleships, something that even in the Second World War the Germans did not achieve (the so-called 'pocket battleships' were in reality, not battleships at all). He did not like the idea of a naval base on the Forth at Rosyth, so this base was not available until 1916, and no other base suitable for the support of the Grand Fleet was ever built.

No one is perfect. Fisher was a man in a hurry as he became convinced that war was imminent. He had to clear away almost a century of complacency from the Royal Navy, and brooked no opposition. A lesser man might have trimmed his sails to the wind, but such a man would not have achieved half as much in the time available. A lesser man would have wasted years and opportunities by introducing changes to ship design one or two steps at a time, but Fisher ploughed ahead and *Dreadnought* was the result. The revolution in warship design that she represented might not have been completed before the First World War broke out, but not only did it happen, but by the time hostilities started, the Royal Navy included many 'super-Dreadnoughts'.

John Arbuthnot Fisher did not simply transform the Royal Navy, he reinvented it.

The Royal Navy to 1900

The navy is an impenetrable mystery surrounded by seasickness.
Admiral of the Fleet Lord Fisher

Despite almost a century having passed, the shadow of Nelson's great victory at Trafalgar in 1805 still fell across the Royal Navy at the dawn of the twentieth century. The victory had been truly great and historic, but the real reason for its continued influence was that so little had happened in the intervening years. There had been the Second Battle of Copenhagen and a naval war with the United States, but not much more. The Army had – apart from its colonial wars, of which the most notable were the Indian Mutiny and the Boer or South African War – the Crimean War, but the Royal Navy's involvement with these had been limited. There was something like a maritime *Pax Britannica*.

While the ships and the uniforms officers and men wore had changed, there had been no major fleet actions over the intervening years to test the readiness of the service for the new weapons and new means of propulsion that had arrived in the meantime. Naval officers of the day still harked back to Trafalgar, the third of Nelson's three famous victories, although, of course, none of them had been there. Not that the Royal Navy had been completely out of touch with these developments. It is all too often overlooked that Trafalgar was Nelson's third victory, after the Battle of the Nile, or Aboukir Bay, in 1798, and Copenhagen in 1801. Indeed, in many ways Copenhagen was a more daring and dashing victory as, since the Danes wouldn't set sail, Nelson sent frigates into the port to ferret them out. Just a few years later, in 1807, two years after Trafalgar and the great Admiral's death, the Royal Navy was back at Copenhagen, using artillery rockets for the first time in the west to bombard the city. Originally invented by the Chinese, artillery rockets had reached Europe via India, where they had been used by the Tipu Sultan's troops against the Duke of Wellington's forces in 1799. Reinvented by Sir William Congreve who test-fired his rockets in 1805, the artillery rocket was effective over a longer range than cannon. The bombardment of Copenhagen on 2–4 September 1807, used incendiary rockets and had such an effect that on 5 September the Danes surrendered their fleet after suffering 200 naval and army personnel killed and another 350 wounded. While as a foretaste of the shape of wars to come, 1,600 civilians were killed and another 1,000 wounded. Having lost the best of its fleet, Denmark was reduced to waging a 'gunboat war' against the Royal Navy. The following year, eighteen 'rocket boats' bombarded Boulogne, setting the town on fire.

The early use of artillery rockets is interesting, for it is ignored when time and time again the supposed ultra-conservatism of the Royal Navy is raised, and this was not the last invention to be taken up quickly.

A clear idea of the power of the service early in the nineteenth century can be garnered from the fact that it possessed 120 ships of the line, against 40 for France, 30 for Spain and 20 for the Netherlands. This was far more even than the Two Power Standard by which the British government began to assess the size of the Royal Navy.

As we will see later, the fate of the Royal Navy was far more to the fore in the hearts and minds of the people at large, as well as the press and politicians, than it is today. Any suggestion of naval weakness was greeted with outrage and protest. Naval achievements were welcomed and great pride was shown.

After France pressured Russia to join the 'Continental System' in 1807, the Russian fleet became another threat to the dominance of the Royal Navy. As the Russian Mediterranean Fleet sailed home after fighting with Turkish forces in September 1808, it was blockaded in Lisbon by the Royal Navy and the crews were only allowed safe passage home after the ships had been surrendered. While the age of diplomacy had begun, at this time, force still counted for more.

'Gunboat diplomacy' accounted for the start of a naval war with the United States. During the continuing war with France and her allies, British interference with neutral shipping had so angered the United States that hostilities between the two countries broke out in June 1812. US policy was to some extent coloured by the ambition to take Canada from the British. The naval actions that followed were mostly minor, with actions on Lake Erie in 1813 and Lake Champlain the following year. This was not a long war, or at least not at full intensity and peace with the United States followed shortly afterwards, so that by 1816, a combined British, American and Dutch naval squadron was active in the Mediterranean against the Barbary pirates who had spread terror from their bases in North Africa. This was the first action that saw the United States involved in the 'Old World', more than a hundred years before US troops were sent to France to fight. British and Dutch ships also bombarded Algiers.

THE AGE OF STEAM AND ARMOUR

While steam made its appearance aboard shipping well before the first passenger-carrying railways, it was at first confined to merchant shipping, and especially canal and river craft. Even so, the last major naval battle to be fought completely under sail was during the Greek War of Independence at Navarino in 1827, when a Turkish and Egyptian combined fleet was confronted by an Anglo-French-Russian fleet led by Vice-Admiral Sir Edward Codrington, RN. The battle seems to have started by mistake, always a danger when there is an armed 'stand-off'. The Turks and Egyptians were heavily outnumbered by the Allies with just seven ships of the line against four each from the UK, France and Russia. Codrington was under orders to engage the enemy simply as a last resort, and negotiations were put in hand when the two fleets met in Navarino Bay on the south-west coast of the Peloponnese peninsula. Boats shuttled between the ships of the two sides, and when one Allied boat was fired on by Turkish troops who mistook it for a boarding party, one of the British ships fired a cannon shot, and soon all of the ships were firing.

A battle then ensued, during which the Turks lost one ship of the line, twelve frigates out of fifteen and twenty-two of their twenty-six corvettes. Turkish gunnery was poor, and even when fireships were used, they caused more damage to their own side than to the opposition.

Twenty-seven years later, during the Crimean War in 1854, many warships were steam-powered, but retained a full set of sails for the practical reason that they were propelled by paddles that were vulnerable to cannon fire. Even when screws replaced paddle wheels, the early coal-fired steam engines used so much fuel that the range of the warships under steam was limited, and so, on longer voyages, sail remained an option, especially since many ships were almost as fast under sail as under steam, given a favourable wind. The paddles also took up so much space on the sides of ships that they reduced the number of cannon that could be carried. It was not until the advent of screw propulsion in 1829 that steam became a viable option as auxiliary power for frigates, and even so the first steam-powered ship of the line did not appear until 1848.

The changes in propulsion were accompanied by changes in armament. First, rifling of cannon improved accuracy, and then in 1821, the Frenchman Paixhans invented the explosive shell, which was so devastating against wooden hulls that there was a rush to introduce armoured plating, initially iron sheets bolted onto the wooden hulls. By this time, despite its numerical strength, the Royal Navy was lagging behind in technology. The French were the first to introduce an all-armoured warship, the frigate *Gloire* in 1859, but during the Crimean War they had used floating batteries. The advent of more accurate gunnery over longer ranges and explosive shells also marked another major and often unremarked change in naval warfare. Nelson had urged his captains to 'engage the enemy more closely'. He was shot by a marksman, not killed by a cannon ball. Cannon fire devastated masts and rigging, cleared decks of men, including gunners, leaving a bloody mess of bones and flesh, but it had little impact on the hull, other than when it blasted through the stern cabins of the captains and admirals and through into the gunnery decks. Exploding shells could sink ships, set them on fire, detonate magazines.

Although war in the Crimea had broken out in 1853, British and French involvement really dated from 1854, when steamships sped the movement of an Anglo-French expeditionary force of 60,000 men. In October, the bombardment of Sevastapol took place, with six screw-driven steamships involved and supported by another twenty-one sailing ships of the line, which had to be towed into position by steam tugs. Beginning at noon on 17 October, the operation was intended to have a crippling effect on the Russian defenders, but the opposite proved to be the case, with little harm done to the defences, while in only six hours, the attacking fleet had many ships badly damaged and 340 men were killed or wounded. The age of the wooden wall had ended and the age of the armoured warship had begun.

Such actions cannot hide the fact that the Royal Navy spent most of the nineteenth century on the sidelines, a massive but untried instrument of power. It could be argued that the policy of maintaining a fleet that was the equal of any two others was the ultimate deterrent, and the (relative) peace of the long Victorian era was the result of this policy. Yet, there were other factors at play. Two major European powers, Germany and Italy, were only just becoming unified national entities, while the United States had still to recognise the potential of sea power, and was in any case preoccupied with the Americas. France took some time to recover from its Napoleonic defeats.

The American Civil War, 1861–1865, did not affect the Royal Navy materiallly, but afloat, as well as ashore, this conflict saw the beginnings of modern warfare. As early as August 1861, Unionist forces used a captive balloon aboard a ship for artillery observation. Mines and submersibles made their appearance, and the famous battle between the armoured ships *Merrimack* and *Monitor* showed that armour could defeat explosive shells, at least of the kind then available. A primitive submarine sank a blockade ship using a 'spear' torpedo; one of thirty-two ships that were sunk by the new underwater weapons of mine or torpedo during this conflict.

RENEWED IMPORTANCE OF THE MEDITERRANEAN

Other changes were also taking place that would influence the deployment of the Royal Navy during the following century. The opening of the Suez Canal in 1869 meant that the Mediterranean, which had become something of a backwater following the defeat of the Ottoman forces at Lepanto in 1571, again assumed strategic importance. Overnight, the Mediterranean had become a vital thoroughfare, more important than at any time since the fall of the Roman Empire. Almost overnight, Gibraltar, Malta and Alexandria became important bases and coaling stations for the Royal Navy.

The 'spear' torpedo had its equivalent in the surface fleet with the advent of the ram, a forward projection on the bows of battleships mainly beneath the waterline. While in the two world wars, warship commanders would, in desperation, ram an enemy submarine caught on the surface, as an instrument of warfare in its own right and in manoeuvres the ram was to prove not just an over-rated weapon, but a hazard to one's own side. In fact, one of the most successful actions in which ramming played a vital part, the battle between Austria and Italy off Lissa on 20 July 1866, saw the Austrian warships 'ram' Italian ships even though none of their vessels had a proper ram, but simply a cut-water formed by the joint of the armour plating. The Italians lost two ships and 612 men, while the Austrians had one ship badly damaged and lost 38 men. One outcome of this battle was the realisation that the ironclads were made vulnerable by the immense weight of the thick armour over the wooden hull – as thick as 24 inches in one example – which made them difficult to handle and top heavy.

The ram was a weapon that belonged to an earlier age, one in which ships made physical contact, getting as close to the enemy as possible. It did not belong to an age in which gunnery ranges were opening up with opposing fleets engaging several miles apart. Not only was the period of close contact past, the rams could be a hazard to other ships when steaming in close proximity. In 1893, the Mediterranean Fleet under the command of Vice-Admiral Sir George Tryon was steaming in two parallel divisions, when Tryon ordered them to reverse course with each column turning inwards, a manoeuvre that required the ships to be a minimum distance apart before it started. Aboard one of the leading ships, *Camperdown*, was Rear Admiral Markham, who soon realised that the distance between his ship and the other leading ship, *Victoria*, with Tryon aboard, was less than their combined turning circles, meaning that they overlapped and that a collision was inevitable unless the order was changed. The state of mind of even senior officers in the Royal Navy at the time was that no one dared say a word, even though the inevitability of disaster was soon apparent to many officers on the bridges of both ships. Tryon alone was oblivious to impending disaster. As a result, *Camperdown* cut through the side of *Victoria*, killing Tryon and 360 officers and men. Had the ships not had rams, the death toll would have been much lower.

Victoria was, incidentally, an example of much else that was wrong with the Royal Navy at the time. Her 16.25-inch guns were so heavy that their muzzles sagged under their own weight and they had never been fired with a full explosive charge.

MENACE UNDER THE SEA

Torpedo development continued apace as it became clear that in most cases, warfare at sea would have opposing fleets farther apart, and that close contact with the enemy would no longer be desirable, or indeed possible, as the range of naval artillery increased. The Austrian Navy attempted the development of self-propelled torpedoes, but it took an Englishman working at Fiume, Robert Whitehead, to perfect this in 1869. The Whitehead torpedo used compressed air and could run submerged at six knots for 300 yards carrying an 18-pound explosive in the nose, and was soon improved by the addition of a gyroscope to ensure that it remained on course. Once again the Royal Navy was quick to investigate the possibilities of this weapon, first buying it in 1870. A variation on the Whitehead was the towed torpedo, or 'Harvey', named after Commander Harvey, RN, which was launched from the deck of a steamship and towed by wire, before diverging from the track of the towing vessel and heading off at an angle of 45 degrees. On reaching the target, it could be exploded by contact, although electric detonation was also possible. Given this unorthodox means of targeting, it is not surprising that the Harvey never fulfilled its promise, and it fell to the rival Whitehead torpedo to score the first success.

Mine warfare also began to make an impact, with the leading proponents being the Russians, but they were also the first to use the Whitehead torpedo in anger when, on 26 January 1878, Russian torpedo-boats sank the Turkish warship *Intibah*. That was the same year that John P. Holland built his first submarine. It was in 1885 that the Swedish submarine *Nordenfelt I*, entered service, not only carrying a Whitehead torpedo in an external bow casing but also being the first submarine to carry a surface armament.

Less successful than rockets or torpedoes was the Royal Navy's early experience with breech-loading guns, which resulted in a number of accidents so that most ships retained a muzzle-loading armament. Debate arose over whether warships should have a central battery of guns, which had replaced the long lines of cannon on both sides of ships as steam had started to take over from sail, or use a turret system, as with the US *Monitor*. The leading British advocates of the turret system, Captain Coles, was allowed to design HMS *Captain*, a turret ship for the Royal Navy, but she proved to be top heavy and capsized in the Atlantic on 7 September 1870. An alternative, the Admiralty's own design, HMS *Monarch*, proved to be more successful. Neither ship would have been a practical proposition as the sail rig cluttered the deck and limited the radius of fire of the guns. It was not until HMS *Devastation* entered service in 1873 that the Royal Navy received its first major warship without sails and with turrets, and she served with the fleet until the early twentieth century.

Even with turrets, forward firing of guns could be difficult with the rise towards the bow of the forecastle, especially as at this stage 'super-firing' – having 'B' turret higher than 'A' turret or 'X' higher than 'Y' – had still to appear.

This was a period when the ideal design for a warship using the new armament and the new propulsive system had still to evolve. Before this could happen, several experimental designs entered service with the Royal Navy, including HMS *Agamemnon* in 1883. *Agamemnon* has been described as one of the ugliest ships to see service with the fleet, with turrets placed amidships on either side able to fire forward and aft. Spurred on by a new Italian warship with 17.7-inch calibre guns and armour plating confined to protection of the machinery, magazines and turrets, the Royal Navy ordered what was the largest warship of its day, HMS *Inflexible*, 11,000 tons, with four 16-inch muzzle-loaded guns, and capable of 15 knots; while she also had anti-rolling tanks and electric light. The new ship carried two 60-foot torpedo boats which for the first time had submerged tubes. The idea of having torpedo boats aboard a larger ship was to be resurrected during the Second World War, but never proved to be a practical proposition.

Despite many innovations being seized upon by the Admiralty, a good example of Admiralty conservatism was to be found in the accommo-dation aboard warships, with that for officers still aft, a reflection of the importance of their being near the quarterdeck with its steering and navigating positions on a sailing ship, but a long way from the com-mand and control positions on a ship without sail.

Other navies were also experimenting with different approaches to warship design. One German admiral described the new Germany's navy as a collection of prototypes.

Under the command of a certain Captain John Arbuthnot Fisher, *Inflexible* saw action in 1882, when the Mediterranean Fleet bombarded Alexandria in Egypt after a number of Europeans had been massacred. Eight ironclads, including *Inflexible*, shelled the fortifications, a difficult target against which ships had traditionally been at a disadvantage, as at Sevastapol less than twenty years earlier. Nevertheless, Admiral Sir Frederick Seymour's force ensured that the forts were eventually sur-rendered, while at one of them the powder magazine blew up under shellfire from HMS *Superb*. Even so, control ashore had to be exerted and the job finished by a naval shore party, again under Fisher, ably assisted by his fellow captain, George Wilson.

One further significant invention was to appear before the century closed. This was the steam turbine, whose inventor Sir Charles Parsons had used when building a small, fast craft, *Turbina*, which gate-crashed the Naval Review of 1897, demonstrating beyond all doubt its superiority over the reciprocating engines then in use. Speed was not the sole advantage of the steam turbine. The new engine had a much lower profile than the reciprocating engines, which on a large ship rose up through the level of several decks. This meant that space existed above the engine for heavy deck armour plating and the lower centre of gravity also allowed heavier armament to be carried. The massive superstructures that were to become a feature of battleships as the twentieth century progressed would not have been possible with tall reciprocating engines.

TECHNOLOGY AND WARFARE

While commanding officer of *Inflexible* at the time of the bombardment of Alexandria, Fisher, already with a reputation as a keen-eyed and outspoken naval officer, was quick to point out that while the gunnery left much to be desired, it was also hampered by dud shells and poor fuses. One shell landed amidst 300 tons of gunpowder without causing the devastating explosion that might have been expected! The lack of big breech loading guns by this time, when the French had already perfected the mechanisms, was a further handicap, leading to an agonizingly slow rate of fire. Fisher's ship had to depress her two twin 16-inch turrets so that reloading could take place.

Other changes were taking place at the same time. For the eighteenth and nineteenth century any ship that 'cruised', or patrolled, was described as a 'cruiser', while in effect most were frigates. During the late nineteenth century, the frigate began to be replaced by the forerunner of the cruiser of the twentieth century. Initially two types of cruiser were developed, the protected cruiser and the armoured cruiser. The former lacked side armour but was built of steel of varying thickness. Protection was provided by locating the coal bunkers at the sides of the ship and ensuring sufficient watertight divisions of the hull. The first two were the *Iris* and *Mercury* of 1877, the first British ships constructed entirely of steel. Armoured cruisers had heavy armour plating and often heavy armament, but this affected speed and endurance, making it impossible for these ships to execute one of the main duties of the cruiser, reconnaissance. The first cruiser action used the smaller protected cruiser and involved the French Navy fighting Chinese forces on the Min River in French Indo-China in 1884. British ship-yards soon established a thriving business building cruisers for many of the world's navies.

A cruiser also featured in the outbreak of the Spanish-American War in 1898, when the USS *Maine* blew up at Santiago in Chile, most probably due to spontaneous combustion by either her coal bunkers or her magazine, but the Americans suspected Spanish treachery. Despite occurring late in the nineteenth century, the Spanish-American War was unremarkable technically or strategically, but it did persuade the American body politic to take a closer interest in naval matters for the first time.

Fisher had become Third Naval Lord and Controller of the Navy in 1892. This was a more than usually distinguished term of office, for he introduced the water tube boiler, thus improving the efficiency of warship propulsion for no extra fuel, and also introduced the destroyer – although these ships were for many years very much smaller and less heavily armed than those of sixty or seventy years later. He also influenced the design of a new major warship which was later to become his flagship on the North American and West Indies Station.

The first genuine major fleet action for the new warships came during the Russo-Japanese War of 1904–1905. As would happen almost forty years later, the Japanese did not declare war first. The surprise torpedo attack on the Russian fleet at Port Arthur on the night of 8/9 February saw two Russian battleships put out of action for several months while a cruiser was also hit. War was not declared until 10 February. At the Battle of the Yellow Sea on 10/11 August 1904, the Japanese won even though they had four battleships against the Russians' six. This was partly owing to superior Japanese tactics and gunnery, but also because the Japanese had overwhelming superiority in destroyers and torpedo-boats, which they used to harass the Russians after darkness fell while their own major fleet units rested. The war concluded with a major Russian defeat in the great naval battle of Tsushima on 27/28 May 1905. The stately progress of the Russian ships from the Baltic to the Far East was marked by paranoia over Japanese torpedo boats,

which led to an 'engagement' between the Russians and British fishing vessels in the North Sea, which nearly brought Great Britain and
Russia to war. Any element of surprise was lost through the necessity
for repeated re-coaling. The balance of firepower looked to be on the
side of the Russians, who had eight battleships against four Japanese,
although the latter had eight armoured cruisers against one armoured
cruiser and three armoured coast defence ships. The Japanese had superiority in destroyers as well as cruisers, plus many torpedo boats which
were to play a crucial role in the battle.

At Tsushima the Russians lost all eight battleships sent to the Far East,
with six sunk and two surrendered, while one coastal armoured ship
was sunk and another two surrendered, three armoured cruisers were
sunk, two cruisers were sunk and three interned, five destroyers were
sunk, one interned and another captured, and four of the eight auxiliaries were also sunk. The Russians lost 5,000 men dead, 500 wounded
and 6,000 become prisoners of war, but only after they had broken into
their ships' vodka stores and consumed the contents – doubtless starting captivity with a massive hangover!

By contrast, the Japanese lost three torpedo-boats, while three battleships and two cruisers were badly damaged. Casualties were 600
dead and wounded. This was a devastating blow: a major European
power had been defeated by an Oriental state using the most up-to-
date weapons of the day.

FISHER AT THE ADMIRALTY

On 20 October 1904, Admiral Sir John Fisher became First Sea Lord,
insisting that the titles of 'Sea Lords' that had been dropped almost a
century earlier be revived and supersede the titles of 'Naval Lords', used
for the naval officers on the Board of Admiralty to distinguish them
from the politicians and civil servants. Having delayed taking up his
appointment until Trafalgar Day, in the end he was so impatient that he
started a day early.

Fisher had already been introduced to the workings of the Board of
Admiralty, having not only been Third Naval Lord and Controller of
the Navy but also Second Naval Lord, responsible for personnel, from
1902. He had already done much to improve conditions for the men
of the fleet. His elevation more or less coincided with a proposal by

an Italian engineer, Vittorio Cuniberti, that the ideal battleship for the Royal Navy would be around 17,000 tons displacement and have an armament of twelve 12-inch guns capable of firing salvoes, with armour 12 inches thick over the machinery spaces and magazines, and be capable of 24 knots. His ideas struck a chord with Fisher, as an aggressive, fighting admiral, who saw no point in low speeds or lightweight armaments. The end result of his thinking was HMS *Dreadnought*, the ship that made all other battleships obsolete. Subsequently all battleshipss would be divided into 'pre-Dreadnoughts' and 'Dreadnoughts'.

Dreadnought was built within a year at the Portsmouth Royal Dockyard. Turbine-powered, *Dreadnought* displaced 17,900 tons, could steam at 21 knots and had an armour belt that was 11 inches thick at its strongest point. Armament consisted of ten 12-inch guns, and, showing the importance attached to this particular weapon, she also had no less than five submerged 18-inch torpedo tubes. Her armament was not all 'big gun', as she had smaller weapons for protection against the dreaded torpedo boat. The feeling of many at the Admiralty was that Fisher had introduced too many innovations in one go, but the nature of the Admiralty was still reactionary at the time. Fisher was a man in a hurry and did not have the time – or, just as important, the budgets – to introduce innovation piecemeal. *Dreadnought* was the first British warship to have the officers' accommodation forward, so that they could be at their posts within minutes.

The only real drawback with such a radical departure from the accepted standards for a battleship was that the Royal Navy found itself starting again from scratch, losing its established advantage over every other navy. With the commissioning of *Dreadnought*, the rest of the British battle fleet became obsolete and the fleet would have to be rebuilt. Inherited fleets no longer mattered, and the availability of funding and possession of a substantial shipbuilding industry would settle the winner in the race to create the twentieth century's most powerful navy. The Imperial German Navy received its first dreadnought, the Nassau-class, in 1907, and this proved to be the start of a desperate Anglo-German naval race.

Aboard *Dreadnought* herself, the ideal of having an all big gun ship soon had to be compromised. Smaller calibre fast-firing guns were also necessary, initially to fend off attacks by torpedo boats as previously mentioned, but such armament was also eventually to prove useful – indeed essential – for anti-aircraft warfare once the concept of high angle, HA, or combined high and low angle, HA/LA, weaponry was formulated.

The next stage in the development of the twentieth-century fleet was the battlecruiser. The original intention was that this type of ship would have as radical an impact on cruiser design as the *Dreadnought* had on the battleship, making all earlier vessels obsolete. First of these was *Invincible*, with eight 12-inch guns and a six-inch armoured belt, and with a far higher speed of 26 knots. The intention was that she should be able to blow any enemy cruiser out of the water, but instead of replacing the cruiser, which continued its own development, the battlecruiser became what more or less amounted to an intermediate type of vessel falling between the cruiser and battleship, intended primarily for scouting and reconnaissance ahead of a battle fleet, and for commerce raiding. In fact, battlecruisers would have made an uncomfortable replacement for the cruisers of the day, many of which were little bigger than Second World War destroyers, and far smaller than today's Type 45 destroyers. The weakness of a battlecruiser was apparent when it encountered an opposing battleship when its lack of armour left it vulnerable. This was not a ship for fleet actions, but that is where it often found itself.

It is debatable whether the battlecruiser ever fulfilled expectations, but as we will find later, Fisher believed that they were the future, and favoured them over battleships.

Larger still were the Lion-class of battlecruisers, with the leadship, *Lion*, launched in 1910, displacing 30,000 tons, heavily armed with 13.5-inch guns and capable of 28 knots. With a sister ship named *Tiger*, types of the class were sometimes referred to as the 'big cats'.

Other changes were taking place. The fear of the torpedo boat had resulted in a counter-measure, the torpedo boat destroyer, and before the First World War broke out, this was already evolving into a larger category of escort vessel, the destroyer. The battle squadrons of the coming conflict were to be escorted by cruisers and destroyers, the former more capable of maintaining station with battleships in the open seas, but the latter having the manoeuvrability necessary for close quarter actions in coastal and offshore waters. Both types of warship carried torpedoes, intended for attacks on larger warships, but while this did sometimes happen with destroyer torpedo attacks, for the most part torpedoes fired by surface vessels were used to deliver the *coup de grace* against enemy ships already crippled by heavy gunfire.

Even though the Admiralty was conservative, by 1900 the Royal Navy did have submarines, with five Holland-type boats in service. Nevertheless, much of the surface fleet was very old and as late as 1890, the training cruiser was a sailing ship. Fisher incurred the wrath of many senior officers by bringing home from the various fleets, squadrons and overseas stations many older ships. Many of the ships in reserve were in a similar condition and were scrapped. The senior officers who had preceded him had confused sheer numbers with efficiency, an extreme case of quantity rather than quality. The problem as previously pointed out was that there had been no major fleet action between Navarino in 1827 and Tsushima in 1905, and the Royal Navy was absent from the more recent and relevant of these battles.

EVOLUTIONS BEFORE EVOLUTION

Fisher inherited a service that had lost its edge since its victories a hundred years or so earlier. Initiative was stifled. In Nelson's day, the commanding officers of frigates did much of the work of any navy, and the old phrase about 'sending a gunboat' more usually meant sending a frigate, not unlike the role of destroyers and frigates in the latter half of the twentieth century. This responsibility and the limitations of communications at the time meant that initiative was necessary and that commanding officers carried a heavy burden of responsibility. The major ships of the line came together for the big set piece fleet actions, in which case the role of the frigate was changed, acting both as despatch vessels and also sailing abeam of the battle fleet so that signals from the flagship could be repeated for the benefit of those ships some miles astern. The late Victorian navy had become obsessed with appearance and with fleet manoeuvres, so that handling the ship successfully and maintaining its place in the formation, fleet evolutions, was more important than being able to fight.

Some commanding officers would have their ship repainted every six or seven months, with others it could be six weeks, and it was common for the more zealous to augment the paint supplied by the dockyard by paying for additional supplies from their own pockets. When HMS *Victoria* was lost, her commanding officer, the future Lord Jellicoe and commander of the Grand Fleet, found that his friends had arranged a collection to compensate him for the paint bought before the ship sailed from Malta. The collection raised £75, equal to about £12,000 in today's values.

The present Sovereign has had just three Royal Fleet Reviews in more than fifty years on the throne, but before the First World War these were far more frequent, with Royal Reviews at Spithead in June 1911, another one at Dublin and finally one at Weymouth in May 1912. The last of these was notable for the arrival of Charles Rumney Samson's aeroplane, which stole the show. The Royal Reviews of the Fleet were the most important of the navy's interactions with the community. Instead of being largely out of sight and out of mind as today, the pre-First World War navy would send ships, sometimes squadrons of ships, into seaside resorts to the delight of the admiring holidaymakers. Before this, in 1891, the Royal Naval Exhibition had attracted 2.5 million visitors in a country with a far smaller population than today.

These were the days of the 'naval scares'. The general population took an interest in the Royal Navy that is all too rare today. Unfortunately the general population, the press and many politicians confused quantity and quality, and Fisher's withdrawal of ships from many overseas stations on the grounds that they were rotting and their crews deteriorating, and the scrapping of others that were too old to be useful, was unpopular and controversial, losing him many potential allies for the political battles of the future.

The fact that warships were deployed as squadrons was significant. A 'squadron' of warships meant major warships, specifically battleships, battlecruisers or cruisers, or today it would mean aircraft carriers. Destroyers, and today frigates, would have been part of a flotilla, not a squadron. There was no preset number of ships in a squadron other than the fact that it had to be at least two, but in the Victorian and Edwardian navy, and later during the First World War, it more usually meant four or five major warships. Flotillas could mean a dozen or more.

Aboard ships, spit and polish was far more highly regarded than fighting capability. Gunnery practice was neglected because it made the ship dirty, and it was not unknown for practice munitions to be quietly dumped overboard. Fisher's great rival while he was First Sea Lord, Admiral Charles Beresford, was a good example of a man who favoured presentation and ceremony over exercises.

Ships did of course become dirty whenever they had to re-coal, a process that took some time with a battleship or battlecruiser requiring some 3,000 to 3,500 tons of coal, with loading largely by hand, apart from the simple hoist that lifted the coal out of the barge or collier, with the entire ship's company loading at the rate of some 300 tons per hour. Ships used less coal when steaming at a relatively high speed and consumption increased at slow speeds. Coaling was necessary every seven to ten days. As an example, *Dreadnought* could carry 2,900 tons of coal and was regarded as being very economical with a consumption of around 300 tons a day. Aboard destroyers, just four or five men would struggle to bring aboard fifty tons of coal, and the ship could be re-coaling every three days if spending much time at sea.

The range and availability of ships improved considerably with the advent of oil firing. Refuelling with oil was cleaner than re-coaling and should have been much quicker, but the Royal Navy was to lag behind the United States Navy in the development of under-way replenishment. RN ships still using a slow system of transfer with the ship refuelling trailing behind the oiler, as naval tankers are known; this situation persisted into the Second World War. The USN developed the abeam method, which was faster and could also continue in fairly rough weather. The widespread adoption of oil as a fuel was delayed in the Royal Navy not so much because of conservative attitudes but because of fears over the security of supplies during wartime. The country had scant natural oil resources of its own at this time, but coal was abundant. A sign of the future, however, was that the Queen Elizabeth-class ships were oil-fired from the start.

2

Jumping Over the Chair

My examination to enter the Navy was very simple, but it was adequate. I wrote out the Lord's prayer and the doctor made me jump over a chair naked, and I was given a glass of sherry on being in the Navy.

Fisher's account of how he joined the Royal Navy in 1854 is of course from a different era, but he was actually being what we would now describe as 'economical with the truth', for he had already passed an examination involving taking dictation of some thirty lines of English, and copied a number of sentences from a morning paper, taken a paper in arithmetic, and an earlier medical examination had been more thorough, giving him a certificate to show that he was free from any physical defects. This was June 1854, and he was just 13 years of age. Fisher had also been nominated, not by the Admiralty as was the standard practice, but by Commander-in-Chief Plymouth, Admiral Sir William Parker, a neighbour of Fisher's godmother, Lady Wilmot-Horton.

This was one aspect of naval life that did not change as much as one might have expected over the intervening years. While nepotism was steadily removed from the service of the crown during the Victorian period, very senior officers did still manage to ensure that their staff contained a fair number of people who were either family or friends.

This meant that the patronage and support of his godmother was important in ensuring that Fisher had a good start to his naval career. It would be wrong to assume that Fisher came from a naval family with a long line of ancestors who had served with the Fleet; like Nelson before him, he came from quite different stock. True, his mother had a grand-father who had served under Lord Nelson at Trafalgar. Nevertheless, his immediate ancestors had little to do with the sea. Further back, the Fishers were an old Warwickshire family whose origins were lost in time, but there had been a Sir Clement Fisher under Charles II, a newly created baronet, who is known to have married a Jane Lane, but the baronetcy almost immediately lapsed for want of £500 to meet the necessary fees. His paternal grandfather was rector of Wavendon in Buckinghamshire, with a brother who had been fatally wounded fighting at Waterloo. Fisher was to treasure the watch that had belonged to his great uncle and which bore the dent of the bullet that had killed him. One result was that Fisher's father, William, was commissioned as a result of his great uncle's dying wish and was despatched to Ceylon in 1831 as an ensign in command of the Governor's Guard. The connection with Nelson notwithstanding, his mother, Sophie Lambe, was the daughter of a wine merchant in New Bond Street. Next door, many years earlier, the young Emma Hamilton had been a housemaid and had scrubbed the front steps.

Sophie Lambe was sent to Colombo in Ceylon, now Sri Lanka, to keep house for her brother Frederick. It seems that she was a welcome addition to the local social scene, with many admirers despite her family having come from 'trade', a mark of shame to some in the new Victorian age. One of her admirers was William Fisher, by this time a captain in the 78th Highland Regiment. They married in April, 1840. Fisher was later to note that his mother 'had only beauty and he [William] had only his splendid body!' This may have been a romantic image coloured over the years, and the photograph of the couple taken some years after the marriage does not exhibit obvious signs of beauty by modern tastes; but there was nothing romantic about his own self-assessment. 'Why I am ugly is one of those puzzles of physiology which are beyond finding out!' In fact, Fisher had almost an oriental appearance and some colouring, something which was not missed by his enemies and was to be used by them against him in later life.

JOHN ARBUTHNOT AS A CHILD

William Fisher enjoyed the honour of being ADC to the then governor of Ceylon, Sir Robert Wilmot-Horton, and could have expected at least a modestly successful military career, but it was not to be. Shortly after his first child, John Arbuthnot Fisher, was born at Rambodde on 25 January 1841, he decided to leave the governor's service. Attracted by the wealth enjoyed by the coffee planters, he bought himself out of the army and purchased a coffee plantation. Unfortunately this was no easy route to wealth, and before long he was in debt, his situation helped little by the growth of his family; Sophie endured eleven pregnancies, losing four of her children in infancy or early childhood. It seems that Fisher was a poor businessman, a poor manager of money and improvident, despite being a kindly man, and that the family and indeed the household was efficiently and effectively managed by Sophie. Despite his later romantic memories and admiration of his parents, when Sophie returned home as a widow and turned to him for financial support, John Fisher came to resent his family's constant demands of him, struggling as he was to bring up his own family on his naval pay alone. At the same time, as his reputation grew, his mother and his siblings assumed that someone so famous must also be wealthy.

'I attribute my present vitality to the imbibing of my mother's milk beyond the legal period of nine months,' Fisher was later to write.[1] Given the high infant mortality rates of the day, and the heat and disease of the tropics, it certainly kept him away from other less nutritious substances for a while. While he certainly was not born with a silver spoon in his mouth, he was nevertheless fortunate in that the governor's wife, Lady Wilmot-Horton, became his godmother. She was wealthy and influential, but soon widowed and returned to her family seat at Catton Hall, near Burton-on-Trent.

Fisher himself left his parents at the tender age of six years, never to see his father again, and was sent 'home' to stay with his Uncle Frederick who had returned to England shortly after Sophie and William had married. Fisher was sent to boarding school at Knight's School in Coventry. From the fact that the headmaster was indeed a Mr J.F. Knight, we can be sure that this was not one of the great public schools, and it was no doubt a destination enforced by his father's poor means. Instead of spending his holidays with his uncle, however, he found himself spending them with his godmother at Catton Hall. Here was a life of comfort and plenty, and the young boy soon fell to fishing for perch on the River Trent, which flowed past the house. He was less lucky with a gun. He quickly mastered the art and became a good marksman, claiming to have been taught to shoot at anything he saw moving, but when he saw the tall grass moving and fired, he shot the butler. Presumably the man survived the ordeal, for which Fisher roundly blamed him, but he was refused any further contact with firearms whilst at Catton.

Despite this youthful misdemeanour, his godmother adored him and indulged almost any of his wishes, other than those involving guns.

It is not clear when Fisher first displayed an enthusiasm for the Royal Navy, but Lady Wilmot-Horton was well-connected. On the opposite side of Lichfield lived the last survivor from Nelson's 'band of brothers', his sea captains, Admiral Sir William Parker, who was appointed Port Admiral at Portsmouth. Within his power were two nominations for entry into the Royal Navy, and when Fisher celebrated his thirteenth birthday, Lady Wilmot-Horton had no difficulty in persuading the Admiral to advance the cause of her young charge. It must have been a moment of absent-mindedness that saw Parker give his second nomination to Fisher as well, the youth having also attracted the support of another elderly lady, a niece of Lord Nelson.

DOUBLY NOMINATED

Doubly nominated, and no doubt doubly blessed as well, Fisher took his examinations and was examined by a naval physician, officially entering the Royal Navy but being sent back to Catton Hall before receiving his appointment as a cadet in HMS *Victory*. When he left Catton Hall in June 1854, he was given a letter of introduction from Lady Wilmot-Horton to Admiral Parker.

At Portsmouth, perhaps surprisingly to the modern reader, formalities were kept to the minimum and Fisher was entertained by the Admiral, something that would hardly have happened in the twentieth century to a young cadet, not even a midshipman. Just thirteen, he arrived at Portsmouth and was given a bed for the night by a naval outfitter. He went aboard his ship, was examined, and then allowed ashore to take his letter to Parker.

'He asked me to dinner,' Fisher later recalled. 'But I told him that I thought that I had better get on board my ship! He was amused and told me to dine and sleep at his house, and he told me all about Lord Nelson, who he had served under a great many years.'[2]

The hospitality continued the following morning, with the Admiral's own coxswain taking him to the *Victory*. This was when harsh reality set in. On arriving aboard he immediately had a bucket of salt water thrown over his feet. There was no shore training, no briefing on the service, it was immediately down to work. The seemingly easy familiarity of the previous twenty-four hours, and even of the entrance process, was soon replaced by a brutal regime in which the cadets learnt as they worked. Cadets holystoned the wooden decks of the *Victory*, and on his first day, the young man saw no less than eight men flogged, fainting at the sight. The commanding officer, Captain C.D. Hay, had been tried by a court martial for flogging an entire crew, but acquitted and left to continue in his ways. The second-in-command, who would be the executive officer today, Commander Alexander Boyle, was clearly from the same mould. His own predilection was for padlocking ratings to a ringbolt before having buckets of salt water thrown over them. His reaction to Fisher was to make him walk the break of the poop deck with a coil of rope around his neck, maintaining that the boy was made to be hanged! The first lieutenant roared at the youngsters like a 'Bull of Bashan' in Fisher's words, although he later gave the boy an orange, a rare treat at the time. Perversely, perhaps, Fisher always claimed that he loved both the captain and the commander. 'Both loved me till they died,' he maintained. 'They were each of them great for war; but, alas! peace was their portion.'[3] One wonders whether such men would have been great in leading their men into war. Nelson, by contrast, was a humane commander.

The great technological changes in the Royal Navy were, for the most part, to occur in the second half of the nineteenth century. Life aboard ship had changed little since Nelson. Without refrigeration, perishable items were soon consumed, and on the long voyages, still under sail for most, the diet soon settled to the dreary routine of salt beef and hard tack, and ship's biscuit that was weevil-ridden, so that sailors habitually came to tap the biscuit to dislodge the weevils before eating. While the bread lasted, rats who had indulged in the ship's bread or flour were caught, killed and cooked, being regarded by the midshipmen as a delicacy. Fisher noted that:

It was a matter of the survival of the fittest among those little midshipmen. In the first ship I was in we not only carried our fresh water in casks, but we had some rare old ship's biscuit supplied in what were known as "bread-bags" [sic]. These bread bags were not preservative; they were creative. A favourite amusement was to put a bit of this biscuit on the table and see how soon all of it would walk away. In fact one midshipman could gamble away his "tot" of rum with another midshipman by pitting one biscuit against another ...

I didn't grow tall because in the days when I went to sea the poor little Midshipmen were kept in three watches with insufficient food … measuring just 4 feet nothing, the poor little boys had to walk the quarter-deck in their "watch-keeping" from 8pm till midnight one night and from midnight to 4 am the following night! And always very hungry all the time! They never had a whole night's rest ever! And their little bellies were never full![4]

Midshipmen were allowed just a basin of water in which to wash, and if anyone spilt a drop of water on the deck, he had to holystone the deck himself. Each kept his own basin in his sea-chest. Old at the time of Trafalgar, *Victory* was almost 100 years old when Fisher joined her, but was still kept ready for sea, and for warfare. Anchors had to be weighed by hand, and each ship had a fiddler to keep the men on the capstans in step during this procedure.

Officers of Fisher's generation nevertheless valued the links between their careers and that of Nelson, through the great flagship and through association with men who had served under the famous Admiral.

Locked into her dry dock at Portsmouth today, in Fisher's day, the great ship remained afloat in Portsmouth Harbour. Many of her officers lived ashore, including Boyle, and it was part of Fisher's duties to take a boat ashore each morning to collect the commander, and later to return him. Some evidence for Fisher's charming of the opposite sex is seen early. In his own words: 'He had a very lovely young wife, and she used to give me Devonshire cream and jam every morning … She really was a very lovely woman – only seventeen.'

'POCKET MONEY'

For all of this, not only were the cadets not paid, but their parents were expected to keep them in what Fisher's father described as 'pocket money'. Fisher would have received little of this, however, for on 15 May 1854, written before he finally joined his ship but received some time afterwards, a letter from his father laid down some ground rules, after first reminding him that he was very poor and with a great many children, so that he could not give his eldest son much pocket money. His father also expressed the hope that Fisher would see some fighting. Fisher was undoubtedly receiving some form of support from his godmother, which was probably as well, for despite his protestations of poverty, his father also wanted him to 'dress well and be very clean in your person and dress'. (Many years later, faced with the fees for the Britannia Royal Naval College at Dartmouth, one father was moved to write to the Admiralty that he could accept that his son might die for his country, but he didn't see why he should pay for the privilege!)

The Victorian era was not one of peace, but the fighting that did take place had little impact on the Royal Navy. Even by 1854, with the Crimean War having started the previous year, the effect of so long a period of inaction was being felt. The Mediterranean Fleet, commanded by Vice-Admiral Sir James Dundas, was dispatched to the Black Sea, while a substantial ad hoc force was raised under Vice-Admiral Sir Charles Napier and sent to the Baltic.

Neither force acquitted itself with any distinction, although both had sufficient numbers of ships and men. Despite the French capturing the island fortress of Bomarsund in the Baltic in mid-August, a pointless exercise as this had to be abandoned when the winter weather came, the main action was in the Black Sea. An Anglo-French-Turkish expeditionary force of 60,000 men was transported from Varna to Eupatoria, landing on 14 September. The Allied forces soon besieged Sevastapol and to assist the armies ashore the Royal Navy joined in a bombardment from the sea, on 17 October. The naval force consisted of six screw-driven ships and twenty-one of sail, with the latter towed into position by steamers. This was clearly not a fleet that could be used in a battle at sea. It was equally ineffectual in the action that followed.

Beginning at noon, the bombardment lasted for six hours and inflicted little damage on the Russians, but received terrible punishment in return, with 340 dead and wounded aboard the ships, and two of the British ships of the line so badly damaged that they had to be towed to Constantinople (now Istanbul), while other ships were also left battered. It began to dawn on the authorities that armoured warships were to be the future. The lesson was not lost on the young Fisher, even though he was safely far away from the action at Portsmouth.

Nevertheless, between 9 and 11 August 1855, an Anglo-French fleet did successfully bombard Sveaborg, a Baltic fortress. On 17 October, an Allied force of ten ships of the line and eighty other vessels hammered the weak fort of Kinburn at the entrance of Nikolaev harbour. Three of the ships were armoured and showed their superiority – but they were French!

SEASICKNESS AND STEAM

By this time Fisher was at sea for the first time, still as a cadet, in the 84-gun two-decker HMS *Calcutta*, having sailed from Plymouth in February. He struggled to find his sea legs, and at first was prone to frequent bouts of seasickness, which left an impression on him for life. Not for nothing did he describe the service as 'an impenetrable mystery surrounded by seasickness'. It did not help that the ship left port to encounter such fierce storms that after a week they were off the Isles of Scilly when they should have been making their way up the English Channel on passage to the Baltic.

His seasickness may well have been the reason for the limited record of his first experience at sea, but it could also be that his duties and the life of the gunroom kept him from his pen. He found time to learn to play the violin, motivated by the attention received in the wardroom by one of his peers who entertained the officers playing popular airs to buy one for himself and persuade a bandsman to give him lessons. He also found time for poetry, including one verse that combined his disdain for the age of sail and his memories of the cruelty of seasickness:

> Now sailors all take my advice
> Let steamships be your motta
> And never go to sea again
> In the sailing ship Calcutta

Whether or not action was expected with the Russians in the Baltic, the *Calcutta* was spared, and by autumn she was back at Plymouth. By the end of the year, *Calcutta* was paid off, but Fisher was not finished with sail as he was sent aboard the *Impregnable*, a second-rate ship of the line which was fifty years old and in terms of technology indistinguishable from *Victory*. Nevertheless, he was simply using the ship as a means of reaching his next appointment, aboard the modern steam screw *Agamemnon* with the Mediterranean Fleet. As with other naval and merchant vessels of the day, *Agamemnon* still had masts and sails, and the steam engines were regarded as auxiliary means of propulsion.

This was not simply a case of the Royal Navy being ultra-cautious. The range of coal-fired vessels was extremely short, and the continual re-coaling would take between eight and twelve hours. It made sense to extend the time a ship could spend at sea by using sail whenever the weather permitted. At this time, the network of coaling stations around the world, or around the British Empire, which was pretty much the same thing, was of course still being established.

The Royal Navy of the day consisted of a small but growing number of modern vessels and a substantial number of ships that would be extremely vulnerable when faced with a well-equipped opponent. It had reached this sorry state not simply because of technological advances – both in propulsion and armaments and hence in ship design and configuration – but because the driving necessity to modernise was missing, and the sole overriding factor for Britain's armed forces then, as now, to be kept up-to-date, had to be war or the threat of war.

By the time he reached the Mediterranean and joined the *Agamemnon*, the chance of seeing action had disappeared with the end of the Crimean War. *Agamemnon* was reduced to acting as a troop-ship, bringing soldiers from the Crimea. Even so, junior cadet Fisher continued to learn seamanship and was instilled with the very basic elements of gunnery. When he finally returned home to England in 1856, he was promoted to midshipman or, in naval terms, a 'snotty', and addressed as 'mister'.

The Mediterranean Fleet was one of the two largest elements in the Royal Navy, the other being what at different times was known as the First Fleet, the Grand Fleet, the Atlantic Fleet or the Home Fleet. The far flung strands of the service were the 'stations', including the North America Station, based in the West Indies, the South American Station, based on the Falklands, and the China Station, based on Hong Kong. At this time, the dominions had yet to create their own navies.

OFF TO THE FAR EAST

Mr Midshipman Fisher sailed for the Far East in July 1856, aboard the corvette *Highflyer*, under the command of Captain Charles Shadwell. War with Russia in 1854–1855 was ended. In 1856, the Treaty of Paris banned piracy and gave the maritime nations the right to pursue their trade on the high seas. At one and the same time, the Royal Navy had to be 'a surety for those proceeding upon their lawful occasions'. Now war with China had started and would last until 1860.

The Crimean War and the Second China War were very different conflicts. Nationalism and expansionisim had been behind the former, a reminder that even before Communism, Russia had been a nation determined upon territorial gain and on inflicting its attitudes on its neighbours. The latter was a trade war, with the Western nations anxious to develop the Chinese market, not simply in order to export the growing range and quantity of products spawned by the industrial revolution, but also to sell the Chinese opium, which paid for British imports from China, including porcelain, silk and most important of all, tea. British plans had run up against Chinese obstinacy, comprised of xenophobia and a sense of superiority over the 'white ghosts', but there was also a fear amongst some Chinese of the debilitating effects of opium on the population. There was also the question of the persecution of Christian missionaries, especially the French Roman Catholics. Similar attitudes to the West were to be found in nineteenth-century Japan, even though the Chinese and the Japanese were no friends.

The First Chinese War, 1839–1842, had been better known as the Opium War, and had been an earlier instance of the European powers trying to penetrate the vast Chinese market. Restrictions on trade with China were eased by the treaty of Nanking in 1842, with British merchants gaining five large ports, the so-called Treaty ports. Other European nations were also granted treaty ports in the years that followed. Nevertheless, Chinese suspicion of foreigners remained an obstacle, as did the demands of local warlords and the weakness of central government rule, as well as widespread corruption.

Freed from the demands of war with Russia, the British and French were able to return to the problems of their relationship with China. On the other hand, the Chinese were again in danger of border disputes with Russia, freed, in their turn from the demands of war with the British, French and the Turks.

While discontent and disputes had rumbled on for many years, the spark that ignited the Second Chinese War was the arrest of twelve Chinese seamen at Canton by Chinese officers from a ship flying the Union flag on charges of piracy. The resulting war lasted for almost four years.

Fortunately for Fisher, his new commanding officer was in complete contrast to those he had met aboard *Victory*. Shadwell was paternalistic, not sadistic, and Fisher gained in experience and accomplished many things, including learning how to handle a small boat in a gale. Shadwell would entertain the midshipmen to breakfast, and according to Fisher, treated seasickness with champagne and gingerbread nuts. Like his men, he slept in a hammock. It was his proud boast that he never had a man flogged in his life.

'I learnt from him nearly all that I know,' recalled Fisher in his *Records*. 'He taught me how to predict eclipses and occultations, and I suppose I took more lunar observations than any Midshipman ever did before.'

Later, in 1859, Shadwell had such faith in the young midshipman that he allowed him to keep lieutenant's watch at sea, but it was a faith that could so easily have been misplaced. On one occasion, Fisher nearly had some of the yards carried away when his ship got caught in a squall, such were the hazards and uncertainties of life under sail. Also unusual for a midshipman, not officially an officer, was his appointment as Shadwell's ADC.

Certainly, Fisher now learnt what it was like to be under fire and showed that he could face this with courage. These were not naval engagements as such, but what could be described as colonial police actions. They found themselves in the many creeks and rivers of the China coast looking for pirates, and coming under fire from pirate strongholds ashore. One such action had Fisher and others in small boats when they came under fire from pirates hiding in a banana plantation on the river bank.

'I remember I was armed to the teeth like a Greek brigand, all swords and pistols, and was weighed down with weapons,' wrote Fisher in his *Records*. 'We took shelter in the banana plantation, but our Captain stood on the river bank. I shall never forget it. He was dressed in a pair of white trousers, yellow waistcoat and a blue tail coat with brass buttons and a tall white hat with a white stripe up the side of it, and he was waving a white umbrella to encourage us to come out of the bananas and go for the enemy. He had no weapon of any sort. So (I rather think against our inclinations, as the gingall bullets were flying about pretty thick) we all had to come out and go for the Chinese.'

The apparently admirable Captain Shadwell was eventually posted back to England, but before departing he asked if there was anything he could do for Fisher, who asked if he could have a set of studs bearing the Shadwell family motto, *Loyal au mort*. He got them, and wore them every day for the next sixty years.

In fact, it seems that Fisher always painted a prettier picture of those whom he admired than they actually deserved. He did on one occasion write about Shadwell having two men flogged and another six being disrated, which apparently upset the CO for a full day afterwards. It does seem that the punishments were fully earned, as one of the men flogged had deserted from a boat commanded by Fisher, and when a party of marines was sent to capture him, he abused their commander, who knocked him down, denting his skull and stunning him. Shadwell told the marine commander that he should have cut the man down with his sword. Compared to that, perhaps 36 lashes was merciful.

THE PEIHO FORTS

For a young man, already having spent more than half his life away from his parents, and then having been taken from the kindly attentions of Lady Wilmot-Horton, life could be lonely. No doubt it was character forming. It was not as bleak as this may seem, however, for many of the wives of expatriate British residents provided a home-from-home for young cadets and midshipmen. In Fisher's case, his unofficial duty foster mother, called 'Mams' by Fisher, was Mrs Edmund Warden, wife of the Far East manager for the Peninsular & Oriental Steam Navigation Company, more usually known as the P&O.

The work was demanding, but there were spells of excitement. Spending their time in coastal waters also meant that the diet was better and more varied. Even so, in bad weather with heavy rain and high winds, not to mention high seas, the galley fire would be out for safety's sake. On one such occasion, Fisher's evening meal consisted of red herrings washed down with beer.

While Fisher's time in the Far East was punctuated by a string of minor skirmishes, a major action came on 25 June 1859, in the battle off the Peiho Forts. The previous year, treaties between the British, French and Americans on the one hand, and the Chinese on the other, had been agreed at Tientsin, with the intention of bringing the Second Opium War to a peaceful conclusion. On 20 June, envoys from the three western powers arrived at the estuary of the River Peiho intent on making their way to Peking to have the treaties ratified. Unknown to them, the Chinese had changed their minds and decided to reject the treaties. Aware that the passage up the Peiho to Tientsin, where the envoys would disembark before travelling overland to Peking, had been hazardous in the past, a substantial Anglo-French naval squadron had been assembled, with modern ships and armament, prepared to force a passage if it proved necessary. The force assembled early, and the crews of the warships found themselves employed in preparations for war, including assembling scaling ladders.

On arrival, it was discovered that the Chinese were indeed prepared to repel the foreigners. There was not one but three booms, or obstructions, behind which were some well-designed forts. The first obstruction consisted of iron piles, and was followed by one of heavy spars of wood, cross-lashed, moored before and aft, behind which was a third obstruction consisting of large timber baulks, tied together and cross-lashed, with iron links, altogether being 120 feet wide and 3 feet deep, made in two overlapping pieces.

The Chinese were asked to remove the booms and allow the envoys to proceed up river to Tientsin, but the requests were ignored. On 24 June, the British commander of the naval squadron, Rear Admiral Sir James Hope, decided to force a way through the booms and capture the forts. He selected nine small gunboats, each of 250 tons, and two larger vessels, dividing this force into two, with Shadwell being in command of the right hand force, amongst which was the gunboat *Banterer*, commanded by Lieutenant John Jenkins, with Midshipman Fisher aboard. The rationale behind this scheme was that a small gunboat could get through a gap in the third boom, although against the current and under Chinese fire from the forts, it would be a hazardous operation.

At 14.00 on 25 June, the attack began. A gunboat pulled up the first boom, allowing others past it to the second boom. At this point, heavy and accurate fire erupted from the forts, which it transpired had forty guns between them.

Hope had joined his light forces in the gun vessel *Cormorant*, and gave orders to engage. The resulting exchange of fire lasted for five hours, but the balance of force was on the side of the Chinese, well-prepared and safely ensconced in heavy fortifications against which the naval fire could make little impression. The small gunboats were vulnerable in the extreme, all the more so once some of them became stuck in the mudbanks at the side of the river, and even the Admiral was wounded.

The fighting was carried by the small force deployed by Hope, as the French lacked craft small enough for the engagement, and the Americans were officially neutral. Nevertheless, one American, Commodore Josiah Tattnall, decided to do something, and was rowed upstream in a cutter to the *Cormorant*, where he found Hope in his cabin lying wounded with a massive injury in his thigh. The crew of his cutter then took over, helping the British sailors manning the guns, unknown to Tattnall below. The Americans then helped to evacuate the British wounded.

Despite the way in which the action was going, at 19.00 Shadwell ordered the assault party of 350 marines and sailors ashore, towed upstream by small steamboats, including, according to one account, Tattnall's. Once ashore, the men found themselves attempting to advance under heavy fire over thick river mud amidst sharp stakes. Men fell under the heavy fire, and some who fell or simply slipped suffocated in the glutinous mud. Shadwell was amongst those wounded, and was evacuated to his ship by Fisher, who had not had an easy time of it.

> I had to fling all my arms away coming back from the forts and was nearly smothered once, only one of our bluejackets was kind enough to haul me out. You sank up to your knees at least every step, and just fancy the slaughter going 500 yards in the face of that fire … right in front of you and on each flank … They had horrid fire-balls firing at us when we landed. I saw one poor fellow with his eye and part of his face burnt right out. If a piece struck you, it stuck to you and regularly burnt you away till it was all gone.[5]

It was to Fisher's credit that while he would often recall the struggle in the Peiho mud, he would seldom mention his part in saving Shadwell. There were other horrors as well, especially for a young man of eighteen years, with the corpses of the fallen aboard his gunboat being thrown overboard to clear the deck space. He saw men dying in agony, and the next day witnessed the medieval horror of the heads of the dead stuck on the walls of the Peiho forts. Half the 1,100 men aboard the gunboats and in the landing party had been killed or wounded.

ROUGH SURGERY AND SMOOTH PATRONAGE

Shadwell had been badly wounded in his foot, and suffered considerable pain. He failed to recover and in October, a retired surgeon examined the wound and advised cutting into it in two places, but deeper than before. Early one morning they gave the unfortunate CO a heavy dose of chloroform and cut the foot right across the bottom and then right down the middle, in each case reaching the bone. The operation completed, the foot bandaged and the chloroform worn off and Shadwell was recovering when the main artery to the foot ruptured and the cabin was filled with blood. They had to remove the bandages and make a further cut to reach the artery, but with no time for chloroform.

'Well, Fisher,' Shadwell remarked later. 'I am afraid I made a great deal of noise this morning.'

After this crude treatment, Shadwell's foot began to improve, and it seemed almost healed by November, but it worsened again by Christmas. At Hong Kong, a Rear Admiral came aboard and told Shadwell to give up his command and sail home in January. The move was seen at the time as one of simple recognition that an officer with a severe wound needed to be sent home for treatment, but unknown to those present until some time later, there had been considerable criticism in the press back in the UK of the failure to seize the Peiho forts. While Hope inevitably had been the target of some of the criticism, the main culprit was seen as the unfortunate Shadwell, and this may have been a factor in his being relieved of his command. Not until the newspapers arrived in Hong Kong, several months old, did this become known to the other officers and midshipmen. This was an early lesson for Fisher regarding the power of the press, and it was not lost on him in later life.

It was typical of Shadwell that he arranged his departure to the benefit of his officers. He dined the midshipmen in his cabin, and they returned the compliment, leading to resentment amongst the members of the wardroom who, of course, ought to have done this. One Christmas Eve, he divided his store of essential toiletries and personal items amongst the midshipmen, and Fisher, in addition to gaining the engraved studs, gained all of Shadwell's books, all leather bound.

For Shadwell, his departure was sweetened by the promise of a ship of the line once he had recovered, and he promised Fisher that he would join him then. Fisher had feared that with the departure of his patron, his fortunes would dwindle and he would be just another midshipmen to Shadwell's successor, but before he left, Shadwell was asked by Hope if he could do anything for him, and was told: 'Take care of that boy.'

Unknown to Fisher, Hope believed that favouritism, or patronage at least, was the secret of efficiency. Fisher was ordered to the flagship, HMS *Chesapeake*, and so began a long and successful association with the Rear Admiral. Once again, Fisher had landed firmly on his feet, and what was originally perceived as being a reversal was quite the opposite.

On his nineteenth birthday, 25 January 1860, Fisher took his examinations for the rank of mate, equivalent to a sub-lieutenant in today's Royal Navy. He had to appear before three captains, and was closely questioned over three days, but Fisher sailed through with flying colours gaining a first-class certificate. Shortly afterwards, the senior post captain on the station told Fisher that he would be 'mentioned to the admiral', and so he was. Hope sent for Fisher and told him that he was very pleased that the young man had passed the examination, so well and because of it, and Shadwell's recommendation, he would become his flag mate, with the promise that he could be assured of his support and patronage. The Admiral was 51 years of age, but at the time officers served long past what would now be considered retirement age – if they survived, of course. Even a rear admiral could also fall prey to the other curse of the Royal Navy at the time, not having an appointment open to him and so being put 'on the beach' on half pay.

It was certainly the case that Fisher impressed those around him, even though they could not overlook his youth. He was shrewd beyond his years, resourceful and industrious, and always first to volunteer, indeed, he never gave his peers a chance. He soon had the same comfortable relationship with Hope that he had enjoyed with Shadwell. This was no small achievement as Hope had a far fiercer reputation than the captain, and the manner in which he conducted himself was not lost on the ambitious Fisher.

'A great man, very stern and stately, the sort of man everybody was afraid of,' was Fisher's description of Hope in later years. 'His nickname was composed of the three ships he had commanded: "Terrible … Firebrand … Majestic".'

'I went all round Hong Kong the day before yesterday with the Admiral in his yacht,' he wrote to Mrs Warden. 'He is an awful old proud fellow, but he is very kind at the same time. Post-captains have to

 Nevertheless, Fisher also had to do his share of running after the Admiral:

> I have nothing to do with anyone in the ship except the Admiral himself, and no mistake, he keeps me going … I have to call him at 5 am, be in his cabin dressed by 7 am, ready to receive orders as to what the different ships are to do. At 8 o'clock I take him a load of papers, which takes me two hours of the previous evening to make out, and follow him like a dog whenever he leaves his cabin. It is very jolly in one way. I can give some of these lieutenants a good snubbing sometimes. They dare not say anything to me, because the Admiral has given strict orders that no one is to interfere with his staff on any pretence what-sum-dever.[7]

Even on what appeared to be a social outing, on 7 February 1860, when they went sailing and went ashore some six miles from their flagship, the Admiral invited Fisher to walk back with him:

> He kept me at almost a run the whole way, he has got such awful long legs. You would never think, to see him walking, that he had a hole in his thigh you could shove both fists into. I had an awful long confab with him and he finished up very jolly. He asked me to dinner. They are very jealous of me on board because I have got into such a good berth.[8]

The favouritism continued, and did cause jealousy not just amongst Fisher's peers but also those who would otherwise have been his immediate superiors. It is clear that in the Victorian Navy, advancement could be rapid and on the whim of a supportive senior officer. Just four days after the outing, Fisher was told by Hope that he had a blank commission to give away, and that he had intended to give it to Fisher. Nevertheless, he had just learnt of a mate who on his way out to the station had jumped overboard to save a man even though the ship was going at 10 knots. Hope wished to recognise the man's bravery, and he was someone who had been a mate for a very long time, so he gave the lieutenant's commission to him. In a letter to Mrs Warden, by this time back in England, Fisher claimed not to begrudge the award as the other man deserved it more than he did. The extraordinary irony was that later, the man in question was to become Admiral of the Fleet Sir Edward Seymour, and one of Fisher's strongest opponents.

CORRESPONDENCE AND LIEUTENANCY

Fisher's correspondence says much about his relationships. He wrote to Ceylon rarely and seems to have written very little to his benefactress, Lady Wilmot-Horden, and never to his uncle back in England, as far as we can see. Nevertheless, even after she returned to England, Mrs Warden received a regular correspondence from her young protégé, although she seems to have been somewhat tardy in replying. He had not seen his mother since he was six, and when at the age of nineteen he was sent a picture, which arrived broken into three pieces, he could hardly recognise her.

On 24 March, Fisher was finally offered the rank of lieutenant, aboard the *Esk*, a ship similar to his previous berth the *Highflyer*, but when it became apparent that the *Esk* would not be taking part in the fighting that appeared to be imminent, he turned it down. It was the right thing to do, gaining Hope's approval while at the same time allowing Fisher to remain close to the Admiral. Nor did he lose much salary or seniority (always based on the date of a promotion) as a result, for he was promoted to Lieutenant on 28 March.

Fisher was thrown in at the deep end in his new rank. He was given command of the *Coromandel* for four days, taking the ship to Canton and then returning. He then joined HMS *Pearl* to take passage to join Sir W.A. Bruce aboard the *Furious* as his naval ADC, but he had to take his share of the duties on the way. On his first night as officer of the watch, some of the ship's sails blew away in a gale.

His arrival aboard *Furious* was an abrupt fall to earth. The ship itself was ancient, a 'horrid old tub' in Fisher's words, and her commanding officer, Captain Oliver Jones, was stern and unyielding. Fisher reported that there had been one mutiny aboard the ship already and that all of the lieutenants were young and still to be confirmed in their rank, a ploy by Jones to ensure that they all were beholden to him to retain their commissions. Fisher recalled in later years:

> He was Satanic … Yet I … liked him, for, like Satan, he could disguise himself as an angel; and I believe I was the only officer he did not

put under arrest. For some reason I got on with him, and he made me the navigating officer of the ship. He told me when I first came on board that he thought he had committed every crime under the sun except murder. I think he committed that crime while I was with him. He was a most fascinating man. He had such a charm, he was most accomplished, he was a splendid rider, a wonderful linguist, an expert navigator and a thorough seaman. He had the best cook, and the best wines ever afloat in the Navy, and was hospitable to an extreme. Almost daily he had a lot of us to dinner, but after dinner came hell! We dined with him in tail coat and epaulettes. After dinner he had sail drill, or preparing the ship for battle, and persecution then did its utmost.[9]

Fisher gained much experience aboard the ship, which was trapped in ice during the winter, and then took him – via a desert island, where he was landed to conduct a survey – back to England. The ship was given the honour of conveying gifts from the Mikado to Queen Victoria, the voyage taking six months. After an absence of five years, Fisher was grateful to be on his way home to Portsmouth.

Furious arrived at Portsmouth on 20 August 1861. His rigid commanding officer unbent enough to give the still young man a glowing report: 'As a sailor, an officer, a navigator and a gentleman, I cannot praise him too highly.'

Notes

1 Kilverstone, Admiral of the Fleet Baron, *Memories*, London, 1919
2 Ibid
3 Bacon, Admiral Sir R.H., *The Life of Lord Fisher of Kilverstone*, London, 1929
4 Kilverstone, Admiral of the Fleet Baron, *Records*, London, 1919
5 Kilverstone, Admiral of the Fleet Baron, *Memories*, London, 1919
6 Kilverstone, Admiral of the Fleet Baron, *Records*, London, 1919
7 Ibid
8 Ibid
9 Ibid

Fighting the Colonial Wars

If you are a gunnery man, you must believe and teach that the world must be saved by gunnery, and will only be saved by gunnery. If you are a torpedo man, you must lecture and teach the same thing about torpedoes. But be in earnest. The man who doubts or who is half-hearted, never does anything...
Fisher, 1872.

Fisher may well have needed the confidence that was implied in Captain Jones' report. He had still to be confirmed in the rank of lieutenant and was immediately sent to the old hulk HMS *Excellent* at Portsmouth. He crammed mathematics and gunnery ready for his examination, having only been examined in seamanship while on the China Station.

Fisher's enthusiasm was undiminished and not only did he pass out with first-class certificates in both subjects, but with the highest marks in mathematics that year, for which he was awarded the prestigious annual Beaufort Testimonial, awarded in memory of Admiral Sir Frederick Beaufort, the famous hydrographer. A more practical award was that his commission was back-dated twelve months, which ensured his future seniority and would be valuable in the future, followed by being appointed gunnery staff officer aboard *Excellent* in January 1862.

It seemed as if Fisher could do no wrong. Perhaps he couldn't, but officialdom had prepared a nasty surprise. Clearly their lordships at the Admiralty had woken up to the fact that the long period of peace was leading to a slipping of standards. The order went out that every lieutenant had to undergo a six-month course in gunnery at the Royal Naval College, and until he had passed that, he would be classified as a third-class gunnery officer. The marks gained in the qualifying exam would determine future pay.

'This did not suit Fisher, for there was nothing third-class about him,' wrote Admiral Bacon. 'He set to work daily after his duties were done, and devoted the evenings to study. In due course, he applied for a special examination, which was granted; he then obtained a first-class certificate, and became a first-class gunnery lieutenant.'[1]

The award for this was substantial, an extra 3s 6d daily, equivalent to £9 today. Though it looks little enough, this was important, as many of his peers had private means, or at least the support of generous parents who were comfortably off. Fisher, by contrast, while still in China had received a further letter from his father in which he once again pleaded poverty, claiming to have been intending to send some money for some time, and eventually managing to send him £10. Again, the other children were the excuse, although he also admitted to bad crops from his estates, but in fact Fisher's father was chronically improvident. Fisher's success in his exams prompted a further letter, dated 14 January 1862, congratulating him and telling him that 'you will continue to prosper' – which seems like a subtle hint not to expect anything further!

Fisher senior had suffered several bad seasons with his coffee crops, but had managed to continue producing a regular crop of babies. One after another, those who survived infancy were sent away, home to England. Fisher had two sisters, Alice and Lucy; two brothers, Arthur and Frank, who became colonial civil servants, finding their way back to Ceylon; while another two brothers, Philip and Frederick, joined the Royal Navy. William Fisher's constant claims that his brood were straining his finances need to be viewed in this light. Once Alice married, she was sent the youngest brother, just four years old, to care for. The one saving grace was that Sophie showed that she had an exceptional business brain, and but for her intervention, it is likely that the family finances would have been even worse. William wanted to send Sophie herself home, but she refused and did not return to England until after William's untimely death in 1866, when he fell from a horse.

Meanwhile, their eldest son continued to train himself. Conscious of his relative youth, he practised comportment and composure. He took walks across Portsdown Hill, where he could be heard shouting orders to an imaginary crew, exercising his voice so that it would have carrying power in a strong wind and authority. Bacon later wrote he was

… rather a terrifying examiner in practical gunnery … He used to stare at his victims without any expression on his face, and only by the movements of the pencil could it be guessed that dots and crosses were being registered with a consequent loss of numbers.

Whenever during a conversation he was analysing or digesting a remark, his lips parted slightly and his face assumed an expression of complete vacuity, which was most disconcerting for anyone who wished to gather information as to how the remarked was affecting him.[2]

HOME, TRAVEL, AND A PLUM POSTING

Back in England, he was able to take friends to visit Lady Wilmot-Horton at Catton Hall and also use her house in Mayfair at weekends. She may have been an indifferent correspondent, but she still afforded him an affectionate welcome now that he was back. Better still, he was able to acquaint himself with three of his brothers, Arthur, Frank and Frederic, two of whom had been born after he left Ceylon, as once again Lady Wilmot-Horton proved herself a friend in need to the Fisher family, taking in the young Fisher males.

At a time when only a select few travelled abroad other than in the service of the crown or one of the great trading companies, Fisher also managed to visit France. He liked Paris, but was not over-impressed with the French. Writing to his aunt:

> I am very much pleased with Paris. But I am exceedingly glad that I am not a Frenchman. From the highest to the lowest they are the most dirty, immoral people I have ever seen. My friend with whom I am staying is a nephew of Marshal Baillaut who is at the head of the emperor's household so I see lots of things which I should not if I had been staying with someone else. I went the night before last to see some grand theatricals (amateur). The actors were all 'bigwigs', two princesses, a marchioness and counts no end ...

It was clear that Fisher was able to work hard and play hard. *Excellent* always had a legendary reputation as a demanding position, whether as a member of the staff or as a student, whether afloat in the old hulk or ashore as in the twentieth century. Even here, Fisher pleased his superiors. When the lords of the admiralty paid their annual visit, a powder boy overheard one of the naval lords, as the service members of the Board of Admiralty were known at the time, ask another whether Lieutenant Fisher was as good a seaman as he was a gunnery man. Never backward, Fisher stepped up, introducing himself: 'My Lords, I am Lieutenant Fisher, just as good a seaman as a gunnery man.'[3]

Very few young officers with the still junior rank of lieutenant would be known to the naval, or sea, lords even today, in a far smaller navy and with far better communications than was the case when Fisher held the rank. Fisher was undoubtedly a hard taskmaster who drove himself even harder than he drove others, but there is always the feeling that he usually happened to be in the right place at the right time. Was it simply chance, or was his presence aboard *Excellent* a reflection of his outstanding success in his examinations? Whether it was because of his position aboard the hulk or his name being known in high places, his next appointment was one that every gunnery officer in the Royal Navy would have died for (some did).

The latest warship was the frigate HMS *Warrior*, the pride of the Royal Navy and the most advanced vessel in the fleet. In March 1863, Fisher became her gunnery lieutenant. The lessons of the Crimea had resulted in many wooden ships being built with a covering of iron, the appropriately-named 'ironclads', the first being the French *Gloire* of 1858, as mentioned earlier. The Royal Navy went one better, and *Warrior* was built with an iron hull. Her steam engines enabled her to overtake any other warship, with a maximum speed of 14 knots, and she could also sail impressively using her three masts. In one sense, she did follow tradition, with her guns spread along the sides – but what guns! She had twenty-six 68-pounders, four 70-pounders and ten 110-pounders, amongst the first breech-loaders in the Royal Navy. She was the first of a class, albeit of just two ships, with a sister, *Black Prince*. Both could destroy even the largest of the old wooden walls, ships of the line. In their day, these two ships were as big an innovation as the future HMS *Dreadnought* was to be, and no doubt had a considerable influence on Fisher's thinking.

Fisher's tenure as gunnery lieutenant aboard *Warrior* was a long one, at three-and-half years. He had substantial delegated authority over those below him, and a free hand to make changes, in part because this was a new type of ship with a different armament. It was here that his radical ideas not only to began take shape, but also to be implemented.

His watchword was always efficiency. He had seen enough of other officers by this time to have become his own role model. He established himself as a firm disciplinarian, but never forgot how to win the friendship of the others in the wardroom. He became an excellent conversationalist and could be playful if the opportunity arose.

His attitudes were matched by those of his superiors, like him hand-picked men with fine reputations. The commanding officer was Captain the Hon. Arthur Cochrane and the commander was George Tryon. As often happens, the well disciplined lower deck had a reputation for being exceptionally boisterous once ashore. On one occasion, Fisher recalled, they all enjoyed too much beer at a reception hosted by the mayor of Liverpool, and the only way he could get them back to the ship was to order them to link arms and march in sections of four to conceal their unstable condition. He was somewhat bemused, but no doubt highly relieved, to be congratulated for their magnificent marching!

Fisher was treated as the baby of the wardroom. This was due in part to it containing a number of mature officers, including Paymaster John de Vries, 'grey-headed', Surgeon Samuel Wells, a 'mature doctor', and Chaplain the Rev Robert Jackson, 'still more mature'. Belying their age, with the help of a number of younger officers they devised their own ship's band. The chaplain played the coal scuttle, the surgeon the tongs and shovel, and the paymaster used the kettle as the cymbals. The younger officers made do with brown paper instruments. They marched through the officers' accommodation playing. Captain Cochrane opened his door and demanded of the sentry what the noise was, and received the reply that it was 'Mr Fisher, Sir!' The CO shut the door. Commander Tryon was less sympathetic, sending a messenger to Fisher to stop the fooling.

Stern disciplinarian Fisher may have been, but his men supported him, and enjoyed being part of an efficient team. *Warrior's* gun drills became a model of speed and accuracy. There was no need for the old gunnery officer's time honoured report of 'Many valuable lessons learnt – no hits!' Fisher was seen by them as a 'character'.

Fisher gained no special favours. Like all members of the crew of a warship at the time, with the exception of the commanding officer and commander, Fisher had to play his part in the messy, tedious business of coaling.

PUBLIC RELATIONS

There must have been many opportunities for a good 'run ashore'. The Admiralty was keen for their pride and joy to be seen as often as possible and in as many places as possible. This did make strategic sense as well, since raising awareness of the potential of a new weapons system was bound to act as a deterrent. It must also have played its part in promoting the shipbuilding industry and the cannon foundries. Early in 1864, she was to be found at Madeira, Lisbon, Gibraltar and Teneriffe, before being ordered home as war loomed, following Prussian threats to the tiny and feeble state of Schleswig-Holstein.

The visit to Lisbon had taken place in March, where *Warrior* was inspected by Admiral Sir Michael Seymour, a demanding and critical officer. Impressed, Seymour told Fisher that he had hardly ever seen a ship in such 'splendid gunnery-order [and that he would] bring it to the attention of the Admiralty.' He was true to his word, and on their return to Portsmouth, a letter of congratulation was awaiting Fisher from the Admiralty. This was a rare honour and once again Fisher was separated out from the crowd.

The following month, the threat to Schleswig-Holstein over, the fleet was at Weymouth, where Giuseppe Garibaldi was a guest and was able to inspect the new ship. Fisher wrote to his Aunt Kate:

We went to general quarters and commenced firing away like fun and went through all sorts of different evolutions with the guns ... First we supposed the enemy on one bow and then on the other; in fact, the enemy was everywhere in the course of ten minutes. The men worked the guns splendidly. I never saw them move quicker before. Garibaldi turned round to me and said he was 'very much pleased indeed,' and he afterwards said it was almost the finest thing he had seen in England.

Before leaving the ship, he told the ship's company that he had 'seen one of the things [he] had set his heart on seeing, and that was the *Warrior.*' I had a good look at him for the Admiral made me go round with him everywhere to explain things he wanted to know about the guns, etc. I thought him looking very worn and done up. I don't wonder a bit about people being so enthusiastic about him, for he has such a noble face and at the same time such a simple manner ...[4]

Exceptional efforts were also made to ensure that the British public also saw the ship. This was before the 'Navy days' at which the public was admitted to naval bases to see the ships, although Royal Reviews were far more common than today and annual exercises were held around the coast. *Warrior* visited not just naval bases, but other ports and anchorages around the coast. On visiting Sunderland, Fisher was surprised to find that 14,000 people had come aboard during just one day. The local authorities and prominent individuals laid on balls and dinners to celebrate the visits. A visit to Leith gave Fisher the opportunity to renew his acquaintanceship with Sir James Hope, who lived twenty miles away near Linlithgow. Hope pressed him to stay for a few days rather than simply visit, but *Warrior* was off to Orkney and then to the north of Ireland to Loch Swilly.

MARRIAGE AND PARTING

This round of public 'engagments' was a rare glimpse of everyday life for the ambitious young officer, a reminder there was more to life than the Navy. The round of visits to ports at home and abroad meant that his ship occasionally returned to her home port of Portsmouth. On one such visit, Fisher encountered Katharine Broughton, the daughter of the Rector of Bletchley in Buckinghamshire, visiting the town with her mother to see her brothers, who were also naval officers. A few months older than Fisher, and able to trace her ancestry back to the Plantagenets, she was undoubtedly a catch. Fisher was charmed by the pretty, dark-haired young woman. He had learned from his father's improvidence and had accumulated savings so that he could afford to marry and to set up home. He proposed, and they married on 4 April 1866. The marriage was to last for fifty-two years, until her death.

Given the demands of the Royal Navy at the time, they could so easily have married and then see Fisher transferred to the China Station for another five-year spell. It was a happy coincidence that his next appointment was ashore at Portsmouth as First Lieutenant of *Excellent* for three years. A furnished house was rented in Portsmouth, and their first two children, Cecil and Beatrix, were born. As First Lieutenant, Fisher was responsible for discipline and administration, but he was also expected to be one of the ship's instructors. Not for the last time, some of those whom he instructed were to reach the highest levels of the service. One of these was later First Sea Lord and Admiral of the Fleet Sir Knyvet Wilson, who recalled Fisher's lectures:

> The main feature was a narrative of the cunning devices he used in order to get the Commander to detail men for gunnery drills instead of employing them in cleaning, painting and polishing the ship. His method, which was highly entertaining as recounted, consisted chiefly in the artful use of judicious flattery, at which he was a past master.[5]

Just as the new ship *Warrior* with its advanced technology had given Fisher a lead over many of his peers, he was also in the right place at the right time when the torpedo was developed into an effective form of armament, as discussed in Chapter One, and he was an early champion of the weapon. As early as 1868, while Whitehead was still working on the device, Fisher published *A Short Treatise on Electricity and the Management of Torpedoes*. He declared that the torpedo was destined to play an important part in naval warfare, giving as his reasons:

> I. Ships as at present constructed are powerless against its attacks, supposing them to get within its destructive area …
> II. The demoralising effect on men from the constant dread of sudden destruction …

This was far-sighted. The ships of the day used their guns as the sole means of attacking other ships, unless one could get close enough for rifle fire from the rigging and to put a boarding party aboard. Nevertheless, the torpedo was still far from a potent weapon at the time, with a speed of six knots and a range of around 300 yards, so it took confidence to support the new weapon and look ahead to a more potent and reliable form. His support for the weapon did no harm, with Fisher being given full responsibility for the torpedo instruction at *Excellent* for his final six months aboard the ship. He hoped next to go to the Admiralty in London, where he could still enjoy domestic bliss, either by moving his wife and young family to the capital, or by travelling home at weekends on the still new Portsmouth 'Direct' route of the London & South Western Railway. In fact, he planned to move to Long Ditton and stay with his younger brother Alfred. He was to be disappointed as he was posted back to the China Station. This was an odd decision by the Admiralty. It was an obvious advantage that he knew China and indeed the wider Far East, but a young officer whose star was in the ascendant might have gained wider experience by being sent elsewhere; to the Mediterranean, or to the North or South American stations, for example.

It was a wrench for both Fisher and Kitty, being parted. He also bemoaned the fact that missing out on an appointment at the Admiralty denied him 'a great lift in the service as one gets to know all the bigwigs so intimately'. Nevertheless, he did come to accept it was the case that he had been 'most extraordinarily lucky so far in everything, so I must expect a disappointment now and then.'

The move to the China Station was not without its compensations. He had been promoted to commander and was aboard HMS *Ocean*, an ironclad. This raises the question why, with experience of *Warrior* and *Black Prince*, was the Royal Navy ordering and commissioning iron-clads? In fact, the ship had been laid down as a wooden two-decker and converted to an ironclad while on the slipway, with almost 2,000 tons of iron plate attached to her sides and the upper deck, all of which adversely affected her stability. Such ships were especially vulnerable in bad weather, and in 1871, another ironclad, *Captain*, capsized in a storm with just eighteen survivors.

CAMPAIGNS (PERSONAL)

Having established a reputation as someone who was not afraid to let his thoughts be known through his *Short Treatise*, Fisher embarked on a campaign to ensure that while he may have been out of sight of influ-ential senior officers, he was not out of mind. He started writing letters to senior officers, mainly at the Admiralty, but not overlooking others elsewhere. This was a risky strategy that could have backfired. He wrote to his former commanding officer, Captain Henry Boys:

> The great failing of the *Excellent* is an aversion to change. I mean large changes. She has seldom led the way, and this is but natural. Everyone on board has so much to do that (unless they are enthusiasts) they only have time to keep up with their work, whereas at Woolwich, at Shoebury, and at Chatham the Staff and the permanent committees which are always sitting at those places are so large that they never fail to remind me of the Athenians and strangers who spent their time in nothing else but either to tell or hear some new thing.[6]

He continued, complaining about the Admiralty's dependence on the War Office for 'almost any species of warlike store, from a 35-ton gun down to a boarding pike and a common shovel'. He had a point. When one cavalry colonel was told that a ship had her main yard 'carried away', he ordered that whoever had taken it should return it forthwith! Fortunately, as with all of his superiors, his relationship with Captain Boys was such that the newly-promoted commander could be frank, and the humour did not do any harm either.

In addition to correspondence, Fisher had pamphlets privately printed, no doubt so that he could distribute these widely. After all, laboriously hand-writing letters, which also needed to be copied, was no easy matter, especially since all had to be done after a hard day as what would now be described as *Ocean's* executive officer. One such pamphlet was entitled *Naval Tactics*, and called for a complete reconstitution of the Royal Navy, from top to bottom, in both personnel and equipment, and abandonment of the tactics favoured in Nelson's day. Again, he had a point. This was written in 1871, but for the rest of the century, and beyond, naval officers would still hark back to Nelson. This was one result of the prolonged peace on the seas. Technological change was taking place, often disliked by officers who, very often, regarded their engineer colleagues as an inferior species; and it was *untried* technological change. There was also an *Addenda* to his original pamphlet on torpedoes, for he continued to experiment.

Modesty was not, and never was, part of the Fisher make-up. He did not hesitate, when an admiral showed him the courtesy of writing a complimentary letter, to copy it and forward the copy to Kitty, writing that she could show it to others if she liked, 'unless you think it is too flattering.' He was also considering sending a copy to Tryon, who was by this time the private secretary to the First Lord, in the belief that it would do him further good. In his vanity, he assumed that a busy private secretary would wave the copied letter in front of his master.

Once again he courted and received the benefits of favouritism, endangering his relationship with his commanding officer by getting into the good books and the confidences of Vice-Admiral Sir Henry Kellet. Nevertheless, in the end, he once again deflected the jealousy of his peers and his immediate superior.

September 1871 marked the end of his second stint in the Far East, but homecoming was at a painfully slow 4½ knots, and the voyage from

Singapore to Plymouth took 164 days. *Ocean* was in need of a refit, but no doubt the calls at Zanzibar, Cape Town and Sierra Leone added to the time. The voyage was not uneventful, even if tedious, because the ship encountered a typhoon off Madagascar. The ship was soon rolling forty degrees each way, which was bad enough, but the weight of the iron plating soon started to pull the sides away from the deck. Two large boats were washed away, although this was commonplace on what was essentially a sailing ship and not unknown in more recent times. Fisher's own quarters on the main deck were flooded, leaving him up to his waist at one time, and he lost two uniform caps overboard as well as a silver ring, which in a letter to Kitty describing the storm, he told her 'was to have been yours when we had been married 25 years!' Not that Fisher spent much time in his cabin, recounting with great satisfaction that the ship at one stage rolled to 41 degrees on one side when he 'was up in the foretop … helping to furl the fore-topsail and it was as much as I could do to hold on …'[7]

BACK TO *EXCELLENT*

The joy of homecoming was clouded by his future prospects. His great desire was promotion to captain, ideally post-captain, but he reflected gloomily that this was unlikely for another five or six years at the current rate. He seems to have had some choice in the matter, but many were surprised when he accepted the posting to *Excellent* as her commander, as this seemed a backward step and an unexciting backwater. Certainly, even today the author has noted that naval officers are often distinctly unenthused by a move from operations to a training post. Fisher's attitude was different, however, as he saw the potential for gaining an outstanding reputation as a torpedo expert. He was not alone in realising the potential of the new weapon, as the Royal Navy had established a torpedo school, HMS *Vernon*, at Portsmouth, which was attached to the *Excellent*. In any case, he wrote assuring his wife that he 'was not going to do anything which takes me off the main line of the profession'.

In fact, one again, fate and fortune were on Fisher's side. Given that the torpedo was a new weapon, the officers passing through the courses he devised and ran at *Vernon* ranged from lieutenants at the start of their careers to post-captains, and he treated them all as if they were midshipmen, returning the more senior some decades back in their service to pulling oars and handling cables. A passion for the Old Testament manifested itself, and a lecture on the Daniell electric cell was prefaced by a picture of Daniel in the lion's den.

Little of this went unnoticed. Once again, Fisher was the man on the spot when members of the Board of Admiralty deigned to pay a visit. The First Lord of the Admiralty, its political boss, visited HMS *Vernon* on 3 October 1873, accompanied by the First and Second Naval Lords (the Second Naval Lord then, as with the Second Sea Lord now, was the member responsible for personnel). The Second Naval Lord, Vice-Admiral Sir Walter Tarleton, noted in his diary that evening:

> Had a most interesting lecture from Commander Fisher, a promising young officer, and witnessed several experiments. The result of my observations was that in my opinion the Torpedo has a great future before it and that mechanical training will in the near future be essential for officers. Made a note to speak to Goschen about young Fisher.'[8]

Goschen was Sir George Goschen, First Naval Lord.

For Fisher the predicted long wait of five or six years for promotion was not to be; for in October 1874, at just 33 years old, he was promoted to captain. Nevertheless, he remained at *Excellent* for almost two more years, until September 1876. He then suffered the uncomfortable experience of spending a short period on half-pay, the curse of peacetime naval officers until the late 1930s.

He was not 'laid up' for long. He was sent on a special assignment to the Mediterranean, where he had not been since his time as a cadet, and then only briefly. This was important, and not just because the Mediterranean Fleet had become one of the most important postings since the opening of the Suez Canal had turned the 'middle sea' into an important trade route, after spending almost three hundred years as a back water following the great Christian victory at the Battle of Lepanto. It was here that a major gap in his experience so far was rectified; he was able to gain experience in fleet sailing. Renewed fighting between Turkey and Russia seemed likely at the time, and he was called upon to share his experience with torpedoes. Vice-Admiral Sir James Drummon, commander-in-chief of the Mediterranean Fleet, also sought his advice on the defence of Malta's famous Grand Harbour, should war break out.

FLAG CAPTAIN

This was followed by a spell as flag captain to Admiral Sir Astley Cooper-Key on the North American Station aboard HMS *Bellerephon*, 'Old Billy', 7,500 tons and fitted with some of the largest guns in the Royal Navy. The two men were no strangers as Cooper-Key had been commanding officer at *Excellent* during Fisher's first spell there, and were close friends. Once again there was an element of favouritism, but the lessons were not to be lost on Fisher, and in later years he was to acquire his own string of favourites, men whose progress he watched and who, while not necessarily working under him, belonged to what became known in the service as 'The Fishpond'. They were to include such prominent figures as Jellicoe.

Flag captain gave him command of a ship, but it was one on which a flag officer, an officer of the rank of rear admiral or above, was present. It meant therefore that the commanding officer was very much at his superior's beck and call. It lacked the status of an independent command, but also gave an able officer the chance to impress one very much his superior. Fisher's reputation preceded him, and those aboard *Bellerephon* were apprehensive. As one midshipman noted:

> The state of the ship was undoubtedly slack. Captain Fisher was not long in letting his opinion be known. He fell the officers and crew in on the quarter-deck; and having told them what he thought of the want of smartness and efficiency, said: 'Now I intend to give you "hell" for three months, and if you have not come up to my standard in that time you'll have "hell" for another three months.'
>
> He was as good as his word. We had drills and exercises all the time ... and in three months the ship was as smart as any in the service. Then the captain, with characteristic energy and versatility, threw himself heart and soul into the amusements of the officers and men.[9]

In his amusements, Fisher was as demanding as in his duty. He would take a couple of midshipmen with him who had to dance with him if no female partner matched his high standards. He would even cancel leave if one of his officers would not dance. He enjoyed the rhythm and the music, the exercise, and the chance to be with women. At Halifax, the North American Station's main base, he would often dance with Cooper-Key's daughter, whistling 'if no better orchestra was available'.

War with Russia loomed yet again, and Cooper-Key was ordered to form a Particular Service Squadron to reinforce the Channel Fleet, moving his flag to the new and larger *Hercules*. It must have come as a disappointment to Fisher when his Admiral became First Naval Lord, as once again he was cast adrift on half pay. Nevertheless, this was of short duration and he was sent back to the Mediterranean Fleet as command-ing officer of HMS *Pallas*, an ancient corvette. This was a mean posting for a captain, and especially one of Fisher's stature, and it was of some comfort that the commander-in-chief, Admiral Phipps Hornby, wrote to him saying that he was obliged to the Admiralty for sending Fisher and looked forward to seeing him. Indeed, Fisher was taken aboard the flagship when the Admiral discovered that the quarters aboard the *Pallas* were in no fit state for her commanding officer. Still, Fisher took command of his ship and it must have been an odd arrangement com-muting between his command and the flagship. Phipps Hornby spent the next six months grooming Fisher for higher responsibilities. These were before the days of staff colleges, and an aspiring flag officer had to be carefully prepared by a senior officer.

Fisher's next appointment was ashore, as chairman of the committee revising the *Gunnery Manual of the Fleet*, a role that must have seemed to be heaven sent. He then returned to the North American Station, once again as flag-captain, on 25 September 1879, aboard the new cruiser★ *Northampton*.

Working up a new ship was a new experience for Fisher, and in peacetime it was an opportunity that could pass by many naval officers. *Northampton* had the added value that she incorporated many innova-tions, but it was still a case of steam *and* sail. One of her lieutenants recorded that:

★ To the Royal Navy, any ship that patrolled or 'cruised' could be described as a cruiser, and it was not until Fisher's death that the Washington Naval Treaty of 1922 defined cruisers as either 'heavy' with 8-inch guns or 'light' with 6-inch guns. Even during the First World War, many cruisers were usually smaller than a present day destroyer such as the Type 45, typically with a displacement of around 3,500 tons. Ships heavier than this were 'armoured' or 'protected' cruisers.

Shortly after commissioning, the *Northampton* proceeded for a week's cruise in the Channel for trial of guns and to test the ship under sail. The amount of work put into that week was prodigious: steam trials under steam alone, trials under steam and sail, trials under sail alone, tacking, wearing, making and shortening sail, gun trials, general quarters, night quarters, searchlight tests, and frequent coaling ship.[10]

Fisher applied his customary energy and single-mindedness to his new ship, and to his new crew. It was also the case, however, that his mercurial character manifested itself, with changes of mood depending on whatever had been achieved, or *not* achieved, in the past five minutes. It was not helped by the fact that Fisher's commander was Wilmot H. Fawkes, a more conventional naval officer and one unaccustomed to Fisher's mania for rapid and radical change. In a letter to his wife he complained of Fisher's unusual approach:

> What strikes me most is a lack of system. I fancy Captain Fisher is a splendid man for each individual thing but does not stick to a routine enough to make things work easily and well ...
>
> I am disappointed with him. Of course he must be wonderfully clever; but I don't admire him as an Officer. He gets into a state on deck and shouts himself instead of telling me what he wants done ... he is more of a scientific man full of torpedoes and inventions and does not attend much to the details of a ship's organisation ...
>
> The Captain is quite disgraceful. He danced nearly every dance with one young lady and every one but two with her last night...[11]

Whatever Fawkes' qualities may or may not have been, with the benefit of hindsight one can say that he was very perceptive. Fisher *was* a man for gadgets and innovation. He was to prove himself in later years as the great innovator rather than the great strategist. He was also a 'one thing at a time' man. Finally, he had long had more than just an eye for the ladies. Certainly, Fawkes was to complain that everything had to be done 'with such a rush that one can't do things properly.'

Nevertheless, in January 1881, at the age of forty years, Fisher had news of his own ship. Once again he was favoured, as his new ship was HMS *Inflexible*, a large new ironclad, and at the time the largest warship in the world. This was a posting that would normally be reserved for a very senior captain. Again he had outstripped his peers.

The appointment was a much needed boost to Fisher's spirits, as he had lost his young brother Philip, just 22 years old, in early 1880. Philip had followed him into the Royal Navy and seemed to be following in his eldest brother's footsteps inasmuch as he was impressing his superiors, and no less a person than Her Majesty Queen Victoria herself had prevailed upon the Admiralty to post him to the training frigate HMS *Atalanta*. This was unfortunate in the extreme as the ship foundered with all hands on 31 January 1880 off Bermuda. This was a peacetime disaster involving the loss of 113 members of the ship's company and 170 cadets. She had been launched in 1844 as HMS *Juno*. Fisher had a softer side and was devoted to his young brother.

Fisher was immediately returned from the North America station – he was in Antigua at the time – to take up his command.

Notes

1 Bacon, Admiral Sir R.H., *The Life of Lord Fisher of Kilverstone*, London, 1929
2 Kilverstone, Admiral of the Fleet Baron, *Memories*, London, 1919
3 Ibid
4 Bacon, Admiral Sir R.H., *The Life of Lord Fisher of Kilverstone*, London, 1929
5 Ibid
6 Ibid
7 Kilverstone, Admiral of the Fleet Baron, *Memories*, London, 1919
8 Bacon, Admiral Sir R.H., *The Life of Lord Fisher of Kilverstone*, London, 1929
9 Ibid
10 Ibid
11 Ibid

4

Command

Though the Queen has already through the Admiralty conveyed her thanks and congratulations to the Fleet at Alexandria, Her Majesty desires me to assure you of the extreme interests with which she has followed the movements of the Inflexible *during recent times, and, in Her Majesty's name, heartily to congratulate you, your officers and men on the successful issue of your action on the 11ᵗʰ…*

The Queen thought little how soon the splendid guardship at Mentone would be actively engaged…

Letter from Queen Victoria's Private Secretary, July 1882.[1]

Inflexible was Britain's answer to developments elsewhere, not an innovation as such. The Italians had introduced two new battleships, *Duilio* and *Dandalo*, with four guns of 100 tons each mounted in a central citadel and armour plate that was 21½ inches thick in places. The Royal Navy could not do less. The result was *Inflexible*, 12,000-tons, and with even heavier armour and four 16-inch guns. Given the adverse effect on stability from the armour plating, the designers had tried to compensate by giving her ballast tanks in an attempt to reduce rolling, while for the first time there was also electric light. Many naval officers viewed both these innovations with suspicion. Once again, she had mast and sails, although not quite a full set as there were just two masts, even though her engines could propel her at 14 knots. Fisher later recalled that even with full sail, they 'had as much effect upon her in a gale of wind as a fly would have on a hippopotamus in producing any movement.'

In truth, she was an ungainly tub. The ship was not just badly designed in many respects, she was also lacking many essential features. Ventilation was poor, and fans had to be installed, along with fresh air leads and cowls. The increasing size of warships and the loss of the old open gun decks, in which men also ate and slept, resulted in passages and compartments, and men took time to familiarise themselves with the layout. This was far from trivial as it affected efficiency, whether it be attending to the sails in a storm or preparing for imminent battle. Below decks it was a maze, and even old hands suddenly could not be sure which direction was fore and which was aft. In what must have been one of the first examples of colour coding, Fisher painted bulk-heads in different colours and used arrows and symbols so that the sense of direction was regained.

This was Fisher's second new ship to be worked up after she was commissioned at Portsmouth on 5 July 1881. It was probably as well that he was now experienced in this important task, for he immediately found himself at odds with the Admiral Superintendent of the Dockyard, Rear Admiral the Hon. Fitzgerald Foley. The ship had to be ready for sea as soon as possible, but Fisher's demands for such an essential item as a navigating bridge was initially refused, as was his request for more water closets, with both these items regarded as unnecessary; while incandescent lamps for lighting were regarded as dangerous. A lesser man would have accepted defeat, but in his drive for efficiency, Fisher simply went over the senior officer's head to the Admiralty, which soon ordered that his demands were to be met.

This was no unusual event. The officer in charge of a naval dockyard always tried to limit the time and expense spent on any one ship, while those aboard who had to live with the ship, navigate her and, when necessary fight the ship, always had a long list of desirable improvements. Even during the height of the Second World War in the Pacific, the commanding officer of the aircraft carrier, HMS *Formidable*, had to send one of his officers to buy additional fire-fighting equipment from a store in Sydney, and then argue with the Captain of the Dockyard to get him to settle the bill. In this case, the two officers concerned were of the same rank, Fisher and Foley were not.

The upshot of this was, of course, that Fisher was very busy with his new command and her demands. Being aboard a Portsmouth-based ship before she was ready for sea should have meant that he could spend time with his family, for they now had children – including two daughters – and the menage had by this time graduated to a small house in Portsmouth's then fashionable resort area of Southsea. It was not to be, and instead of being reunited, separation was in effect prolonged except for the occasional fleeting visit or snatched weekend.

INFLEXIBLE IN THE MEDITERRANEAN

No doubt it would have been a welcome development if *Inflexible* had been assigned to the Channel Fleet, but it was not to be. In October 1881, she was sent to join the Mediterranean Fleet, where Admiral Sir Frederick Seymour was commander-in-chief. Seymour was the complete antithesis of Fisher; ultra-conservative and hide-bound, trapped by tradition.

The long voyage through the Bay of Biscay to Gibraltar, which, on this occasion, was more unwelcoming than usual, gave Fisher and his officers sufficient time to bring the ship up to a high standard of fighting efficiency. This was not enough, for Seymour was more concerned with the ability of the ship's company to handle the sails efficiently, and in this they lagged behind other ships in the fleet. With his customary zeal, Fisher concentrated on improving their performance, so that before long they were the best in the Mediterranean Fleet, and known as the 'smartest ship'. Again, we find Fisher managing to make the best of the situation and win the approval of a superior with whom he had little in common.

It is commonly believed that Queen Victoria never went abroad, but she did. In 1882, she visited Mentone in the South of France from 18 March to 15 April, and *Inflexible*, as the newest and smartest ship in the Mediterranean Fleet was despatched to act as guard ship. This was not the first time that Fisher had met Her Majesty, having first been introduced to her when she visited the *Hercules*, which was reinforcing the Channel Fleet, in 1878. Nevertheless, despite receiving notification of Royal approval on the previous visit, this was the occasion when Fisher became closely associated with the Royal Family, with shipboard inspections and ceremonial, and an invitation to visit Osborne House on the Isle of Wight when Her Majesty was in residence and Fisher at Portsmouth.

Fisher wrote to his wife Kitty with an account of his meetings with the Queen. His letters were always addressed to 'My Darling Heart', and were loving but always concise. He would use terms of affection that would be regarded as extravagant today in many of his letters, but which were more commonplace in Victorian and Edwardian times. 'My Darling Heart' for his wife perhaps does not seem so romantic when seen next to 'My Beloved' for the wife of a colleague, or his writing to the wife of the journalist, J.A. Spender: 'You are like that very lovely woman who knew me and I didn't know her who said, "The moon looks on many rivers, the rivers look only on one moon!'"

HEALTH WORRIES

After Queen Victoria left for the long railway and Royal Yacht journey to England, *Inflexible* sailed for Malta. It was at this time that he began to worry about his health. Later, it was to become a preoccupation. Middle age arrived much earlier in the late nineteenth century than is the case today, and Fisher had undoubtedly put on weight, although he was hardly rotund. He was also experiencing the first twinges of gout, complaining about a 'horrible tingling pain' in his legs when he got out of his bath. Part of the problem was the lack of exercise and, of course, the lack of fresh food and the abundance of alcohol; while in the days before concerns about tobacco, he smoked numerous cigars daily. He started reading books about gout and diseases of the skin, cut out wines and spirits for a short period and cut back to two or three cigars daily. He did not stay away from drink for very long, but afterwards always avoided heavy drinking and his cigar consumption remained low.

The recommended 'cure' for gout, more a case of alleviating the symptoms than curing it, was to drink only water, and to avoid carbo-hydrates, including potatoes and sugar, and pastry, and to avoid salt and pepper. Fisher wrote to Kitty telling her that he was off to the butcher to be weighed as he had been told to watch his weight. From this time onwards, he was to take the waters at spas such as Marienbad in Bohemia, and became interested in medical matters.

A welcome diversion from this increasing preoccupation with himself came shortly afterwards, with a crisis in Egypt to which the Mediterranean Fleet was sent to intervene. It was important that the Suez Canal should be protected. Not for the last time the crisis was created by nationalist elements within the Egyptian Army, with one officer, Arabi Pasha, accusing the Khedive of being a pawn of the British and French. The Khedive was ousted from power, but British and French intervention saw that Arabi himself was overthrown. He returned on 27 May to establish a dictatorship. His taking power led to riots and 68 Europeans were slaughtered while British and French residents fled the country. French naval units lay offshore during June and July before being withdrawn, while nationalist forces began to build fortifications at Alexandria. On 10 July, Seymour was ordered to issue an ultimatum to Arabi, demanding that work on the fortifications must cease and that the forts be surrendered within 24 hours. The Mediterranean Fleet's eight battleships were lined up on the evening of 10 July to emphasise that the demands would be enforced if necessary.

At 7 a.m. on 11 July, the signal for general action was hoisted aboard the flagship *Invincible*, and the *Alexandra* fired the first shot, aiming at a battery near Fort Ada. The Egyptians returned the fire almost immediately, and continued to fire despite the bombardment being brought down upon them. *Inflexible* played her part, but the 16-inch guns were unpleasant companions, with Fisher recording that they 'blew the cap off my head and nearly deafened me'. The Egyptian fire was more effective than many would have expected, with shells passing over the ships, and before long a shell had hit the port quarter close to the waterline, causing a leak in the bread room. Worse was to come, for thirty minutes after this, a 10-inch round from the battery close to the lighthouse killed the ship's carpenter, Channon, and wounded three other men including Lieutenant Jackson. In fact, the British ships took a battering, but for the most part damage was limited to the superstructure, masts and boats. While the Egyptians were outgunned, it took ten hours to subdue the forts. Fisher's ship laid down accurate fire, but half the shells failed to explode.

Inflexible was fitted with a new invention, an electric searchlight, and after darkness this was used to sweep the sea and shore looking for drifting mines or even a torpedo attack. The following morning, fire was renewed until the final fort raised the white flag of surrender. Landing parties were then sent to occupy the ports.

Elsewhere, the outbreak of hostilities led to widespread rioting and looting in Alexandria itself, with European-owned houses and business premises destroyed. Arabi stationed forces outside the city, and in response Seymour sent Fisher ashore in command of a party of sailors and marines. While not anticipating such a responsibility, since he had written to Kitty reassuring her that he would be kept safely aboard his ship, Fisher welcomed the role. His force was outnumbered by the nationalists, whose forces had been strengthened by the arrival of Bedouin tribesmen.

A mate with the leading party wrote:

About 1 a.m., Captain Fisher proceeded to inspect our outposts beyond the Maharun Bay Gate. He arrived without warning, and so suddenly that one of the gun's crew fired at him with a revolver. I knocked up the man's arm and the bullet went over Fisher's head. He took no notice of the occurrence, but merely inspected the gun, etc. He then told the officer to expect an advance of a large number of Arabi's followers during the night, and that the post must be held at all costs, remarking, finally, in a jocular way, 'You can't miss 'em. You've only got to put in the ammunition and off it goes.' Then he disappeared as silently as he came.[2]

Despite the fact that his health was beginning to crumble, there was no sleep for him or any of the officers ashore. With an old friend, Captain Arthur Wilson, Fisher even managed to assemble an armoured train using some old sheets of iron found lying around and mounting a 40-pounder gun on a railway wagon. This was intended for armed reconnaissance and is believed to have been the first ever armoured train. It remained in service when British troops arrived to relieve Fisher's shore parties. When journalists also arrived, the armoured train was the star attraction, and Fisher was credited with it, bringing his name in news reports before the British public for the first time. This prompted the letter of congratulations from Queen Victoria. His activities ashore also resulted in him becoming a CB, Commander of the Bath, but he was angered that Wilson did not receive the same award. The train, widely credited to Fisher alone, had been in fact a joint venture between the two friends.

So closely associated with the train was Fisher, that in late July, when the press reported that the officer in command of 'the ironclad train' had been wounded and his foot amputated, his wife immediately jumped to the conclusion that it was him. Apparently the story also caused dismay and concern at Court. By this time, Fisher was safely back aboard his ship.

Or perhaps not so safely. On 22 August, he was struck down by dysentery in a particularly fierce attack. He was given eight pills of ipecacuanha and opium every four hours for two days. This was a drastic course of treatment as the proper course was meant to be one pill, but overdosing and therefore poisoning the patient with ipecacuanha – derived from the root of a South American shrub and intended to have a purgative effect – was seen as the treatment. The remedy was almost worse than the disease, with constant sickness.

The alarm caused throughout the Fleet was considerable, with Seymour putting a suite of cabins aboard his flagship at Fisher's disposal, or as an alternative offering to send *Inflexible* anywhere if he intended to remain aboard. There can be little doubt that baking in an iron shell in the heat of the Eastern Mediterranean with poor food and, by modern standards, inadequate ventilation and sanitation, was hardly conducive to a cure, but where could he go? Fisher stayed aboard his ship, and his ship stayed at Alexandria.

He recovered, but much weakened, he needed convalescence and this meant remaining aboard his ship, during which time he lay on a sofa in his day cabin. Despite being weak and no doubt dehydrated from his illness, he did not stop work, and started to plough through the backlog of administration that had piled up not only during his illness, but while he had been ashore with the armoured train. He also found time on 12 September to write a treatise on the shortcomings of his ship, compared with the Italian *Dandalo*, which he had had the chance of inspecting. He thought an improved design would be fifty feet longer and with a false keel of two feet, which would give an extra three knots speed.

At the end of the month, *Inflexible* was sent to Malta, only for Fisher to suffer a relapse on arrival.★ The second bout was far worse than the first and he was not expected to survive. The First Lord, Lord Northolt, signalled that he should come home: 'We can get many *Inflexibles*, but only one Jack Fisher.' The Queen sent a message of sympathy. Fisher was beginning to recover by this time, and concerned that, weak though he was after a second severe illness, relinquishing his command would have an adverse effect on his career. In any case, he would have to pay £50 for the journey home and did not have the money, while everyone else assumed that such a senior officer would have sufficient means, so no one thought of offering it. He wrote to Kitty explaining that there was so much to do, and he had new officers to settle in.

In the end, spurred on by the concern amongst all those around him, including a letter from the lower deck wishing him well and looking forward to him being amongst them once again, he relented, and sailed

★ It could have been the variety of the dysentery known as 'Malta dog', a cure for which was discovered by an army doctor early in the twentieth century.

for England on 9 November 1882. He had to be carried aboard on a stretcher, drifting in and out of consciousness, and in one brief moment of lucidity, he overheard a doctor saying that he would never reach Gibraltar; this was probably the best medicine that the doctor concerned could have given, for Fisher being Fisher he determined to prove the doctor wrong.

He returned home and as soon as he was well enough, he was pressed to join Queen Victoria at Osborne House, with the concession that at dancing he could, as an invalid, wear trousers rather than tights. His wife Kitty and eldest daughter Beatrix, aged fifteen, were also invited to join the party for luncheon, followed by a drive with one of the other guests. Fisher himself saw the Queen often, usually at dinner and afterwards. He remained at Osborne until March 1883 and in early April was ready to return to active service.

Notes

1 Bacon, Admiral Sir R.H., *The Life of Lord Fisher of Kilverstone*, London, 1929
2 Ibid

5

Ashore

*'He was never the same man for two days together,' wrote a naval journalist.
'But all that he did he always did wholeheartedly ... The story is told that he
had two tablets by his bedside – one with a red pencil, which meant "urgent",
and the other with a black pencil – and that in the night he would wake and
make a note on one or the other of the tablets or ask his wife to do so.*[11]

Fisher had by this time enjoyed a series of successful commands and
had seen action at Alexandria both ashore and afloat, although he never
actually engaged in a naval battle. His experience of leading a landing
party may well have encouraged him to become such an advocate of
amphibious operations in the period immediately before and during
the First World War. Certainly, he was successful, but the circumstances
of such successes were unconventional for a Royal Naval officer.

His experience and his passion for technology and innovation
meant that he was probably more valuable to the Royal Navy ashore
working on weapon development than afloat. Even if he had been
left at sea along with the other 'salt horse skippers', he would have
seen little naval action because of the long naval peace enjoyed by the
Victorians. There was also the question of a suitable appointment, for
he was a little too young to become a rear admiral, the lowest rank
of flag officer. The intervening rank of commodore provided relatively
few posts.

For all of his drive, energy and enthusiasm, and his deep-rooted conviction that *he was right*, certainly at this stage of his career, Fisher never
assumed that he knew everything. This was an unusual feature in the
Royal Navy at the time, and not only in the service but in other walks
of life. If someone, no matter how junior, had experience or ideas of
value, Fisher would listen. He did not simply use his subordinates or his
advisers; he never pretended that a good idea was his alone. These were,
and remain, rare qualities.

Arriving ashore in 1883, Fisher was the man that the service needed, but many did not recognise it at the time. This was a turning point in his career and in the history of the Royal Navy. There was another change as well. So far, Fisher had by one means or another, won over superiors who had a completely different outlook from himself. Seymour in the Mediterranean was a particularly good example. From 1883 onwards, Fisher became something of a 'Whitehall warrior', and began to make enemies. One officer wrote that: 'There is undoubtedly a useful dash of the savage in Fisher's nature.'

Fisher started his campaign at Portsmouth, where, on 6 April 1883, he took command of HMS *Excellent*, returning to the ship for the fourth time. This time, he was in a position to make changes:

> What was called the 'forty years routine' was in full swing: practically nothing had altered for forty years, since the *Excellent* had been made the Gunnery School. All the firing practices were carried out with old smooth-bore guns. The establishment was crowded with 'deadheads', ie pensioners who occupied accommodation to the exclusion of active service ratings, who should have been there for training. All the gunnery methods were antiquated; the whole place was in a state of Rip-van-Winkleism.[2]

The pensioners had to go, and Fisher ensured that they went, suffering a crescendo of complaints, but there was at last accommodation for the active service ratings. Modern quick-firing guns were installed. It was here that he met two of the early members of the 'Fishpond', John Jellicoe and Percy Scott, as young lieutenants, who endeared themselves to him by sharing his ideas.

It was Scott who had done much to improve the performance of the young gunners, and who had the idea that a new gunnery school be founded on Whale Island although at the time, the 'island' was nothing more than a massive mound of mud excavated during the dredging of Portsmouth Harbour. Fisher immediately took up Scott's proposal, and never one to think small, expanded it, so that ashore a new purpose-built gunnery and torpedo school was founded and the mud flat was more deserving of its 'island' definition.

MAKING CONNECTIONS

That was not all. He started to make connections outside the service. For some time he had been a friend of William Stead, the editor of the Liberal-supporting *Pall Mall Gazette*. It was a relationship of mutual admiration. This was the start of Fisher's association with the press, and it was to be a mixed one. He admired those journalists who shared his views, and had unreserved scorn for those who did not, no matter how well they argued their case. Fisher came to know and became known to politicians. One of these was a close friend of Stead, the Hon. Reginald Brett, later ennobled as Lord Esher. Described by some as a Machiavellian figure who did his work behind the scenes, Brett was to become a counsellor and sounding board for Fisher in later years, as well as an advocate in his dealings with politicians. In front of the scenes Brett was Secretary to the Office of Works and Deputy-Governor of Windsor Castle, yet despite such a mundane position as public works, he was a man of considerable influence, especially on defence. With Fisher's plans for Whale Island in mind, Brett was undoubtedly a worthwhile ally at the time, but it was also the start of a long relationship and in his later years, Fisher would have done well to heed the advice of his friend.

Stead and Brett were barometers of public opinion, men who knew when to say, or write, the right thing. A third associate for Fisher was H.O. Arnold-Foster, initially a student of military and naval matters, but later Secretary of State for War. This gave Fisher a connection with the War Office, the department that controlled the British Army. This was to be useful in the years that lay ahead, as inter-service rivalry is nothing new, especially when budgets are stretched.

Yet another opportunity to maintain the Royal connection soon presented itself to Fisher. During his period in command, he had the future King George V pass through *Excellent* for six months, graduating as a lieutenant. Once again, Queen Victoria was in touch, wanting to know how the young man, her grandson, had done. Fisher was able to assure her that 'His attention to his work and the manner in which he has performed all his duties has been all that your Majesty could desire.' In fact, the young Prince George hadn't come out with top marks, and so Fisher was moved to write privately to Queen Victoria's secretary the following day: 'Prince George only lost his first-class at pilotage by 20 marks. The yarn is that one of his examiners, an old salt-horse sailor, didn't think it would do to let him fancy he knew all about it.'[3]

THE FIRST NAVAL SCARE

Despite the long years of peace and the alliance with France in the campaigns against Russia and then Egypt, the British were still suspicious of their nearest neighbour. Both countries were still engaged in empire-building, or protecting. The French were increasing the pace of naval shipbuilding, while the Russians were showing increasing hostility towards India. In 1884, Russian troops were sent into Afghanistan, and senior officers talked openly about the desirability of taking India. Certainly, this would be one way of giving Russia the warm water ports that she craved, and which was a permanent feature of Russian policy regardless of the form or colour of the government.

Concerns over the strength of the Royal Navy began to surface. This was the first of the 'naval scares' of the period before the First World War. Certainly there was much to be concerned about. After all, had there not been, Fisher would not have made such an impact and would not have been nearly so pressured in his work.

The difficulty for Fisher was that these concerns manifested themselves as accusations against the Admiralty, first by Arnold-Foster and then by Stead. In fact, it was the former who suggested to Stead that his newspaper should run a series of articles sensationalising the perceived poor condition of the Royal Navy. Arnold-Foster promised to provide the information if Stead himself should lend his personal authority to the campaign by writing the articles himself, although Arnold-Foster would write the first one. Despite his position, Arnold-Foster knew that they needed reliable information, and using Brett as an intermediary, they approached Fisher.

Fisher did not need convincing, despite the risk to his career. His experience and knowledge was broad enough not to be confined to gunnery, munitions or his beloved torpedoes.

The first of Stead's articles appeared on 15 September 1884, and was signed by 'One Who Knows the Facts', as the start of a series on 'The Truth about the Navy'. The truth was that despite the country's wealth having increased by 40 per cent since 1868, and the merchant fleet by 30 per cent, the country was spending less on the Royal Navy. French warships and armament were said to be superior to those of the British, more torpedo boats were desperately needed, the main naval bases were undefended, and the merchant ports were completely wide open to attack.

Lord Northolt, First Lord of the Admiralty, placed himself in a vulnerable position in July 1884, before leaving for Egypt. In the context of a debate on the vulnerability of large ironclad ships, he made a statement that suffered from the curse that haunts every politician, it could be quoted out of context against him: 'The great difficulty the Admiralty would have to contend with if they were granted £3,000,000 or £4,000,000 tomorrow for the purpose referred to would be to decide how they should spend the money.'

These sums would amount to £200 million or £260 million today, but that does not give a true value, as defence expenditure in the meantime has suffered from technological inflation. It would be closer to present day reality to add an extra three noughts to each of the figures quoted for equipment costs, while manpower costs have risen perhaps a hundredfold.

To an extent that would not be possible today, this campaign started a debate in the rest of the newspaper world, and became a more pressing subject of conversation than the crisis in Egypt and the Sudan. There were other allies as well, who cranked up the debate, but these had strong vested interests.

'It is surprising that so much apathy should be displayed regarding the unprotected state of our commerce,' declared Sir William Armstrong at the annual general meeting of his shipbuilding, armaments and engineering company (later Vickers-Armstrongs). 'There is at present a well-founded scare about the state of our Navy.'[4]

Protests from such interested parties might be expected. Even the personal vilification of Lord Northolt, who was in Upper Egypt when the campaign started, can be understood in this modern light. What gave it an edge, and would surprise people today, was that the Poet Laureate, none other than Alfred Lord Tennyson, intervened and made a contribution to the debate, and the first and third stanzas of a poem, published in *The Times* on 23 April 1884, addressed to Lord Northolt became widely quoted:

You, you, *if* you have fail'd to understand
The Fleet of England is her all-in-all
On you will come the curse of all the land,
If that Old England fall,
Which Nelson left so great.

You, you, who had the ordering of her Fleet,
If you have only encompassed her disgrace,
When all men starve, the wild mob's million feet
Will kick you from your place
But then too late, too late.[5]

Within the Royal Navy, professional officers felt betrayed then, and not
for the last time, by the First Naval Lord, Admiral Sir Astley Cooper-
Key, who had done so much for Fisher's career in the past. It was more
or less common knowledge that his protégé was behind the series in
the *Pall Mall Gazette*. Today, this would be described by lobby correspondents as 'briefing against' his superior. It is an interesting reflection
on the changes over more than a century that today any naval officer
who behaved in this manner would be sacked. Then, while many of
Fisher's peers were shocked at how ruthless this ambitious and single-
minded officer was being, nothing was done. Fisher himself treated
the charges that he was behind the campaign with disdain. In fact, he
was nOt behind the campaign in the sense that he was its originator,
but he was the informer. He survived most probably because many of
his superiors felt that Cooper-Key was weak and ineffectual as First
Naval Lord, a classic example of a good man being promoted to his
level of incompetence.

Cooper-Key was not slow to defend himself, but his arguments
were ineffectual and out of step with the mood of the nation. The First
Naval Lord believed in moderate increases in armament, arguing that
sudden increases only stimulated arms races as potential foes attempted
to do the same. It could be said that there was some truth in this, but it
would also be easy to steer a battleship through the argument as it was
a prescription for inaction. The big fear of a sudden large increase was
that it brought extra costs of its own without a commensurate increase
in equipment or effectivenesss.

'It is rumoured at Portsmouth that I am opposed to the increase
in the Fleet,' he wrote to Fisher's superior, the Commander-in-Chief
Portsmouth, Admiral Sir Phipps Hornby, on 2 December 1884. 'I wish
to disabuse *your* mind on the subject. If you had seen what I had written, heard what I have said at the Board, you know that I have been
disturbed about the absurdly small sum the Government are asking
for … [But] I have always deprecated asking for a very large sum for

shipbuilding purposes – it will only induce other Nations to make another start.'[6]

This was a messy and contradictory response to the debate, otherwise one would have liked to believe that the First Naval Lord was simply being discreet.

Eventually, even Fisher must have felt that discretion was the better part of valour, and so was not displeased when in June 1885, Phipps Hornby was ordered to form an expeditionary fleet for possible action against Russia in the Baltic. He moved aboard the battleship HMS *Minotaur* as a member of the Admiral's staff. Fortunately – or unfortunately, as many lessons might have been learned that would have served the Royal Navy well during the First World War – the crisis blew over within a few months and the expeditionary fleet saw exercises but no action. Had the two navies met in the Baltic (or anywhere else for that matter), the outcome would have shaken Victorian society to its roots. The Royal Navy not only needed ships, it needed modern armament. The biggest breech–loader was just 6-inch calibre, above which the main armament of the largest ships consisted entirely of primitive muzzle-loaders, which were not only slow to reload, but also exposed the gun crews to enemy fire every time they reloaded. The Russian ships were all equipped with modern breech-loading guns. Again, the shells and fuses were far below any acceptable standard, largely owing to the fact that the Royal Navy still had no control over its guns and ammunition, which remained with the Royal Artillery. One troubling aspect of this arrangement went beyond the technical, as the money for naval ordnance was included in the estimates for the War Office and so the Admiralty had no idea just how much ammunition would be available in wartime, and if ground forces were also deployed in combat at the same time, one can easily guess who would have priority.

In the meantime, Northolt had returned and Parliament had granted an extra £3 million, which led to the start of construction of two new battleships and thirteen new cruisers.

VISITING MARIENBAD

The following year, with the effects of the dysentery still causing him trouble, Fisher made his first visit to Marienbad in Bohemia, part of today's Czech Republic. A former dance partner suggested it, and Fisher recalled later: 'In three weeks I was in robust health ... and I never again had a recurrence.'[7]

In the years that followed he visited Marienbad most years, sometimes alone, sometimes with his family. It was not simply the waters that he took, he also took the opportunity to meet and 'brief' many of the famous and influential who also visited, vastly widening his circle of acquaintances, including leading politicians who travelled from Britain to take the waters. It was no trivial short break, however, as he usually spent three weeks at the spa, and it took a large slice of his annual salary, which would have been around £660 per annum at the time. Costs were kept under control as far as possible, and the frugality included second class railway travel:

> I got breakfast for tenpence, lunch for a shilling and dinner for eighteenpence and barley water for nothing and a bed for three and sixpence ... I did a three weeks' cure there, including the railway fare and every expense for twenty-five pounds ... I preserve to this day the details of every day's expenditure.[8]

Another move was imminent, and on 1 November 1886, he said goodbye to *Excellent* and to Portsmouth, to move to London as Director of Naval Ordnance, DNO. While in theory this gave Fisher control over the guns and mines, and, of course, torpedoes, he was still beholden to the Army. This had to be remedied. In the meantime he quickly elevated his title to 'Ordnance and Torpedoes'.

'I came to the definite conclusion that the ordnance of the Fleet was in a very bad way,' he recalled. 'The only remedy was to take the whole business from the War Office, who controlled the Sea Ordnance and the munitions of sea war. A very funny state of affairs.'[9]

He was in the right place at the right time to change all of this. Lord Salisbury the Prime Minister and the new First Lord, Lord George Hamilton, were inclined to share his views. Hamilton had done much to advance Fisher, even though his admiration was tempered by recognition of his volatile nature, 'His self-advertisement and ... his likes and dislikes of others ... his absorption in the idea of the moment made his grip of the future very fitful.' Clearly Fisher's former commander aboard *Northampton*, Wilmot Fawkes, had been very perceptive!

An inter-departmental committee was set up under the chairman-ship of the Prime Minister, the Secretary for War, W.H. Smith, the First Lord of the Admiralty and the Director of Ordnance at the War Office, Brigadier-General James Alderson, who happened to be the Prime Minister's brother-in-law. Fisher's recollections of the meetings of the committee were that he suffered from a very bad cold, much worse than the one from which Alderson was suffering, but that his sufferings went un-remarked while the Prime Minister 'slobbered over Alderson'. More important than this lack of sympathy, the outcome was that the Admiralty regained control of its ordnance. Unfortunately, the War Office, having lost the battle, then dragged its feet and it took no less than twelve years, from 1887 to 1909, before the transfer was complete. To be fair to Fisher, he handled the negotiations with considerable diplomacy, earning Salisbury's approval and managing not to make an enemy of his opposite number at the War Office.

INDUSTRIAL CONNECTIONS

It was inevitable that given greatly increased powers and responsibility for the development of naval armaments, Fisher started to come into close contact with leading figures in the industry. Some of these he befriended, notably Josiah Vavasseur, the technical director of William Armstrong. Vavasseur's main interest was gun mountings, leaving the design of the weapon itself to Sir Andrew Noble, a partner in the firm. He invented a device that absorbed the energy of gun recoil, allow-ing simpler and lighter gun mountings to be used, and coincidentally allowing smaller ships to mount a heavier armament. The two men became close friends and visited each other's homes. Although based on the Tyne at Elswick, Vavasseur had an estate in Norfolk at Kilverstone Hall, near Thetford. Having no children of his own, he took a liking to Fisher's son Cecil, eighteen years old in 1886, and in 1913 named him as his heir on condition that when the second Lord Fisher should inherit his estate when he died, he and his heirs should adopt the name Vavasseur.

From 1887 onwards, Fisher began to receive increasingly attractive offers to leave the Royal Navy and work for one or another of the great industrial giants. Then, as now, having someone not just with drive and determination, but with an understanding of how the main customer thought and who had the contacts to make winning business easier, was an attractive option for industry. Lord George Hamilton persuaded him to turn the first one down at a time when Fisher was feeling bitter. Some of the later offers were, in his words, 'beyond the dreams of avarice'. They must have been, to a man without private means, in contrast to many of his his peers, and this became even more of a problem as he rose in seniority and was also being pressed by his relatives for money. In fact, his mother lived humbly in London mainly on an allowance provided to her by Fisher. He was also scrupulous about giving a portion of his income to charitable causes.

Fisher lived through a period of great naval technical progress, more than during the previous 300 years. The progress lay in the design of ships, their propulsive systems and in their armament, as well as in the projectiles used. In 1887, he visited Portsmouth from the Admiralty to see a demonstration of a new 4.7-inch quick-firing gun, which fired ten rounds in less than 50 seconds.

Within just a few years, the torpedo had developed from something moving at a water snail's pace to a potent weapon that could manage 30 knots, which meant that the warships of the day could not run away from it. It had a range of 1,200 yards, two-thirds of a statute mile, and could still carry a 200-lb warhead. In response, battleships had to hoist thick nets, sometimes known as 'crinolines', to protect themselves whilst at anchor. This made dropping and weighing anchor a more time-consuming business.

The pace of naval shipbuilding during the late 1880s remained slow and orders were far fewer than the Northbrook programme might have suggested. With hindsight this was a blessing, with fewer ships to be condemned to obsolescence by the advent of the Dreadnought-class, but at the time it was a risky strategy. Just speculate on what might have happened if, at the height of the Boer War, the Dutch or the Germans had decided to intervene, especially since the latter resented having their ships searched for contraband by the Royal Navy. Or consider an engagement with the Russian fleet that set sail to the Far East for the great defeat at the hands of the Japanese at Tsushima, and which nearly provoked a war by firing on British trawlers in the North Sea.

Fortunately, this lull in the shipbuilding programme soon started to be rectified, with Lord George Hamilton's Naval Defence Act, 1889.

This measure voted the Admiralty the then massive sum of £21.5 million for no less than seventy vessels, which was far more than the Royal Navy was looking for, and also undertook the modernisation of bases and dockyards. The driving force behind this largesse was quite simple, the rumour had started that the Royal Navy could no longer meet the 'Two Power Standard', which meant that it had to be twice the size of the next largest fleet. It came at a time when auxiliary sails were no longer specified, ships were built of iron and not clad with it, and guns were placed in turrets or barbettes fore and aft.

ADMIRAL SUPERINTENDENT AT PORTSMOUTH

Fisher was sent back to Portsmouth in 1891 as Admiral Superintendent of the dockyard, reporting to the commander-in-chief Portsmouth. He was promoted to the rank of rear admiral. This was less exciting in many ways than a sea-going appointment, but it suited his interests.

Fisher had a chance to influence the construction of the first of the Naval Defence Act battleships, HMS *Royal Sovereign*, herself costing the almost unthinkable sum of almost £7 million. This was a period when many naval vessels were built in the great dockyards at Portsmouth, Plymouth and Chatham, something that ended during the 1960s. Inevitably, most of his subordinates at Portsmouth were civilians. The dockyard workers were notoriously unproductive, but Fisher intended to rectify this, and he started at the top:

> The methods he used were peculiar to himself. One important official was hard to move out of his office. Fisher wanted him to visit and personally supervise the building sheds more often; but to this he demurred. One morning, Fisher sent him a note to tell him that he had heard that there was going to be a vacancy at Trincomalee (in Ceylon), for which he was eligible. That was all! But according to all accounts that official was seen, within two minutes of receiving that note, sprinting down to the building sheds.[10]

For someone who had spent his entire life since he became a teenager in the Royal Navy, Fisher's grasp of industrial efficiency was remarkably enlightened and forward looking. The first point is obvious but essential. 'If you build two ships in the same time as it formerly took to build one, then you want half the number of slips and half the plant,' he would explain none too patiently to those around him, who had to listen. 'Therefore you effect a great saving in capital outlay and depreciation; moreover a ship gets into commission earlier, and your Fleet therefore is stronger; and instead of a ship being almost obsolete by the time she is commissioned, she is in the prime of her power.'[11] He didn't waste time, and the *Royal Sovereign* was the first to be built under the Fisher-effect.

> One way he had of encouraging the workmen was to find out quietly from the charge hand the names of one or more of the men who were working on the *Royal Sovereign*. A little time afterwards he would pass one of them and say, 'That's right, Thomas Williamson, glad to see you digging out so well.' 'Goodness gracious me, the Admiral knows my name,' the man would think, and the report went round the yard that the Admiral knew the names of all the men. The net result of such craft and energy was that the *Royal Sovereign* was ... built in just two years.[12]

Even greater progress was made in speeding up refitting and repair work at Portsmouth. The time taken to lift out and replace the heavy gun of a battleship was reduced from two days to two hours. This was achieved by Fisher having a table and chair placed on top of the turret and having his lunch served there, declaring before he started that he intended to stay there until the work had been completed!

Notes

1 Hurd, Sir Archibald, *Who Goes There?* London, 1942
2 Bacon, Admiral Sir R.H., *The Life of Lord Fisher of Kilverstone*, London, 1929
3 Hurd, Sir Archibald, *Who Goes There?* London, 1942
4 *The Times*, 2 October 1884
5 *The Times*, 23 April 1884

6 Colomb, Vice-Admiral P.H., *Memoirs of Admiral the Rt Hon. Sir Astley Cooper-Key*, London, 1898

7 Kilverstone, Admiral of the Fleet Baron, *Memories*, London, 1919

8 Kilverstone, Admiral of the Fleet Baron, *Records*, London, 1919

9 Ibid

10 Bacon, Admiral Sir R.H., *The Life of Lord Fisher of Kilverstone*, London, 1929

11 Ibid

12 Ibid

The Whitehall Warrior

Build few and build fast,
Each one better than the last!
Fisher

Fisher's spell at Portsmouth was all the more impressive for being very short, and on 1 February 1892, he returned to the Admiralty as a Vice-Admiral to take up the post of Third Naval Lord and Controller of the Navy. This was a post with a wide remit and he was to hold it until early 1897, an amount of time that would be regarded as unthinkable today, yet it meant that a man could see his work bear fruit – or wither on the vine. Far too often today, such people are moved on before their mistakes become apparent.

Development, design, construction, maintenance and scrapping of everything from the smallest items of equipment to the largest battle-ship were all part of his responsibilities, no matter where in the world it might be. He dealt with contractors and designers, so had to be above suspicion, and also had to have the judgement necessary to decide just what innovations were worth making and what practices or equip-ment would have to be abandoned. He was in constant contact with the political establishment, and for the most part he came to despise it, although, as with the press, he also discovered those for whom he could express admiration and even affection.

Given his increasingly exalted rank, however, he was also to become more brittle and unforgiving in his dealings with those around him. His bluntness went beyond simple rudeness, describing one Chancellor of the Exchequer, Sir Michael Hicks, as 'a perfect beast, without a single redeeming feature'. In his defence, it can only be said that this was a man in a hurry, and it is clear that there was much to do and no guarantee that the long period of peace in Europe could continue. It was fortunate that when he started in his new role, the First Naval Lord was Admiral

Sir Frederick Richards, for whom he had considerable respect, and that he felt the same about the First Lord, Lord Spencer, of whom, ironically enough, Fisher indicated that one of his virtues was 'He never hurt any man's feelings'.

He came to the post at a time of international tension. In the Far East, the Chinese and the Japanese were at war. In the west, old rivalries and enmities were changing, with tension between the United Kingdom and France renewed, although relationships with Russia were better. An unknown quantity was the arriviste nation, the newly united Germany, but the often belligerent stance adopted by one of the largest of the new nation's constituent states, Prussia, gave little hope that relationships would always be good. In the African colonies there were uprisings and revolts, especially in South Africa. Relationships with the United States would also deteriorate later in the decade. Protected from Europe by the North Sea and the English Channel, the country had a small volunteer army compared to the large conscript armies of most mainland European nations, with British troops augmented by locally-raised forces throughout the Empire. The key to this situation was still thought to be the presence of a navy capable of matching the next two most important navies in the world, the 'Two Power Standard'. This insistence was not as extreme as it might seem, as the Royal Navy had to maintain a worldwide reach, and at any point it might be overcome by an opponent able to concentrate its forces, be it in the Mediterranean, the Baltic or North Sea, or the Pacific.

A clear signal of German intentions was not long in coming after the end of Fisher's term as Controller. In 1898, a Naval Act established a programme of construction and expansion of a substantial German Navy.

A NEW NAVAL SCARE

It was during 1893 that a justification for Fisher's haste and impatience emerged. This was the third of the naval scares of the 1880s and 1890s that had started with the revelations in the *Pall Mall Gazette*, with the speculation over failing to meet the Two Power Standard being the second.

Relations with France had been poor for some time, while the renewed rivalry between Britain and France had been aggravated by the colonial ambitions of both. It was still possible for a European power to annex territory, even territory with a settled form of government, without anyone raising an eyebrow. At the same time, there were unwritten rules. The European colonial powers could only absorb so much at a time and there was a process for taking territory. Early in 1893, France declared her intention to annex Siam, now Thailand, and when the Siamese seemed hostile to the idea, in May she declared war on the country. What became known, oddly, as the 'Mekong Crisis' (since the river of that name only touches Thailand before flowing into the sea through Vietnam) was the result, and Britain and France nearly came to war.

The timing was unfortunate as the results of the 1889 Naval Defence Act were still building. Worse, it followed the collision in the Mediterranean that had resulted in the loss of the battleship *Victoria* with most of her ship's company, including Vice-Admiral Tryon, commander-in-chief of the Mediterranean Fleet, while the battleship *Camperdown* was badly damaged. Tryon had been the commander aboard HMS *Warrior* when Fisher was a young lieutenant. The relative superiority of the British over the French fleet was for a period substantially reduced, especially in the Mediterranean. This brought home to the British public just how fragile the country's lead was. Once again, there was pressure to build more ships during the second half of 1893. There had been a change of government, and Lord George Hamilton was on the opposition benches and able to move a motion calling for 'a considerable addition' to be made 'at once' to the Royal Navy. The response from Gladstone, 82 years old and heading his fourth Liberal administration, was that no one should be in any doubt about the 'distinct supremacy of Great Britain'.

This was more serious than the usual Parliamentary slanging match. Fisher once again was working away behind the scenes, so that soon hints emerged of resignations from the Board of Admiralty. More than this, he wrote a letter to Austen Chamberlain from the Admiralty in which he referred to the Chancellor of the Exchequer, Sir William Harcourt in uncompromising terms.

'Sir William Harcourt told an unmitigated lie when he said that the professional officers of the Admiralty were satisfied with the present condition of the Navy,' wrote Fisher. 'We don't intend to stand any repetition of such misrepresentation of our views, and further we will not stand much longer delay in dealing with pressing naval requirements.' In the end, as Fisher recorded: 'We got the ships and Mr Gladstone went.'

Harcourt had been one of those who changed sides in the prolonged debate, suggesting that the cost of strengthening the Navy could come from new taxes, including a graduated death duty. Social reforms were also postponed.

On 8 December 1893, a naval construction programme amounting to £31 million was announced by Lord Spencer, which covered seven new battleships, no less than thirty cruisers and 112 torpedo boats and destroyers.★ This programme was changed slightly in the months that followed, to nine battleships of the new Majestic class, and incredibly, all were laid down over a period of sixteen months.

Fisher's reward for behind-the-scenes agitation and manipulation was hardly such as to discourage him. He was appointed Knight Commander of the Bath, KCB, on 26 May 1894.

The shipbuilding programme that resulted would not be possible today, but even at the height of late Victorian industrial power, when British shipyards were *the* world's largest and built more ships than any other nation, resources were stretched as they never had been, and never were again, in peacetime. Workers in shipbuilding and armaments, and of course in the iron and steel industry that underpinned their production, found themselves in a dominant position and demanded higher wages, and when these demands were not met, industrial unrest followed. There was also unrest amongst top industrialists, with rivalry

---

★The destroyer was a creation of the late nineteenth century and emerged originally as the 'torpedo-boat destroyer', reflecting the universal anxiety amongst the world's naval leaders over the potency of the fast torpedo boat and, of course, its armament. Fisher is credited with coining this term in a memo of 8 August 1892. Before this, large warships had been fitted with quick-firing guns, and classes of 'torpedo-boat catchers' were built, but these were a failure, being too slow and clumsy. The original destroyers were small and fast, often less than 1,000 tons displacement. Sizes were beginning to grow before the First World War, and continued during the conflict. When the fleet went to sea, the battleships would have a screen of cruisers, while these in turn were given a protective destroyer screen.

between the then independent Armstrong and Whitworth and accusations that the Controller – Fisher – was giving too much of the work to the state-owned Woolwich Arsenal. There were other controversies as well. The *Pall Mall Gazette* had a new editor, and he published what Fisher described as 'a tissue of misrepresentations about battleships as compared with the French'.

BIRTH OF THE DESTROYER

In fact both the French and the Russians were building what seemed to be fine ships for the day, although many of the French designs were somewhat unorthodox. While many worried about the effect on Britain's vast maritime trade of French commerce raiders, there was also evidence that this was what the Russians had in mind, building cruisers that were superior in speed, armament and endurance to those of the Royal Navy. Typical of these was the *Rurik*, with the exceptional displacement for a cruiser of 10,900 tons. There was also an early experience of the late twentieth-century anxiety about fast missile-armed vessels, in that not only were torpedo boats getting bigger and faster, they were also cheap enough for many smaller nations to buy and give themselves a chance of striking at a superior fleet. Even a major maritime power such as France had 220 torpedo boats, some of them small enough to be transported by rail so that they could be moved between the Atlantic and Mediterranean coasts quickly.

So, the torpedo-boat destroyer was born. The first was built by Alfred Yarrow, HMS *Havock*, and was just 240 tons, carrying a 12-pounder and three 6-pounder guns, as well as three torpedoes, and managed more than 26 knots on trials. The next ship from Yarrow, *Hornet*, could make 28 knots and became the world's fastest ship for a period. Life aboard these fast warships was exciting for those on deck, but with their 3,500-hp engines, still fuelled by coal, as many as twenty-eight men could be attempting to work together in the heat and noise of the engine room. If such a small vessel was hit by a torpedo or struck a mine, there would be no survivors. Nevertheless, these frail craft did the job for which they were intended.

Despite having everything that he could want, Fisher was still conniving. No single company could produce all that was needed, and at the same time not every company could match the quality of work and the inventiveness of the best. Unknown to Yarrow, Fisher distributed copies of the detailed engine drawings to the firm's competitors when awarding contracts. Yarrow's technological lead was lost overnight, and the company guessed what had happened. The company brought the matter into the open by advertising in the press, offering £200 for information that would identify the culprit. Embarrassed, the Admiralty offered compensation, which Yarrow rejected, but the Secretary to the Admiralty Board then issued a statement acknowledging Alfred Yarrow's work. As always Fisher was unrepentant. He argued that Admiralty contracts were so important and prestigious, and backed by the facilities of an experimental establishment, that any short-term losses were outweighed by the longer-term relationship. In fact, it was to take the First World War for such a means of working to be recognised, when additional production of one company's designs would be built by its competitors. While the friendship that had been developing between Fisher and Yarrow waned as a result of the Controller's actions, later Fisher did help to get the shipbuilder a baronetcy.

UNDER PRESSURE

The next controversy was the water-tube boiler, sometimes referred to as the small water-tube boiler. This had been invented by the Frenchman Felix du Temple★ and enabled a small quantity of water to be heated so that sufficient steam pressure could be gained in just an hour, as well as saving weight. They offered higher working pressures and were more efficient and economical as well. Fisher was ecstatic:

> A Fleet that is always ready to go to sea at an hour's notice is a splendid national life-preserver! Here comes the water-tube boiler; without

★ Felix du Temple (1823–1890), a French naval officer, was also involved in aeronautical experiments, building a steam-powered aeroplane. In 1874, a young sailor who had volunteered for the mission, drove the machine down-ramp to make the first take-off by a full-sized heavier-than-air powered flying machine, but merely made a powered hop to which the down-ramp run must have contributed. Nevertheless, the lack of sustained controlled flight did not prevent many from claiming this as the world's first flight.

previous notice or even an inkling, we have been ready in an hour with water-tube boiler ships. You can't exaggerate this![1]

His enthusiasm was not widely shared at first. Much of the resistance was from the old school of naval officers who had never quite accepted the end of sail and were immediately suspicious, if not downright hostile, towards anything new. They must have felt vindicated when the first examples of the new boilers proved troublesome and rectification work expensive. The shortcomings of the old boilers were immediately forgiven and forgotten once the new boilers suffered a defect, no matter how trifling. The major engineering companies saw them as a threat rather than an opportunity, as it meant re-equipping their workshops and retraining their workers, neither of which would be cheap and would displease their shareholders. Already it was the case that British industrialists kept their plant working for too long, rather than updating it. This was to prove a major weakness in terms of productivity and national competitiveness apparent during the late nineteenth century and for much of the twentieth.

It took the discovery that both the French and the Russians were using the boilers in their new ships before Fisher could persuade the Admiralty that they must be fitted to the new class of battleships, as well as in the *Powerful* and *Terrible*. What became the 'Battle of the Boilers' continued even after the return of a Conservative government led by Lord Salisbury in 1895, and the matter was still unresolved when Fisher left the Board to become Flag Officer North America and West Indies in 1897, when he was succeeded by his friend and armoured train collaborator, Arthur Wilson. He had already been promoted to Vice-Admiral on 8 May 1896, on a salary of £1,460 pa. The new First Lord, George Goschen, and Wilson eventually succumbed to the hostile reaction to the new boilers and agreed to a committee of enquiry, which eventually found in favour of the new boilers. In the meantime their introduction was delayed for ten years, leaving the French and the Russians with ships that had superior steaming qualities.

The Belleville water tube boiler had indeed needed further development to enhance its reliability, but there were also far too few engineers capable of getting the best out of it. The use of higher steam pressure also created difficulties, as Fisher later explained in a letter to a later First Lord:

The whole Pith of the matter in our difficulties with the water-tube boiler lies in the fact that we suddenly went to a pressure of 300-lbs and the workmanship did not keep pace with the increase of pressure, hence tons and tons of water going unperceived up the funnel through an infinity of leaking joints ... Surely we must expect great difficulties when we have capsized everything. We have put the water where the fire used to be and put the fire where the water used to be, and some of us think everything ought to go on just the same![2]

TIME WITH THE FAMILY

Fisher's time in Whitehall gave him the longest continuous period with his family of his career. This was fortunate as his children were of an age when they started to leave home. Cecil had joined the Indian Civil Service in 1890, but in 1895 he came home on a long leave before returning. Beatrix, his eldest daughter, became engaged that year to Captain Reginald Neeld, RN, while Dorothy accompanied him to Marienbad and then to Switzerland, returning home via Paris. They managed to stay at Marienbad for three weeks for just £24, but it entailed a knight and a rear admiral using second class railway travel. A letter home from Fisher to his 'Darling Heart' Kitty told of the poor time-keeping of the European railways, as a result of which they struggled to maintain connections, and even when they did so, their luggage got left behind, so that they arrived at the spa and were without luggage for several days. Railway travel across Europe was not for the faint-hearted, and it appears that there was no question of them affording a sleeping car.

Marienbad seems to have been the only place in Europe to appeal to him. Geneva was 'most overrated', and didn't compare with Portsmouth for shopping, while the lake at the foot of Mont Blanc did not compare with Plymouth Sound for beauty!

Notes

1 Bacon, Admiral Sir R.H., *The Life of Lord Fisher of Kilverstone*, London, 1929
2 Ibid

7

Commander-in-Chief

War is the essence of violence.
Moderation in War is imbecility.
Hit first. Hit hard. Keep on hitting.
Fisher, 1899

After spending five years battling in Whitehall, it was with relief that Vice-Admiral Sir John Arbuthnot Fisher, KCB, accepted the appointment of Flag Officer, North America and West Indies in December 1896. He took up his position in the New Year. He knew that he would return to a more senior appointment at the Admiralty in due course, so that his career would continue its upward path. While this was a sea-going appointment, and his first for fifteen years, it was also one that was accompanied. Lady Fisher was able to stay at Admiralty House in Bermuda while the fleet spent the winter months showing the flag in the Caribbean, and then at Admiralty House in Halifax, Nova Scotia, when the fleet spent the summer months in the cooler waters of the north. For most senior naval officers, this would have been a welcome break and for one in Fisher's reduced state of health, one during which to recuperate. But not Fisher.

His flagship was the battleship *Renown*, one that incorporated many of his own ideas. She had four 10-inch guns and ten 6-inch quick-firing guns, as a result of Fisher telling the Director of Naval Construction, William White, in 1892 that he wanted a ship with 'the lightest big gun and the biggest secondary gun'.

While he was anxious for action, this was the posting least likely to provide it. Nevertheless, he would make his presence felt amongst the crew not just of his flagship, but of every ship on the station. The ship's company of the flagship dreaded his appearance, when every man would stand stiffly to attention, hoping not to be noticed. As usual, Fisher expected to find inefficiency and sloppiness, and he was not to be disappointed! He famously demanded a review of all seamen ashore at 07.00 in Antigua, and was furious when he found that many were not wearing hats. The culprit was found to be an officer, Lewis Bayly, who had failed to notice the order in a signal from Fisher:

> I did not notice this, Fisher was furious, and as soon as he returned on board … he made a signal asking whose fault it was. I implored the Captain to say it was mine, but he said he was responsible for everything in the ship, and replied accordingly. Fisher signalled for the Captain to repair on board the Flagship, and again asked the same question by signal, to which I answered that it was mine. He then made a long signal by flags placing me under arrest, and ordered all ships present to repeat it. The effect as a display of flags of all colours was beautiful, while I wondered what would happen next. There followed a letter ordering me to give my reasons in writing for directly disobeying the Commander-in-Chief's order. I replied that it was due to my carelessness and stupidity. There was nothing left for Fisher to do, about an hour after, he made a signal releasing me from arrest.[1]

This was typical of Fisher's sense of the dramatic, and his ability to humiliate publicly any officer, no matter how senior, who did not meet his exacting standards. 'When an officer had committed himself,' recalled another officer. 'The saying used to be, "Will he go home on the *Alpha* or the *Beta*?" – the two regular passenger ships from Bermuda for England. As a rule, the delinquent had no choice.'[2]

The same officer also recalled that if anyone needed help, or if any of the young midshipmen were sick, whenever possible Admiralty House became a sanatorium, under the gentle control of Lady Fisher. Fisher also continued to show his playful nature, remaining an enthusiastic dancer and a very demanding partner. His wife's presence notwith-standing, he continued to seek the most beautiful partners for the dance floor, providing that they could live up to his standards, and stand the pace of a long night on the dance floor. He also took an interest in sport, one way of keeping sailors in a peacetime fleet busy, and keenly supported the flagship in contests between ships, threatening to join the team next time if they ever lost. Fortunately, this seems to have been in jest.

1. Fisher as a rear admiral during the early 1890s – one of the better tempered photographs of him.

2. Fisher as a vice-admiral in his day cabin aboard the battleship HMS *Renown* during the late 1890s. (IWM Q22156)

3. Although this photograph was supposed to date from 1907, Fisher is in the rank of vice-admiral, to which he was promoted in 1896. (Royal Naval Museum)

4. Fisher again as a vice-admiral, wearing the old-style of smaller cap that was commonplace at the time; it was not until the First World War that the current style came into vogue. (IWM Q22155)

5. Admiral Lord C. Beresford in later life.

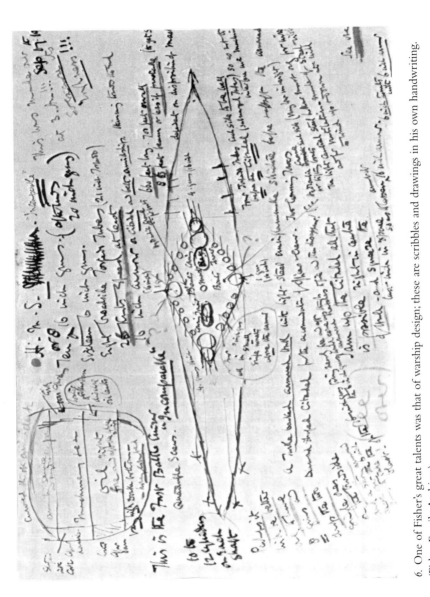

6. One of Fisher's great talents was that of warship design; these are scribbles and drawings in his own handwriting. (Fisher Family Archives)

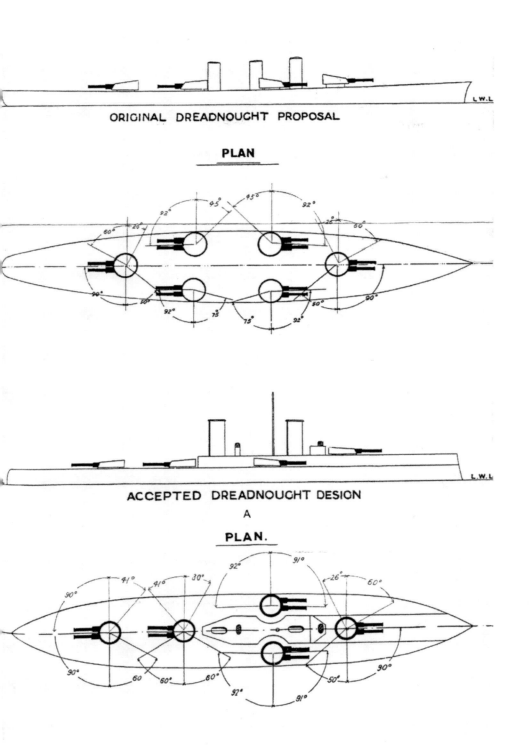

ORIGINAL DREADNOUGHT PROPOSAL

PLAN

ACCEPTED DREADNOUGHT DESIGN

A

PLAN.

Two stages in the design of his masterpiece, HMS *Dreadnought*, the first modern battleship.
(Fisher Family Archives)

8. *Dreadnought* at an early stage of construction in the Royal Dockyard at Portsmouth, where she was built in a year. (Fisher Family Archives)

9. *Dreadnought* as completed, making all other battleships obsolete, but also ensuring that other navies ha a chance to catch up on the Royal Navy. (IWM Q21184)

10. Fisher had a penchant for publicity and was well known to the press, which welcomed his appointment as First Sea Lord in 1904. This is a cartoon from the *Daily Express*, showing Nelson climbing back onto his column after getting ready to climb down and take over. (*Daily Express*)

11. A pair of 12-inch guns – broadside of HMS *Dreadnought* – the all big gun warship. (George Grantham Bain Collection)

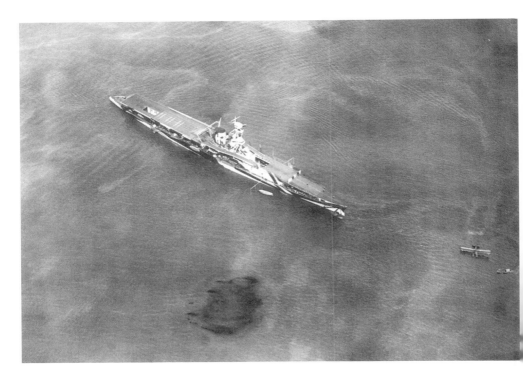

12. Furious was the first to be converted to an aircraft carrier, initially having a flying-off deck forward, and then later a landing on deck was built aft. This is her in 1918. She was later modified to have a through deck. (IWM Q19557)

13. This cartoon from the *Pall Mall Gazette* commented on Fisher's 'Navy Bill', clearly seeing him as a wise old bird. (*Pall Mall Gazette*)

14. Fisher smiling as an admiral of the fleet, the highest rank in the Royal Navy and one which no longer exists for serving officers.

15. Famous for scrapping ships that 'could neither fight nor run away', Fisher was a ruthless moderniser, as this cartoon by Strube shows. Even Neptune couldn't feel safe!

16. At the height of his power Fisher became involved in an increasingly public conflict between his protégé, Rear Admiral Sir Percy Scott, and his rival, Lord Charles Beresford. Scott and Beresford are portrayed here as naughty schoolboys, while the German Kaiser approaches in the background. (*Punch*)

17. 'Weeding the British Navy: fit subjects for Admiral Fisher's proposed rejections.' (*London Illustrated News*, 3 December 1904)

18. With the trenches in place Germany's best chance of victory would be to starve Britain into submission through U-boat attrition, a threat that Fisher had presaged.

1 As designed in 1915, with 15-inch or 18-inch guns forward and aft

2 As completed in mid-1917, with a hangar and flying-off deck forward

19. Fisher's other creation when he returned to the Admiralty was the *Courageous*-class of 'light battlecruisers', designed to have shallow draft so that they could support an ambitious and unrealistic plan for an invasion of Germany's Baltic coast. These were to have a twin 15-inch turret fore and aft, but one, *Furious*, was intended to have a massive 18-inch gun fore and aft, with the latter retained when she received a flying-off deck. (Author's Collection)

20. The light battlecruisers *Courageous* and *Glorious* at sea with a destroyer between them. Made redundant by the Washington Navy Treaty of 1922, these ships were later converted to aircraft carriers, a move of which Fisher would have approved. (IWM SP727)

21. Winston Churchill as First Lord of the Admiralty. (IWM Q93275)

22. Admiral Jellicoe on HMS *Iron Duke.* (IWM Q55499)

23. Beatty with King George V on HMS *Queen Elizabeth*, Scapa Flow, July 1918. (IWM Q19840)

24. Lord Kitchener leaving the Destroyer *Oak* to lunch with Admiral Jellicoe on the *Iron Duke*. Within hours Kitchener was lost at sea with most of the crew of the *Hampshire*. (Mansell Collection)

THE NAVAL BATTLE: FORCE THE GERMAN FLEET WOULD NOT FACE.

PHOTOGRAPH BY CRIBB.

"WHEN THE MAIN BODY OF THE BRITISH FLEET CAME INTO CONTACT WITH THE GERMAN HIGH SEAS FLEET, A VERY BRIEF PERIOD SUFFICED TO COMPEL THE LATTER, WHO HAD BEEN SEVERELY PUNISHED, TO SEEK REFUGE IN THEIR PROTECTED WATERS ": A BRITISH SUPER-DREADNOUGHT BATTLE-SHIP FIRING A BROADSIDE.

25. 'The naval battle force the German Fleet would not face.' A British super-dreadnought battleship firing broadside. (*Illustrated London News*, 10 June 1916)

A SPAT WITH FRANCE AND USN APPLAUDED

Given the time taken for orders to reach the Fleet from the Admiralty, Fisher had more freedom of action than his twentieth-century successors would have enjoyed. When relations between France and Great Britain reached yet another crisis, this time over control of Egypt, he was able to take the *Renown* to Gibraltar so that he did not miss any fighting. This was not as hazardous an escapade as it might seem, as French naval strength in the West Indies consisted mostly of minor warships that could do little more than colonial policing and showing the flag. The ships he left behind were, if hostilities broke out, to seize the French colonies in the Caribbean, while they were also to seize the penal settlement at Devil's Island to take Captain Alfred Dreyfus, unfairly imprisoned on trumped-up charges of treason, and then land him secretly in France to 'so weaken the Government'. This was a wild and unrealistic plan, and one that would undoubtedly have rebounded on poor Dreyfus – later cleared and released – had it gone ahead as it could have compromised his position completely.

The storm over Egypt blew over, and to Fisher's intense disappointment his command had to be bystanders during the Spanish-American War of 1898. His ships had to stand by to protect British interests and subjects during the war, but while the United States enjoyed British support, to the consternation of the other European colonial powers, there was no involvement in the fighting. After Admiral Samson defeated the Spanish under Admiral Cervera in Santiago Bay on 3 July 1898, Fisher invited the Americans to Bermuda the following day. As the US fleet sailed in, the band aboard *Renown* played American patriotic tunes and Fisher held a banquet for Samson and his senior officers at Admiralty House. There were the inevitable speeches, but Fisher thought that Samson's was the best he had ever heard. It was brief and to the point: 'It was a damned fine old hen that hatched the American Eagle!'

THE HAGUE PEACE CONFERENCE

Fisher may have been concerned that being on the North American and West Indies Squadron, he was in danger of being out of sight and out of mind. Perhaps that was another reason why he was so keen to be at Gibraltar. He need not have worried. He was summoned back to

London so that he could attend the Hague Peace Conference in 1899, joining the British delegation.

The Hague Peace Conference was an abortive attempt to curtail the arms race, and especially the naval arms race, that was preoccupying the major powers. The Conference was mainly supported by Russia, which realised that it could no longer keep pace with the expanding military spending of France and Germany, with pressure from revolutionary movements at home also forcing the Tsar's hand. The call for a conference was met by widespread cynicism. No one dared oppose the Conference for appearing to be a warmonger, and the British Prime Minister, Lord Salisbury, was amongst those who believed that there was a danger that there would be a 'terrible effort of mutual destruction which will be fatal for Christian civilisation'. At first, the aim was for a conference that would result in an international treaty outlawing war. This would be unrealistic today, and it was even more of pipe-dream at the time. The objectives were watered down and the agenda called for the banning of certain types of weapon, and what amounted to an armaments standstill for a fixed period. The Conference was set to begin on 18 May at The Hague.

Such a conference was then without precedent. These were the days before the United Nations and its laughably ineffectual predecessor, the League of Nations. Alliances had come and gone, changing as national priorities changed. The major powers eyed each other with suspicion. The United Kingdom had even been at war with the United States in 1812, although it is often forgotten that fairly soon after, in 1816, a combined British, American and Dutch naval squadron had ended the tyranny of the Barbary pirates in North Africa. War with France had ended in 1815, but despite intervals when the two countries collaborated, as in the Crimean War, the two nations had come close to war on many occasions, even as recently as the year before the Conference.

It was while he was at Admiralty House in Bermuda on 22 March 1899, that Fisher had received a telegram from the First Lord ordering him to serve as British naval representative at the conference, where the delegation would be led by Sir Julian Pauncefote, the British Ambassador in Washington, who would be heading a team that also included Sir Arthur Peel, a former Speaker of the House of Commons, Sir Henry Howard, the British Minister to The Hague, and the military representative, Major-General Sir John Ardagh. When the conference ended, Fisher was to become commander-in-chief of the Mediterranean Fleet, at that time the most important sea-going appointment in the Royal Navy.

Even Fisher realised that these two appointments meant that he was passing over many other officers senior to him, and that this was bound to provoke jealousy. In fact, Lord Salisbury had not forgotten Fisher's performance at the meetings on naval ordnance. He knew that this was a man who would fight his corner, and that when put into a situation that required diplomacy, would be relied upon to exercise it.

Despite his quest for action, Fisher knew that war was wasteful and that the consequences could never be foreseen. Some have suggested that he actually hated war, but this argument is in conflict with his apparent appetite for it. Nevertheless, Fisher knew that once war broke out, it could not be humanised: 'You might as well talk of humanising Hell!' he declared.

A DOOMED ENTERPRISE

Set in the *Huis ten Bosch*, House in the Wood, and the summer residence for the House of Orange, the Conference was doomed from the start. This should have been obvious to those attending and was to some. The British and French might have been content to see a standstill in armaments, the Russians over optimistically hoped for reductions, but the Germans were strongly opposed to any standstill. Germany was determined to develop its armed forces so that the country was unchallengeable. The country intended to retain its gains from the Franco-Prussian War of 1870–1871, and to show that a unified nation was stronger still, while a longer term ambition was for this continental power also to become the supreme naval power. Industrial capacity was another factor in these calculations. Germany did not have the shipbuilding capacity of Great Britain, and intended to catch up.

Fisher was his usual self. Good company (and still a tireless dancer) away from the conference table, he was unremittingly grim in his appraisal of the Conference objectives. He even outdid the Germans. William Stead, covering the conference for the *Manchester Guardian*, wrote that 'He was a bit of a barbarian who talked like a savage at times, to the no small scandal of his colleagues.'[3] In Stead's autograph book, Fisher wrote: 'The supremacy of the British Navy is the best security for the peace of the world.' He added later that if a nation was ready for instant war with every unit of its strength, peace was inevitable. Nevertheless, the phrases used also included 'intend to be first in, and hit your enemy in the belly, and kick him when he is down, and boil your prisoners in oil (if you take any) and torture his women and children'. Talking like a savage indeed!

'Suppose that war breaks out, and I am expecting to fight a new Trafalgar on the morrow', Fisher told Stead in reference to a proposal that neutral colliers should be allowed to proceed unmolested.

> Some neutral colliers attempt to steam past us into the enemy's waters. If the enemy gets their coal into his bunkers, it may make all the difference in the coming fight. You tell me I must not seize these colliers. I tell you that nothing that you, or any power on earth, can say will stop me from sending them to the bottom, if I can in no other way keep their coal out of the enemy's hands; for to-morrow I am to fight the battle which will save or wreck the Empire. If I win it, I shall be far too big a man to be affected about protests about the neutral colliers; if I lose it, I shall go down with my ship into the deep and then protests will affect me still less.[4]

Throughout, Fisher's stark realism was in contrast to the ideals of many of the delegates, diplomats with little or no experience of war. He made it clear that the launching of projectiles from balloons, the use of submarines and of poison gas were the weapons of the future – the first aeroplanes had still to fly – and that in a future conflict, civilians would be in the frontline. This last should not have come as a shock to the delegates. In Europe and Asia, civilians had always been in the front line as armies battled across the countryside, and the concept of civilians being spared the rigours and hardships of war was the happy consolation of an island nation that had not been invaded for 800 years.

It seems that alone amongst the delegates, the Germans were the most realistic and open. They told Fisher that the British fleet was useless and that they would sink it with their destroyers and torpedo boats. The warning was taken seriously.

The Conference ended on 28 June, giving Fisher just two days to get to the Mediterranean to rejoin *Renown*, once again his flagship, but from 1 July as Commander-in-Chief of the Mediterranean Fleet.

BACK TO THE MEDITERRANEAN

The Royal Navy at the time had no great concentration of power in home waters. The Channel Fleet operated as far south as Gibraltar, and earlier Fisher had pressed for it to be able to come to the aid of the Mediterranean Fleet if that should come under pressure. The defence of the Realm relied upon the mobilisation of reserves, with many ships manned by men drawn from shore establishments and others manned entirely by reservists. That many of these ships were obsolete, or at best obsolescent, was to be a problem that Fisher would have to face later in his career.

Fisher's hopes to take full control of the Royal Navy were to be postponed, however, for in August 1899, with the retirement of Admiral Sir Fredrick Richards as First Naval Lord, Admiral Lord Walter Kerr became his successor. Not for the first time, Kerr had taken a post coveted by Fisher. To Fisher, this was a serious blow, because in another five years, he would be close to retirement and unlikely to be chosen. He was determined not to let this interfere with his dream. Retirement at the time was not 60 for officers of flag rank, but 65, while today officers that do not reach flag rank retire at 55 or, for junior officers, 50.

Once again Fisher embarked on a programme of exposure of the service's weakness and weaknesses, and of self-promotion; always a risky strategy. It was also to be conducted without hindering his plans to reform and improve the Mediterranean Fleet. This, the single largest concentration of British naval power, was to be hit by a whirlwind. He started as he meant to go on. It was the custom for each commanding officer to visit the flagship to pay an official visit to the new commander-in-chief, and then for the c-in-c formally to visit each warship, returning the visit to each of his commanding officers. The visits usually lasted thirty minutes:

Fisher swept away this waste of time by directing all the Captains to assemble on board his flagship at 10 am, and there he received them all together, the whole ceremony lasting only half an hour. He then called in turn, for three minutes only, on board each ship, so that all the official visits were ended and the conventions satisfied in a single day by 1 pm.'[5]

This same breathless approach extended to the conduct of official dinners and exercises, with torpedo nets deployed, the decks cleared for
action, the bow anchor dropped, and the ship's company sent away, as if
the ship was sinking, and then brought back again, all within a couple
of hours. Having stirred everyone up, Fisher then left them to clear up
the mess. Exercises were conducted with such realism that if there was
just one collision between the small torpedo boats, Fisher was happy.
Instead of ships steaming between ports at a stately 10-knot economical
cruising speed, Fisher had them steam at 15 knots, maximum speed for
many of his ships, which meant hard work in ships with reciprocating
engines and coal-fired boilers. Most ships would only face this sort of
ordeal every six months, just to test the engines and the engine room
personnel, but with Fisher it was a routine event. Critics accused him
of excessive wear and tear on machinery, and of wasting fuel, but Fisher
wanted to ensure that his ships would always be ready for the demands
of war, and if the machinery was not up to such constant hard work,
then it was up to the designers and builders to ensure that machinery
was produced that would be so.

Even commanding officers were not spared. He would visit a ship
and set the captain off on some exercise, and while this was being
supervised, he would suddenly turn and say: 'A torpedo has struck your
ship on the starboard quarter', and then watch his reactions and the
orders that would be given in such a dire emergency. In fact, Fisher
was obsessed with attack by torpedo. This was not unrealistic at the
time, even without his conversations with the German admirals at The
Hague. After a major exercise he wrote to Lady Fisher:

We only had two collisions – with the destroyers – but a near shave,
about 70 feet, between the *Royal Oak* and the *Ramillies*. It was really
all most exciting and was as near war as it could be. I never had any
sleep for 48 hours, nor did anyone else, and not much rest for 4 days,
so we were all pretty well done for at the end. We had a final battle
between the two parts of the Fleet, one against the other, all hands
firing like mad, and it was a splendid sight ... The destroyers all dashing about like mad in the middle of it and torpedoing everyone!

Such manoeuvres were not without result, with the ranges at which
gunnery practice was conducted rising from a mere 3,000 yards to 6,000

yards, and in some cases as much as 7,000 yards. Officers who did not reach Fisher's exacting standards were sent home. This came as a great shock. Failures that some flag officers might have overlooked, or at worst might have earned the culprit a reprimand, resulted in a brief interview with Fisher concluding with them being sent home. This seemed harsh, but Fisher reckoned on men wanting to be part of a first-class fleet. He also took specialist officers into his confidence, and sought their advice, especially the younger men less hidebound by tradition and open to new thinking about new weapons and new threats. This also boosted morale and loyalty. The aim was always that 'The Mediterranean Fleet should be kept constituted for instant war.'

This was a period of rapid change and improvement in naval gunnery. The Mediterranean Fleet gunnery officer, Captain Percy Scott, was a man in Fisher's mould, being an innovator and a perfectionist, and also being intolerant of failure. He was the right man for Fisher and made the longer ranges possible. It is not clear who took the initiative in this, but these were two men who could work well together.

IN SPLENDOUR BUT STILL SCHEMING

Fisher was not blind to the comfort and needs of his officers and men, or his own. His day cabin represented a luxury hotel suite and his barge was claimed to be 'the envy of the German Emperor'. He had a special fore-top-gallant mast fitted to his flagship so that his was the flag that flew highest. When the Fleet visited Mediterranean ports, showing the flag, he behaved like a potentate. Once again his posting was as accompanied as a sea-going command could be, with his wife and those of his family still to fly the nest housed in splendour at Admiralty House, Malta, or able to follow the Fleet in the Admiralty yacht, *Surprise*. All this, on just £1,500 a year, although he would also have received £1,642 in 'table money' for entertaining. In comparison, his son, Cecil, by this time a judge in the Indian Civil Service, was earning £2,000 a year.

None of this inhibited Fisher in his propaganda war with the Admiralty. His strategy was to attack from three sides. The first was his direct assault, while he also mounted two flanking attacks, one through his friends in political life and the other from his friends in the press. He saw the threats as coming from the French at Toulon in the South of France and Bizerta in Algeria, and from the Russians coming through from the Black Sea. In his view, even the magnificent Mediterranean Fleet was inadequate to meet the French threat, and he needed more of every kind of warship.

It should not be assumed that Fisher was alone in his quest to ensure that the Royal Navy was supreme on the world's oceans. There was an active Navy League, constantly lobbying, and many sections of the press also campaigned for more warship building. Indeed, the cause was taken up by many sections of the popular press; papers that today would be more interested in the standard of celebrity ballroom dancing thatn the Two Power Standard. This was also a time when newspapers did not simply have defence correspondents, they had experienced correspondents for both armed forces; and at the other end of the press spectrum was the naval correspondent of *The Times*, James Thursfield. Fisher maintained a lengthy correspondence with Thursfield to acquaint him with the weaknesses of the Mediterranean Fleet, which had had many of its cruisers withdrawn to maintain the blockade of South Africa to prevent the Boers receiving supplies. Another ally was a freelance journalist, Arnold White, who pleased Fisher by writing an article that prophesied an early defeat for the Royal Navy, and that the effects would be 'irretrievable, irreparable, eternal'.

Fisher even went so far as to remind White that repetition was the secret of journalism. Though he seemed to be unaware that an active freelance journalist can be worth several staff writers, with greater freedom to get his work widely published, and indeed, a pressing economic need to do so.

If the fear of warfare with the French seemed ridiculous almost on the eve of the *Entente Cordiale* and with two world wars in which Britain and France would be allies, this was still the period of colonial rivalry and Britain and France had spent much of the previous 700 years at war.

Certainly, Fisher saw the threat as real. Not only was Britain seriously weakened by the Boer War, the conflict and the earlier British support for the United States in its war against Spain had left the country isolated. At the beginning of the twentieth century, the United Kingdom did not have one reliable ally in Europe, and her interests were by definition at odds with those of the other great colonial powers.

'IN A DANGEROUS POSITION'

While at Malta in May 1901 Fisher wrote to the Earl of Rosebery, the former Liberal Prime Minister:

> We are in a dangerous and a serious position in the Mediterranean ... Because instead of seeking the French Fleet to bring it to action, I have got to seek reinforcements coming from England. The ancient and glorious role of the English Navy will be reversed: the tables will be turned; it will be the French Admiral from Toulon falling on the English Admiral in superior force or chasing him with malignant glee!

Fisher saw a partial solution to the crisis in the Mediterranean in cultivating an alliance with Turkey, which could block the Russian fleet in the Bosporus and prevent it steaming into the Mediterranean. He got on good terms with the Sultan, and deplored the lack of support from London. He also came to see the Germans as a greater threat than the French, partly because of his experience at the Hague Conference, and felt that an alliance with France would be beneficial. He was being remarkably prescient. Poor British handling of the relationship with Turkey was to be a factor in that country allying itself with Germany during the First World War, while Germany certainly did of course prove to be the real threat to both Britain and France, and Russia too, as events were to prove.

In the event of war, the Channel Fleet was supposed to reinforce the Mediterranean Fleet, providing that it could get past French ships based at Brest or Lorient. Until Fisher, however, no one had given thought to joint exercises and the practicalities of this wartime working relationship. It was fortunate that the new commander of the Channel Fleet was none other than Fisher's old friend and collaborator in the armoured train venture, Rear Admiral Arthur Wilson. The two men were complete opposites in character, but worked well together. The joint exercises involving the two fleets went ahead, and were greatly enjoyed by Fisher:

> We had a splendid day yesterday manoeuvring the whole Fleet together, and it was a wonderful sight. A passing P&O liner stopped to see it ... We had arranged it, of course, long before, and I had rehearsed it many times, so I felt pretty sure it would come off well

when the time came to put such a mass of ships through it. *We just mount up to fifty vessels*, which is a big lot to work together.[6]

Fisher's other manoeuvres continued, and as his letters became more revealing and more vitriolic, he began ending them with the injunction to 'BURN' or 'DESTROY', but he was not ordering naval officers and these instructions were largely ignored by the recipients.

In October 1900, William Waldegrave Palmer, Earl of Selborne and a son-in-law of Lord Salisbury, succeeded Lord Goschen as First Lord of the Admiralty. Fisher and Selborne were to work closely for many years, and once again this was a meeting of opposites. Selborne was patient and diplomatic, Fisher was impatient and undiplomatic to the point not just of rudeness, but even slander. His correspondence with Selborne was hectoring and could have been counter-productive, while he wrote to Thursfield that 'A strong hand is wanted at Headquarters and … *the strong hand is not there now!*' It says much about Selborne that he asked Fisher to write to him privately on any problems he discovered, doubtless hoping that this would prove to be a safety valve and reduce the pressure from the press and Fisher's political allies. Naturally, Fisher took advantage of this opening. He even went so far as to write to Selborne that he would find the correspondence advantageous. No false modesty with Fisher! He wrote in one of his early letters:

I hope that you will forgive me, and kindly remember that I have the rope around my neck, and if we don't beat the French I shall be hung or shot like Admiral Byng! … *We want more ships of all classes*, with their adjuncts in the shape of officers, men, etc … in this year's estimates, *there is not a single destroyer to be built.*[7]

This could be taken as permissible. After all, a senior naval officer should feel free to advise his political superior on maritime matters, and indeed, it is his duty to do so. It was even just acceptable to tell the First Lord that the Royal Navy was 'criminally deficient' in many warship types, but it was going beyond the bounds of decency to write:

My good friend Walter Kerr (First Naval Lord) is kind enough to suggest in his last letter to me…that I may perhaps find myself in his place and will look foolish to find myself unable to meet these demands!

I don't expect to find myself in his place, but you will see from this remark of his that my pertinacity in urging what I think to be imperatively necessary tends to place me at loggerheads with him.[8]

What this means is 'I don't get on with my boss and so I am going over his head.' People have been sacked for less. What was completely unforgivable was that Fisher then broke the confidence with the First Lord by leaking the correspondence to Thursfield on the grounds that 'Lord Selborne ... seems to be bent on obtaining all we require; but I have no doubt that a little "stiffening" from outside in the shape of one of those "do-your-duty-or-you'll-catch-it" leading articles in *The Times* will help him ... just about this time, when the Estimates are being roughed out in Cabinet meetings!' He was completely open in his criticisms of Kerr to Thursfield, even going so far as to write: 'I bless the wisdom of our ancestors in having a civilian First Lord, as Lord Selborne is far more alive to the great issues at stake than his chief naval adviser'.[9]

In March 1901, Selborne took both Kerr and the Director of Naval Intelligence to Malta to see the new dockyard, or at least that was the official reason. It could also have been that taking a keen interest in the Royal Navy was politic, for King Edward VII had come to the throne in January. The real reason was to discuss with Fisher the issues that he had been raising. Inevitably, according to Fisher the resulting discussions became 'very heated'. One victim of this was Captain Reginald Custance, Director of Naval Intelligence, for from this time on the relationship with Fisher became one of enmity. Kerr stuck to his guns, and Selborne found it difficult, indeed impossible, to overrule the First Naval Lord in front of an inferior, and so Selborne was also tarred with the same brush by Fisher. He wrote to Lord Spencer: 'I hope I may live to see you again First Lord, being in my opinion *the best the Navy ever had!*' He wrote in similar vein to Lord Rosebery.

FRUSTRATION – AND A RIVAL

Fisher was, undoubtedly, frustrated. By this time he had spent almost two years in the Mediterranean and his fleet was no stronger than when he first arrived. Indeed, thanks to the predations caused by the Boer War, it was weaker in many respects. He gave little credence to

Selborne's promise that ships would be sent from England in an emergency.★ There was another edge to this. Kerr was a Roman Catholic and suspected by Fisher of being a 'slave to the Roman Catholic hierarchy' who would want to have their man stay at the top. Roman Catholicism was still regarded with suspicion by many in Britain at the time.

By now, all sense of discretion had been abandoned and even the patient Selborne rebuked the troublesome Admiral, writing that he seemed to have no confidence in the Admiralty. He was promptly assured that Fisher did *not* have confidence in the Admiralty, writing that 'I know your intentions are good, but Hell is paved with good intentions.' Even Kerr started to bite back, and complain about the lack of discretion. To be fair, even Fisher began to worry when the *Daily Mail* ran a series of articles based on what Fisher had considered to be confidential briefings. He complained about these to Thursfield, and then immediately communicated the undoubtedly 'top secret' information to him that in war, the Mediterranean and Channel Fleets would be combined. Lesser men would have been imprisoned, even hanged, for less. In Fisher's case, he was promoted to Admiral on 2 November 1901.

Such an atmosphere was bad for discipline, in which Fisher, paradoxically, was such a believer. It also flushed out other discontented senior officers, of whom the most notable was Rear Admiral Lord Charles William de la Poer Beresford.

Beresford and Fisher belonged to the same generation of naval officers, and both had proceeded to the very highest levels of the service. There any similarity ended. Fisher had made his own way without help from his family, although he had enjoyed the initial impetus provided by his godmother, Lady Wilmot-Horton. Beresford had inherited wealth and the self-assurance that came from a privileged background, as well as good looks and good health. Fisher's health had been poor for some years by this time, and he could never have been described as handsome. Both were well connected, but Fisher had acquired his

★ Very perceptive of him. A similar promise was given to Australia and New Zealand between the two world wars when concerns about Japanese ambitions were raised. When the time came, the ships were otherwise engaged.

connections over many years while Beresford had gone to school with the future Lord Rosebery and Lord George Hamilton.

Another advantage enjoyed by Beresford was that at one stage he actually became a member of Parliament, which was possible while he was on half-pay as he was not enjoying an office of profit under the Crown, and while most naval officers, including the always hard-up Fisher, feared their periods on half-pay, Beresford welcomed the opportunities for hunting and socialising that they brought.

The Royal Navy of the day had been large enough to keep these two men apart for most of their careers. They had been together during the bombardment at Alexandria, and Beresford, who remained afloat while Fisher and Wilson went ashore, received even more public attention. There were those who believed that Beresford stood as good a chance as Fisher of becoming First Naval Lord.

It was simply asking for trouble for Goschen to appoint Beresford as second-in-command of the Mediterranean Fleet, flying his flag in HMS *Ramillies*, under Fisher. Some have suggested that putting two such strong-headed and impetuous officers together was thought to be a means of cancelling each other out, that peace would reign. They were wrong. Coincidental with Fisher's campaign, Beresford mounted one of his own, some even suggest that this was done to compete with his superior. Certainly, Beresford was far more open in his criticisms than Fisher. Some blame Fisher for keeping his second-in-command at a distance, treating him with reserve. Fisher felt that Beresford was over-promoted and a playboy, who had gained his rank because of his background and his connections. Both men felt that they had the answer, indeed *were* the answer, for the future of the Royal Navy. They had that much in common.

Outright warfare between the two men was to wreck both of them in years to come, but the origins of the rift were probably to be found during their time in Malta together. Lord Chatfield wrote of clashes between the two men in his memoirs:

One forenoon, Lord Charles had sent his signalman ashore to the Corradino for signal exercises. He had not asked permission as he should have done by the station orders, an oversight and not a deliberate intention. The Fleet signal officer informed the Commander-in-Chief.

'Make a signal to the *Ramillies*,' ordered Fisher. '*Ramiliies'* signalmen to return to their ship immediately. Report in writing why station order No. – has not been obeyed.' To make such a signal to his second in command was unwise. The Fleet took in the signal and pricked up its ears. That evening Malta was talking of it … There was a rift in the lute. But a storm was shortly to ensue compared to which this was but an April shower.

A few months later the Fleet was returning to Malta at the end of the first summer cruise. Admiral Fisher always led in first in the *Renown*, and walked up to the 'Baracca', a vantage point whence he could watch every ship come into the difficult and narrow harbour and turn round 180 degrees before securing bow and stern to her buoys. It was a fine test of the nerve and skill of their Captains. Rapidity in every task was the order of the day. Charles Beresford was a fine seaman and anxious that his division should be smarter than others. His Flag-Captain, unfortunately, was not one of the best ship-handlers. When the *Ramillies* came in, she had to secure to two buoys in Bighi Bay, the outer anchorage, a fairly easy task. He made a mess of it, got his ship stuck across the harbour and delayed the entrance of the second division. 'Jacky' lost his temper and signalled to the second-in-command: 'Your flagship is to proceed to sea again and come in again in a seamanlike manner.'[10]

Chatfield, later Admiral of the Fleet, saw this incident as 'a lamentable example of bad leadership.' It was typical of Fisher, however, and not the first time that he had publicly humiliated a senior officer.

For himself, Fisher had, by this time, come to play down his chances of becoming First Naval Lord, as we have already seen in a letter to Lord Selborne. He was covering himself against failure and at the same time giving himself free rein to criticise. Nevertheless, for once in his life, it was not what he said or wrote that mattered. He did indicate to the Board of Admiralty that he would welcome a shore appointment. Even he found commanding the Mediterranean Fleet exhausting. On 9 February 1902, Lord Selborne wrote to him, inviting him to become Second Naval Lord, the member of the Admiralty responsible for personnel. The offer was a generous one, and Selborne had the sense to remind Fisher that he or his successors reserved to themselves the right to decide just who would succeed Kerr when the time came, and, no less important, to tell him that any disagreements that they might have during Fisher's term of office as Second Naval Lord, had to be kept within the Board. Whether or not Fisher had learnt any lessons during his time in the Mediterranean, his First Lord most certainly had.

Notes

1 Bayly, Admiral Sir Lewis, RN, *Pull Together*, London, 1939.

2 Bacon, Admiral Sir R.H., *The Life of Lord Fisher of Kilverstone*, London, 1929

3 Ibid

4 *Review of Reviews*, February 1910.

5 Bacon, Admiral Sir R.H., *The Life of Lord Fisher of Kilverstone*, London, 1929

6 Ibid

7 Kilverstone, Admiral of the Fleet Baron, *Records*, London, 1919

8 Ibid

9 Ibid

10 Chatfield, Admiral of the Fleet Lord, *The Navy and Defence*, London, 1942–47 (2 vols)

Second Naval Lord

Rest assured there will be no faltering at the Admiralty! I wrote in chalk on one of my colleague's doors, 'Remember Lot's wife! No looking back now!' And he has taken the hint!
Fisher to James Thursfield, 26 December 1902

Fisher believed in the benefits of favouritism, or patronage, practised it himself and had been on the receiving end more than once during his career, particularly while a junior officer, but even as a captain. Now he had the benefit of being the favourite admiral of a sovereign who had been trained by the Royal Navy and loved the Royal Navy. He was also an intelligent monarch with a keen interest in foreign affairs. This was a case of the country having the right royal man at the right time as the international situation became much more difficult. There were many who expected a major European war within the decade, or at least shortly afterwards.

That Fisher was no great respecter of persons was clear, and he even fell out with His Majesty King Edward VII on occasion. He refused to allow him to be rowed out in a pulling barge at a naval review, instead offering a steam-powered barge, which provoked a fit of Royal pique. Fisher responded in kind, and then some. He earned a rebuke: 'Would you kindly leave off shaking your fist in my face.' Fisher's behaviour at times went far beyond the permissible and he was indeed fortunate that there were those around at the highest levels prepared to tolerate it. This was a man who was prepared to protest that in defeat there would be a rope around his neck, but who behaved in a manner that seemed guaranteed to lead him to just that end.

Fisher's friendship with the Sovereign was important, and acted not just as a safety valve but as a final guarantee against Fisher's wilder plans. Nelson had sent frigates into the harbour at Copenhagen in 1801 when the Danish Fleet refused to come out and fight, and, when, some years later, Fisher suggested that it was time to 'Copenhagen' the German Fleet in its bases without warning, just as the Japanese had done to the Russians in the Far East in 1904, the King replied: 'Fisher, you must be mad!'

Fisher's behaviour could also be eccentric on occasion, and could be so to the point of rudeness. On one occasion he was being driven with the King in a carriage when he spotted a beautiful woman. Fisher recalled:

> I was driving with him alone, and utterly carried away by my feelings, I suddenly stood up in the carriage and waved to a very beautiful woman who I thought was in America! The King was awfully angry, but I made it much worse by saying I had forgotten all about him! But he added, 'Well! Find out where she lives and let me know,' and he gave her little child a sovereign and asked her to dinner, to my intense joy![1]

Such behaviour flew in the face of court etiquette, and it showed incredible tolerance on the part of Edward VII.

Fisher's return to the Admiralty meant that most senior naval officers – and those members of the press and those in political life with an interest in naval matters – once again saw him as Kerr's successor as First Naval Lord. Fisher, meanwhile, saw the potential of his new role. Just as he had turned the procurement and maintenance organisation upside down, he now intended to do the same for the navy's personnel.

'I HAVE NO WORK'

The problem was that while on paper and to outsiders the Second Naval Lord was in charge of personnel, there were distinct limitations to his authority. Fisher was anxious to change this and immediately set about securing the right to control the appointment of all officers, regardless of rank. Some accounts maintain that he did this by stalking the corridors of the Admiralty with a notice announcing 'I have no work' hung around his neck. This was hard to believe as he often started work shortly after 4 a.m. He had a private secretary, Sir Charles Walker, who was amazed at the pace at which Fisher could get through his routine work, reading the pages of a report almost as quickly as he could turn them over, and then writing his opinion on the cover. He never dictated letters, leaving Walker to handle the routine correspondence, while his own correspondence was handwritten.

Seadog Fisher continued to practise his old tricks. He not only continued to bombard the First Lord with his opinions, but maintained his correspondence with politicians and journalists, to whom he now added members of the Royal family. Despite his well-defined role covering personnel – which was indeed occupying most of his time, as during the second half of the year he was planning nothing less than a complete transformation of naval training – he continued to push his thoughts on tactics and on the design of warships.

While the Royal Navy had undergone greater change during Fisher's career than during the preceding 300 years, training of both officers and men had changed little. This is not to say that he objected to everything that tradition had brought to the Royal Navy. Fisher believed unreservedly in two things: the sea as a schoolroom and in starting new entrants young. He demonstrated his faith in the system in a letter to Lord Knollys, private secretary to Edward VII:

> Of all the systems of education ever devised by the wit of man, nothing approaches or ever can approach the education of the sea in giving self-reliance, fertility of resource, fearlessness of responsibility, and the power of initiative. These four great qualities are the habits of mind required for fighting people, for, as has been truly said, they are the four great Nelsonic attributes, and gales of wind, fog, the imminence of great danger, and the uncertainty of life from hour to hour (which uncertainty any night a collision may produce!) all of them conduce unconsciously to train the tender lad to become a brave and resourceful man.'[2]

Work began on the new scheme on 10 June 1902. By late August, Fisher was able to tell Selborne that he was 'getting on splendidly with all the investigations as to what is involved by the alterations in entry and training of officers and men, as set forth in the print, and hope to have every detail cut and dried by the time Parliament meets.' Optimistically, he declared that the 'mountains of the future are the molehills of the past!'

The service in fact simply reflected the class divisions of the society of the day, but a complication came in the distinction between the engineer and the executive, between what Michael Lewis in *The Navy of Britain* defined as those who 'make her go' and those who 'fight her'. Many argue that this was because the engineers were as unwelcome aboard ship as the smelly, noisy and hot engines themselves, but in fact the distinction simply reflected an even earlier one, between the fighting sailors and those who sailed the ship, with the old sailing ship having a lowly sailing master in addition to the captain or the commanding officer.

Nevertheless, it was a fact that that the first engines appeared in a British warship in 1837, but it was another ten years before the first commissioned engineering officer appeared. They were often referred to as 'engine drivers', and on many ships were forced to eat in their own mess, and it was not until the closing years of the nineteenth century that their status was elevated. The improvement came partly as a new generation of naval officers, unfamiliar with the days of sail, emerged, and also as the engines themselves improved, becoming more sophisticated, and the engineers thus became more highly qualified. Fisher himself used to recount the story of a chief engineer called Brown:

> Brown worried the First Lieutenant of a ship ... to exasperation by telling him that he ranked before him when on shore or when going in to dinner. 'Look here, Brown,' said the First Lieutenant, 'it don't matter what rank the Admiralty like to give you, and I don't care a damn whether you walk into dinner before me or after me; but all I know, Brown, is that my Ma will never ask your ma to tea.'[3]

This amused Fisher, but also irritated him. It is highly likely that only an officer with experience of *not* having had a privileged start, good connections and a fine school, could have been so aware of the need for reform. As he wrote to Arnold White, the freelance journalist:

> The old navigating class in the Navy. It was splendid, but dissatisfied, and unrecognised. They were extracted from a different social stratum and couldn't mix any more than oil and vinegar, and were kept in separate bottles all their time in the Service. But a magician arose and said, 'Let's have no class distinctions! Enter them all as midshipmen, and those who show an aptitude for navigating they will take it up'; and the result has been splendid; and it's a matter of fact that

fewer ships have been lost or grounded since this scheme came into maturity than ever known before in the history of the Navy. *So let it be with the Engineers.* Enter them as midshipmen on the Naval College at Dartmouth, put 'em all into the same bottle! And at a suitable time select those for engineering duties, give high special pay, higher than we now give to the Gunnery, or the Torpedo, or the Navigating Lieutenants, and you will then have no lack of Engineer officers of a higher calibre perhaps than at present.[4]

THE FISHER-SELBORNE SCHEME

The Fisher-Selborne Scheme, which was announced on 25 December 1902, saw the solution being that officers and seamen, engineers and marines, should all be of one company; joining, being educated and training together, after which engineering would be treated as a specialisation just as navigation, gunnery and torpedoes had become. The intention was that engineering officers, initially lieutenants (E), would, like lieutenants (N), lieutenants (G) and lieutenants (T), (respectively, navigating, gunnery and torpedoes) be able to rise to the upper reaches of the service.

Implementation began in 1903 and that same year was also notable for the creation of the Royal Naval Volunteer Reserve, RNVR, to augment the Royal Naval Reserve, RNR.

Even for gunnery and navigation students there were problems to be resolved. Many, including Fisher himself, had to be convinced that the traditional means of training entirely at sea was no longer suitable. Fisher initially rejected plans for converting the main officers' training school, the Britannia Royal Naval College at Dartmouth, into a public school, but the difficulty facing him was that while training was best done at sea, teaching was better done ashore. The Britannia Royal Naval College had been based in hulks, including the old HMS *Britannia* herself, on the tidal reaches of the River Dart at Dartmouth, but by the end of the nineteenth century these old ships had outlived their usefulness. Sanitation was poor, and in the prevailing conditions discipline was difficult to enforce. The new shore-based college, offering a four-year public school type of education, was opened in 1905, but the need to move young cadets away from the hulks was so pressing that from September 1903 cadets went to a junior college at Queen

Victoria's former residence at Osborne on the Isle of Wight, staying
there for two years and then moving up to *Britannia*. So cadets spent
two years each at Osborne and Dartmouth, followed by six months in
a training cruiser, before joining the fleet as midshipmen. Midshipmen,
'snotties' to the rest of the Royal Navy, had an officer's cap badge but
were not officers, and occupied a no man's land between ratings and
commissioned personnel. They did not join the officers in the wardroom, but instead messed in the gunroom; contemporary photographs
show this being something like a prefects' common room. They were
still under training, learning much of the practical side of their craft,
and had no equivalent in the army or, for that matter once it came into
existence, the Royal Air Force. Their duties consisted mainly of assisting the officers of a ship, but there were some tasks assigned to them
alone. One of these was commanding the picket boat, which provided a
shuttle service between ship and shore, and for many a young man this
presented a challenge, not just in navigating safely in an often exposed
and choppy anchorage or a busy harbour, but in dealing with drunken
sailors often old enough to be their father.

The Fisher-Selborne system was originally intended to take lieutenants at the age of 22 years and train them as engineers at the Royal
Naval Engineering College at Keyham. Intention and outcome
did not tally, with only one midshipman in twenty volunteering for
engineering, largely, many suspected, because of pressures put on the
youngsters by snobbish parents. The attitude of the parents was understandable. Anyone with a naval connection knew that navigation and
gunnery were the only worthwhile nautical arts and that naval officers in general looked down upon engineers, who were never quite
regarded as being gentlemen. Many argued against the scheme, saying
that the Royal Navy was going to pot and would become a service of
'plumbers and greasers', ignoring the fact that much of what was being
proposed already occurred in the United States Navy. Nevertheless, it
finally became clear that a different approach was needed; but it was
not until after the First World War that midshipmen were selected
for engineering and sent on the long four-year engineering course
at Keyham.

Within days of the scheme being announced, Fisher was delighted
to have the support of twenty-four captains and commanders. What
also surprised and delighted him was that he had the open and whole-
hearted support of his rival, Beresford.

WARRANT OFFICERS' APPEAL

Nevertheless, there were still gaps to plug. In the Victorian Navy, it had been virtually impossible for ratings to become officers. In theory, warrant officers could be promoted to the rank of lieutenant for gallantry in action, but it was not until the golden jubilee honours of Queen Victoria in 1887 that two warrant officers received this promotion. The result was that warrant officers could spend as much as thirty years in the rank, and pressure for reform built up in the service. This eventually found expression in the monthly *Naval Warrant Officers' Journal*, which pressed their case. An opportunity seemed to arise in 1890 when the then First Lord, Lord George Hamilton, announced that the Royal Navy was short of a hundred lieutenants, causing the warrant officers to issue 'An Earnest Appeal for Promotion from the Ranks, Royal Navy,' pointing out that many were already performing the duties of sub-lieutenants and lieutenants. Despite strong public support, the government opposed their ambitions and the extra hundred officers were all RNR officers transferred from the Merchant Navy. Another warrant officer, Thomas Lyne, was commissioned for gallantry during the Boer War in 1902, and eventually became a rear admiral, the first from the lower deck since John Kingcome in 1818. From 1903 onwards, warrant officers could expect to be promoted to lieutenant, but it took Churchill, as First Lord, to formalise this some years later in 1912, encouraged by Fisher, then in retirement.

While engineer officers carried executive titles such as lieutenant or commander, they did not have the curl on their rings or stripes until 1915, but did have purple cloth between the rings, while surgeons had red, paymasters white and instructors blue, but without the curl and without executive titles, having instead ranks such as assistant paymaster or surgeon, and these did not receive the executive curl until 1918. Paymasters were general administrators, since secretaries were members of the paymaster branch. Instructors had blue cloth between their rings.

Fisher did his best to ensure that the influential members of the press and politicians were on his side to ensure that the scheme enjoyed a good start. Once again, he courted royalty and had the Prince of Wales on his side. This became particularly important when some tried to undermine the scheme, and as early as April 1904, there was a proposal that cadets should spend an extra term of six months at *Britannia*.

Prince George saw this as 'disastrous' when it was 'high time in fact for them to be at sea getting in touch with the Service'.

Mention has been made of favouritism in action and of the 'Fishpond'; that group of rising naval officers basking in Fisher approval. Beresford was to be the most notable absentee from the Fishpond, which really started to come into existence during the winter of 1902–1903. Probably the most famous member of the Fishpond was John Jellicoe, the future commander of the Grand Fleet at the Battle of Jutland. The announcement of the Fisher-Selborne Scheme was the catalyst that started the Fishpond. If you openly supported the scheme, you were 'in' and enjoyed official approval; if you objected you were 'out'. Many rising stars found their hopes dashed, and were left behind. One of these was Captain Reginald Custance, the Director of Naval Intelligence. Another was Captain George Egerton, a specialist in Fisher's favourite weapon, the torpedo. After a meeting at the Admiralty, he was called into Fisher's room where the Admiral shook his fist at him and said: 'If you oppose my Education scheme I will crush you.' This was no idle threat, even though Egerton had a point, which he repeated, that torpedo lieutenants could not be trained in just three months. Progress for those who were outside the Fishpond was slow and difficult, and woe betide those who crossed Fisher's path, as Egerton discovered when the great man became Commander-in-Chief, Portsmouth, while he was in command of the torpedo training school, HMS *Vernon*.

There can be little doubt that the abrupt imposition of the scheme alienated many who might have become converts, and also accounted for some of the shortcomings of the scheme that could have been modified or avoided. On the other hand, the state of naval training lagged far behind the technological developments of the Fleet. If one believed that war was imminent, changes had to be made and made quickly. Nevertheless, not only in the abbreviated training of torpedo officers but in the neglect of the Royal Marines, the scheme had its weaknesses and omissions.

Fisher was also able to preside over some major changes in the reserves for the fleet. In 1901, the long considered but also long deferred (it had first been mooted in the 1850s) Royal Fleet Reserve had been formed. In an emergency, it brought together officers and ratings who had recently left the service, including those who had retired, so that men with experience of modern ships and weapons were on hand. In 1903, the Royal Naval Volunteer Reserve was formed, in part from the Royal Naval Artillery Volunteers, to provide a nucleus of citizen sailors who could also be called upon in an emergency. Part of the reason for this was that the Merchant Navy, which had grown from 6 million gross tons of shipping in 1875 to more than 19 million tons at the turn of the century, had seen its British manpower drop over the same period from 182,000 to around 152,000. The Merchant Navy had provided the manpower of the Royal Naval Reserve, but its strength was judged to be inadequate to give the Royal Navy the personnel it would need in wartime.

CHANGES IN WARFARE

It became clear that Fisher's continued presence at the Admiralty was doing little to repair relations with other senior officers. Having been commander-in-chief twice and effectively number one, it was also clear that continued existence as a number two at the Admiralty sat uneasily with him. In March 1903, Fisher was sent to Portsmouth as Commander-in-Chief. The move was welcome to Fisher, not only for the reasons already mentioned, but also because it gave him the opportunity to ensure that the scheme was implemented in the important area of his new command, which would include Osborne, *Vernon* and *Excellent*.

Before he left London for the south coast, he gave a rare public speech at the Royal Academy dinner, promising his audience just three minutes, and delighting them with thirty minutes. He started with a brief reference to his early days at sea, followed by a concise review of the changes in warfare and a brief mention of the Army:

> Look at the submarine boat and wireless telegraphy. When they are perfected, we do not know what a revolution will come about. In their inception they were the weapons of the weak. Now they loom large as the weapons of the strong ... but the great fact which I come to is that we are realizing, the Navy and the Admiralty are realizing, that on the British Navy rests the British Empire ... We are different from continental nations for no soldier of ours can go anywhere unless a sailor carries him on his back. I am not disparaging the Army! I am looking forward to them coming to sea with us again as they did in the old days. Why, Nelson had three regiments of infantry with him at the Battle of Cape St Vincent.[5]

In August 1903, the chairman of Armstrongs, the major north-eastern engineering, shipbuilding and armaments manufacturing company, offered Fisher £10,000 a year to work for him. This was more than double his naval salary while at Portsmouth.

Notes

1 Kilverstone, Admiral of the Fleet Baron, *Memories*, London, 1919
2 Ibid
3 Bacon, Admiral Sir R.H., *The Life of Lord Fisher of Kilverstone*, London, 1929
4 Ibid
5 Kilverstone, Admiral of the Fleet Baron, *Records*, London, 1919

9

Back to Pompey

I honestly believe I can be of more service at Portsmouth as Commander-in-Chief than as Second Naval Lord, especially in view of inaugurating Osborne, new boy's and men's training, organization of barracks, and above all, 'nucleus crews'. At all events ... I will make them miserable who prevent it!
Fisher to Lord Selborne, 5 March 1903

Fisher arrived at Portsmouth in summer 1903, having decided in January that the new school at Osborne would open that August. A contractor appointed by the Admiralty said that the work would take three years, but Fisher found an old acquaintance from the United States was in London – an American building contractor – at the time, and he promised Fisher that the work would be completed for King Edward VII to open the school on 4 August. It was done, with a few days in hand. Meanwhile, Fisher had persuaded Alfred Ewing to leave the University of Cambridge and become the first Director of Naval Education, with a sharp reduction in salary.

Fisher took up his appointment on 31 August. He was definitely not out of sight at Portsmouth, with frequent visits to the Admiralty, despite the great naval base having a remarkably poor railway service to London at that time with just four 'fast' trains a day taking more than two hours for the 74-mile journey. More important, in late September, he was invited to join the King and Queen at Balmoral, where they were hosting the King and Queen of Italy. Despite the important royal guests, he was given the best suite in the castle and at dinner on the first evening sat next to King Edward, with the two men conversing all evening.

Conversation with His Majesty was no idle chatter. In 1903, the Sovereign of course wielded more power and influence than is the case today. The King wanted Fisher to be the First Naval Lord, and made it clear that his spell at Portsmouth would be short. Fisher wrote to his daughter Beatrix: 'He asked me with a merry twinkle in his eye how long I intended to stop at Portsmouth! I told him that, subject to the King's pleasure, I understood that it was a three years' appointment.'[1]

'DAMNABLE, DOMINEERING AND DICTATORIAL'

The King also spent a considerable amount of time in meetings with Fisher late into the evening, asking him for his advice and opinions on matters of defence. Even Fisher became concerned at some of the advice he was giving, but everything was done on condition that only His Majesty, the Prince of Wales and the King's Private Secretary would be privy. Almost as difficult for Fisher, the King had asked him some six months earlier if he would consider joining a committee to reform the War Office. This was at one and the same time a compliment and a tremendous danger. To have a senior naval officer commenting on how the British Army should organise its headquarters was almost unbelievable. There were other problems as well. The Admiralty and the War Office were not mirror images of one another. Unlike the War Office, the Admiralty was also an operational headquarters. Local commanders-in-chief and flag officers could be, and were, bypassed and orders could be given to the commanding officers of individual ships. The British Army gave local commanders in the field considerable delegated responsibility, and there was no question of the War Office bypassing a corps or divisional commander to give orders to the commanding officer of a battalion. Whilst at Balmoral, the King raised the issue again.

A committee of just three men was proposed, with the promise that those of its recommendation that were accepted would be implemented quickly. As the news began to leak out, Fisher's naval friends pressed him not to take part, with one writing to him, 'entreating me not to serve on proposed Committee, as he says it will cause endless ill-feeling and bitterness among the soldiers!'

The poor performance of the British Army during the Boer War had resulted in a committee of investigation, which produced a report that was, for the most part, favourable to the Army. A minority report by Viscount Esher, was critical. It was Esher, who was the King's closest adviser on defence matters, who had the idea for a committee of just three, which he would head. Of course, the problem with Fisher was that he was anti-Army, regarding the Royal Navy as the 'First, second, third, fourth and fifth line of the nation's defence', and the Army only 'as a projectile to be fired by the Navy!' Fisher had not forgotten the (perceived) poor performance of the Army during the Crimean War, and it seemed that nothing had changed in half a century. He had actually written to Esher: 'The military system is rotten to the very core! You want to begin *ab ovo!* The best of the Generals are even worse than the subalterns, because they are more hardened sinners!'

Inevitably, Fisher joined the Committee, chaired by Lord Esher and with the third member Colonel Sir George Clarke, Governor of the State of Victoria in Australia. Clarke was later to become secretary of the Committee of Imperial Defence. Interestingly, he was also a critic of the Fisher-Selborne Scheme, but was accepted by Fisher despite this. The sole serving Army representative was the committee's secretary, a young and able soldier, Lieutenant-Colonel Gerald Ellison. Known officially and inevitably as the Esher Committee, many in the services nicknamed them the 'dauntless three', although a future prime minister, Sir Henry Campbell-Bannerman described them as 'Damnable, Domineering and Dictatorial', although to whom each of these three epithets applied is not clear today. Any one, or all three, could certainly have been aimed at Fisher himself.

Fisher believed in a meritocracy. He was not opposed to wealth or position, and was delighted when his son became the heir to Vavasseur's fortune, and he himself enjoyed the opportunities to mix with the great and the good in Victorian and then Edwardian society. Fisher, however, really did not believe in inherited wealth, and he had worked hard to advance himself. He believed in the professional and in professionalism, not amateurism. War was too important to be a hobby, a side interest. He was appalled by what he saw at senior levels in the British Army. He was not surprised that Boer guerrillas, fighting a highly mobile war, had nearly brought it to its knees. Most of all, he was shocked to find that the worst thing someone could say about a brother officer was 'professional'. He wrote to Esher in frank disbelief: 'They call Clarke "one of those damned professional soldiers!"' This was the reality; the Army was a social institution, with competition to get into a good regiment, rather than a fighting machine.

The Committee got off to a slow start, as Clarke had to sail from Melbourne, a voyage of about six weeks. The initial work consisted of correspondence between Fisher, still at Portsmouth, and Esher in

London. Many of the generals giving evidence to the Committee journeyed to Portsmouth to see Fisher and were entertained at Admiralty House, and he took the opportunity to share his thinking with them and discuss his ideas. Inevitably, Fisher saw the Army as a small, highly mobile, striking force that could be landed by the Navy to create chaos behind enemy lines. This really was what the Royal Marines were to evolve into. It ignored the realities of a major continental war, or of the needs of occupation after a victory. Once again, he saw the Army as an extension of the Navy. Despite this, it seems that he made some converts amongst those who took the trouble to see him, possibly aided by the fact that he played down his own involvement as being 'Esher's facile dupe' and 'Clarke's servile copyist'. Only someone without close contact with Fisher would believe that!

Typical of Fisher's thinking was a letter he wrote to Esher on 19 November 1903:

> The Navy embarks it and lands it where it can do most mischief! Thus the Germans are ready to land a large military force on the Cotentin Peninsula in case of war with France, and my German military colleagues at The Hague Conference told me this comparatively small military force would have the effect of demobilising half a million men, who would thus be taken away from the German frontier. They never know where the brutes are going to land! Consequently, instead of our military manoeuvres being on Salisbury Plain and its vicinity (ineffectually apeing [sic] the vast Continental Armies!), we should be employing ourselves in joint naval and military manoeuvres, embarking 50,000 men at Portsmouth and landing them at Milford Haven or Bantry Bay! This would make the foreigners sit up! Fancy, in the Mediterranean Fleet we disembarked 12,000 men with guns in 19 *minutes*! What do you think of that! And we should hurry up the soldiers! No doubt there will be good-natured chaff! Once we embarked 7,000 soldiers at Malta and took them round and landed them elsewhere for practice, and I remember having a complaint that the bluejackets said, 'Come on, you bloody lobsters! Wake up!'[2]

Given the numbers involved in Fisher's thinking, this was not so much a question of using the troops as marines, but of operating on a scale only achieved by the United States Marine Corps during the Second World War in the Pacific. Later, when he returned to his favourite, and in many ways strongest area of naval affairs, technology, he allowed his imagination to run ahead of what was realistic in the same way.

The Committee made rapid progress, almost certainly due to having just three members. The main thrust of its recommendations were already agreed by January 1904, with Fisher and Esher settling the detail of the planned Army Council, meant to be the equivalent of the Board of Admiralty.

The Committee's recommendations were put into not one but two separate reports, sent on 11 January to the Conservative Prime Minister, Arthur Balfour. The reason for this was that the first report dealt with defence overall, while the second dealt specifically with the War Office. While this meant that the Committee had gone beyond the letter of its remit, the ability to think beyond the immediate problems of one service was good, and the concept was sound.

COMMITTEE OF IMPERIAL DEFENCE

A Committee of Imperial Defence was already in existence by this time, but the Esher Committee felt that its remit should be expanded so that it could 'deal with the complex problems of Imperial Defence'. It was proposed that it should have a staff of seconded naval and army officers who would 'obtain and collate information from the Admiralty, War Office, India Office, Colonial Office and other Departments of State'. This meant that for the first time every aspect of the Empire's defences would be coordinated rather than working as separate compartments. It was not enough even to coordinate the efforts of the Admiralty and War Office, as there was a separate Indian Army and locally-raised troops in the colonies, as well as growing forces in the dominions. The improvement in communications with the invention of the telegraph meant that no longer was it desirable to allow decisions that could plunge the nation into all-out war to be taken locally, and coordination had become feasible and necessary.

The second report dealt with the Committee's original brief, the organisation of the War Office. An Army Council was proposed based on the Admiralty Board, with the Secretary of State for War as its Chairman and equivalent to the First Lord of the Admiralty. This was the more complex of the two reports and it dug deep into the organisation and administration of the Army.

Fisher wrote to Esher:

We don't want dull dogs for this new scheme. WE MUST HAVE
YOUTH AND ENTHUSIASM, as you and Clarke know far better
than I do, the whole military system is rotten from top to bottom
(*more rotten at the top than at the bottom*). And it is only by the agency
of young and enthusiastic believers in the immense revolutions that
must be carried out that our scheme can bear fruit.[3]

The King and the Prime Minister accepted the preliminary reports
immediately, but the latter had reservations about some of the detail
in the second full report on the War Office. While Esher and Clarke
showed signs of compromise over their recommendations, Fisher was
having none of it; it was to be a case of the Government accepting both reports in their entirety or nothing at all. He managed to
strengthen the resolve of the other two members and they threatened
to resign *en masse* if their recommendations were not accepted. The
three men were interviewed by a Cabinet committee representing
interested departments. In the end, almost everything that the Esher
Committee recommended was accepted, with just a few minor items
rejected or delayed, and the structure of the War Office underwent
dramatic change over the remaining months of 1904.

Fisher now started to go beyond the work of the Committee; in fact
it is strange that one of the matters not covered was the education and
training of future Army officers. He wrote a letter in confidence to
Lord Knollys, the King's Private Secretary, confident that it would be
seen by His Majesty:

It is my unalterable conviction that the real secret of military efficiency rests absolutely, wholly and solely on the age of entry and
system of training of the Officers of the Army, and on nothing else!
We have evolved a most logical and lucid system for administering
the Army, but Arnold-Foster★ will tell you we are actually at our wits'
end to find in the whole of the British Army suitable officers to fill
not only the few administrative posts in the new scheme but also

★The then Secretary of State for War.

the Military Commands ... In the analogous case in the Navy there would be literally *hundreds* of suitable officers to choose from!

He wanted nothing less than an Army replica of the Osborne-*Britannia* training scheme.

RUTHLESS, RELENTLESS AND REMORSELESS

Meanwhile, back in the Royal Navy, Fisher was having difficulty in ensuring that his plans for the service were being implemented precisely as he would have wished. There were no half measures with Fisher. Even senior officers could, and did, lose their appointment if they did not do as he wished. One of his successors as Director of Naval Ordnance, DNO, Rear Admiral Angus MacLeod, had reservations about some of Fisher's plans for the Navy's gunnery. In October 1903, he was summoned before the great man at Portsmouth:

'You are trying to wreck my plans regarding gunnery,' Fisher accused.

'No, I am not,' replied MacLeod. 'But as DNO it is my duty to express an opinion.'

'You know people talk of the three R's,' retorted Fisher. 'My three R's are Ruthless, Relentless and Remorseless. Anyone who opposes me I crush, I crush.'

MacLeod later recounted this episode to Admiral Sir George King-Hall, who included the story in his book, *Sea Saga*, saying that Fisher had become 'quite fierce, and glared'.[4]

Other developments were proceeding apace. The most fashionable weapon of the day was the torpedo and, as touched on earlier, during the late nineteenth century this had come to be delivered by small, fast torpedo boats. A practical submersible had been invented in the United States by John Holland, and the first ordered by the United States Navy in 1898 could operate at up to five knots while submerged and carry a single torpedo. This was followed by a larger craft capable of operating over several hundred miles and carrying two torpedoes. Often criticised for its conservatism, the Admiralty hastened to order such vessels to be built under licence in the United Kingdom, and Vickers built five Hollands just after the turn of the century, and in 1903 started to produce an improved type, known as the 'A'-class.

The murmurings of naval officers once again echoed the attitudes displayed as steam came to replace sail. Critics highlighted the limitations of the submarines, seeing their limited capabilities as confining them to the defence of anchorages and harbours, but at the same time worried about their becoming a threat to the battleship, which, if the submarine gained credibility, would be of limited value. There were those who saw Fisher's endorsement of the submarine as the prime cause for Germany embracing the concept during the First World War. Nevertheless, Fisher had already highlighted the importance of the submarine during his speech to the Royal Society, and indicated that in future its capabilities would grow. Some, such as Fisher's long-time friend and railway collaborator Arthur Wilson, actually proclaimed the submarine to be 'underhand, unfair, and damned un-English!' However, Fisher wrote a report after witnessing the first submarine flotilla at exercises in the Solent list that described their advantages in glowing terms:

This Whitehead torpedo can be carried with facility in Submarine Boats, it has now attained such a range and such accuracy ... that even at two miles' range it possesses a greater ratio of power of vitally injuring a ship in the line of battle than does the most accurate gun ... There is this immense fundamental difference between the automobile torpedo and the gun – the torpedo had no trajectory: it travels horizontally and hits below the water, so all its hits are vital hits; but not so the gun – only in a few places are the gun hits vital, and those places are armoured.

The submarine must revolutionise naval tactics for this simple reason – that the present battle formation of ships in a single line presents a target of such a length that the chances are altogether in favour of the Whitehead torpedo hitting some ship in the line even when projected from a distance of several miles ... Imagine even one Submarine Boat with a flock of transports in sight loaded each with two or three thousand troops! Imagine the effect of one such transport going to the bottom in a few seconds with its living freight!

Even the bare thought makes invasion impossible! Fancy 100,000 helpless, huddled up troops in frightened transports with these invisible demons known to be near.

Death near – momentarily – sudden – awful – invisible – unavoidable! Nothing conceivable more demoralising![5]

No less a person than Lord Esher accepted Fisher's assessment and noted that it would be difficult to exaggerate the revolution in naval warfare and strategy that would result.

ROYALTY VISITS PORTSMOUTH

While at Balmoral in October, it had been arranged that King Edward VII would visit Portsmouth, although this did not take place until early the following year, in mid-February 1904, when the King and Queen stayed at Admiralty House in Portsmouth for three days. The weather that winter was bad, but fortunately, for two out of the three days of the visit, it was fine. Fisher had already enthused the Prince of Wales about the potential of the submarine, and now it was the King's turn. It says much for this particular monarch that he tolerated a lengthy lecture by Fisher on the advantages of the submarine, then an almost word for word presentation one evening by the captain in charge of the embryonic submarine service, and then the following day, visiting a submarine for the first time, almost the same again by an enthusiastic young officer. His assistant private secretary who accompanied the Royal party recalled later that he felt inclined to say: 'We know all about that,' but His Majesty not only listened attentively, but encouraged the young officer by asking questions as if hearing about the submarine for the first time. Inevitably, Fisher also ensured that a visit to Osborne was on the agenda, something that would have been relatively easy to organise from Portsmouth as Queen Victoria had ensured that there were landing facilities at Osborne House for the Royal visits that crossed the Solent from Gosport's Stokes Bay. Not only did the King see the school, but he also visited the convalescent home, a facility that was to outlast the school. He also toured HMS *Victory*, and saw the cockpit where Nelson had died and which had been restored under the supervision of Lady Fisher. Perhaps the most exciting part of the visit was the demonstration by an armoured car equipped with a Maxim gun, and a demonstration of rifle training, by Captain Percy Scott, the commanding officer of HMS *Excellent*.

The following month, the Prince and Princess of Wales visited Portsmouth, and theirs was a longer stay. The Royal party embarked in HMS *Mercury*, an old cruiser adapted for the occasion, leaving the Princess of Wales and Lady Fisher behind as the weather was not good.

The Prince saw manoeuvres in the English Channel and a mock attack by submarines. Wisely, the commanding officer had taken Fisher's chief yeoman of signals and the signal staff from *Victory*, so when a problem arose and Fisher declared that he did not think much of *Mercury's* signalmen and was told that they were his own staff, the Prince was delighted and declared: 'He rather got you there, Sir John.'

A great deal of effrot was put in to remind the Prince of his own naval days, including a lunch of pea soup, salt pork and plum pudding. He was also treated to a trip aboard a submarine, which dived and then surfaced, much to Fisher's relief. This was no light or safe undertaking at the time. The early submarines were primitive and mice were kept in cages to register the quality of the air; rather as miners of the day would have taken canaries down in the pits. Of one submarine commander during the manoeuvres, Fisher recorded: 'Yesterday all the mice died in their cages and two of his crew fainted, but the young Lieutenant of the submarine didn't seem to care a damn whether they all died so long as he bagged the battleship he was after.' On another submarine, an explosion made the interior 'hell' in Fisher's words, and it was this craft that took the Prince of Wales below the waves. Within days, it became clear just how hazardous had been the dive, when the Royal Navy suffered its first loss of a submarine, with no survivors. The submarine *A1*, the first of the improved class that had entered service in 1903, was busily engaged in carrying out a mock attack on HMS *Juno* when she was struck by the Castle Line steamer *Berwick Castle*. Her master mistook what was to him a strange craft for a torpedo – which rather suggests he should have taken better avoiding action.

In May Fisher was told formally that he would be returning to the Admiralty as First Naval Lord, but he insisted on his appointment taking effect on 21 October, Trafalgar Day. This was the fulfilment of an ambition held for many years and on which even he had given up at times. He was sixty-three, almost too old for the promotion. Many who knew him felt he already ran the Admiralty, even while at Portsmouth.

He did not go quietly, however. Awkward to the end, when Selborne told him that he would be succeeded at Portsmouth by an officer unacceptable to him, he stoutly declared that he would remain at Portsmouth and that Selborne would have to find another First Naval Lord! This was ungracious and ungrateful. Fisher also haggled over his pay, stating that the King had told Selborne that Fisher would save the country millions, but, he complained to Lord Esher, they jibed at giving him a few hundred pounds extra. He had a point. The peculiar naval pay structure meant while at Portsmouth as commander-in-chief, he received £4,000 pa, but as First Sea Lord, his salary dropped to £2,600. The compromise arranged was that Fisher would become the King's personal Naval ADC, which would give him a welcome extra £400 annually, but this nearly did not happen as the King felt that it would make him appear a favourite, and it seems that intervention by Lord Esher was finally necessary to secure the additional appointment.

Perhaps it was just as well that Selborne left the Admiralty in due course, but even this was not without its problems as Fisher made clear just who he could work with, and who he would not; he wrote to Esher:

> I could not serve with Walter Long, so if he comes in I shall clear out, but Onslow I should love. I told the King last year that he was the man to succeed Selborne ... I told him that the First Lord of the Admiralty should be a peer, so as to give him much more time than the House of Commons allows ... he quite agreed ... he said to me how would Lord Tweedmouth do as First Lord on a change of Government, and I agreed with him.[6]

It was now that Fisher began to make use of the inhabitants of the Fishpond. These were to be the naval officers that Fisher would entrust with key positions in the service. Perhaps it was a reflection of his declining health, or an identifable personality disorder that had fuelled his resentment at not having power, privilege and fortune to advance his career, but he started to become obsessive about personalities from this time onwards. It could simply have been the side effect of having such tremendous power. Certainly, he never lost the sense of insecurity that his shaky start in life had given him, regardless of rank, of honours, of connections, and he spent much time looking for reassurance.

Some officers did manage to steer clear of the Fishpond and of Fisher's critics, and make progress, but it could be extremely difficult. One such was Captain Rosslyn Wemyss, who had been responsible for much of the early success of the college at Osborne. He held the ambition to become Naval Secretary, even though there were many officers senior to him also interested in the appointment. Fisher offered it to him after indicating that there were many senior to Wemyss who ought to be given preference, and also made it clear that the condition on which it was being offered was that he should be completely subservient to the

First Naval Lord. Despite wanting the post, Wemyss rejected the offer on such conditions. The result was that he never again was in contact with Fisher. Fortunately, this did not upset his future career as he eventually reached the rank of full admiral.

One protégé of Fisher was Prince Louis of Battenberg, who had married a granddaughter of Queen Victoria and joined the Royal Navy. To Fisher, Battenberg was another link with the Royal Family, but Fisher did respect him both as a sailor and as an administrator. Fisher even began to investigate just where he could place the Prince even before he returned to the Admiralty, placing him in command of a cruiser squadron in home waters so that he could move to the Admiralty with a history of having had an independent command. Battenberg was also able to reassure Fisher, telling him:

> As to your not coming as SNL, that is absurd ... Your position in the Service and in the Country is now such that no First Lord, Liberal or Conservative, would dream of taking anyone but you. The King and the Prince of Wales moreover are determined about it.

Meanwhile, as they waited for Fisher's arrival, the existing Board of Admiralty found themselves almost powerless, with the members still holding office but unable to take, still less implement decisions. Fisher made matters worse by refusing to disclose his plans and policies while he bided his time at Portsmouth, and held to his planned date for the move. On 2 August he even went so far as to write to the hapless Selborne telling him not to lay down any fresh battleships until he could lay his plans before him! There was one exception to this, for he insisted on and succeeded in changing the titles of the Board members from naval lords to sea lords, titles that dated from 1613 but which had been changed early in the nineteenth century.

Notes

1 Kilverstone, Admiral of the Fleet Baron, *Records*, London, 1919
2 Ibid
3 Ibid
4 King-Hall, Admiral Sir George, *Sea Saga*, London, 1935
5 Kilverstone, Admiral of the Fleet Baron, *Records*, London, 1919
6 Bacon, Admiral Sir R.H., *The Life of Lord Fisher of Kilverstone*, London, 1929

10

First Sea Lord

He may be a very clever fellow, but he abolished Jamaica.
Sir Frederick Richards.

Having insisted that he would take up his post as First Sea Lord on Trafalgar Day 1904, and having refused to budge earlier even though he could have done so and avoided wasting time, perverse to the end, he started on 20 October, a day early. This showed a fine instinct for making an impression, but with scant regard for the existing members of the Board of Admiralty who could do nothing, and certainly felt unable to make decisions.

Fisher's working schedule as First Sea Lord remained as gruelling as during his earlier appointment as Second Naval Lord. When in London he rose at his home at 16 Queen Anne's gate, off St James, between 4 and 5 a.m. He made his way to the Admiralty via Westminster Abbey, where he would spend some time in prayer and meditation, and arrive at his desk by 6 a.m. On some occasions, he would be there by 4.15 a.m. His objective was to get some hours of work in while the building was quiet. Some say he managed three hours of productive work in this way, but it could have been more as senior officers and officials usually arrived at around 10 a.m. Nevertheless, even Fisher needed to be sustained, and he usually left his desk at around 9 a.m. to walk home where he enjoyed a substantial cooked breakfast with his family. He would spend some time with his wife and daughters and read the newspapers before returning to work. Lunch was frugal, unless he was entertaining or being entertained, nothing more than biscuit and a glass of lemonade. He finished his working day and returned home at around 19.30, bathed before dining with his family, and then retired to bed at 21.30. When the King heard that Fisher continued his routine on Sundays he wrote on the back of a menu: 'Admiral Sir John Fisher is to do *no* work on *Sundays*, not go near the Admiralty ... By command, Edward R,' and ordered it to be conveyed to Fisher that he take one day a week off. Fisher boasted to his wife about having worked sixteen-hour days.

Fisher's appetite for paperwork was undiminished despite his advancing years. He left most of the routine correspondence to his secretary, as before, and quickly put his thoughts in handwriting on official reports. His own correspondence was handwritten by himself, and he seldom had documents typed and even rarer was his use of the telephone, a piece of equipment that he seems to have disliked.

Nevertheless, as First Sea Lord he was constantly meeting people and having long lunches with politicians or journalists, foreign naval officers or dignitaries, and there were the inevitable social events in the evenings. He continued to be a welcome guest at country houses at weekends. He also spent time visiting naval establishments and attended the trials of new weapons or inspected new warships under construction.

Although he continued his trips to health spas, and had visited Marienbad before taking up his appointment as First Sea Lord, he all too frequently succumbed to winter colds. He was treated by the King's Physician Extraordinary, who gave him 'some mixture ... and I've hardly coughed since!' as he wrote to his wife, who was out of town at the time.

FRUGALITY, PRAYER AND RETRIBUTION

The house at Queen Anne's gate was run on lines of strict economy – this was nothing new for Fisher and given the demands of his unmarried daughters and the rest of his family, together with his lack of private means and considerable 'workaday' expenses, it was necessary. On one occasion he announced that he was going to close the house for a fortnight, and that his daughters should visit friends!

Despite his occasional tyranny, intolerance and his lack of forgiveness or consideration for the thoughts and feelings of others, there was a strong religious element in Fisher's life. He could on occasion listen to as many as four sermons in a day, despite a not very solemn warning from the Dean of Westminster that he might suffer from spiritual indigestion:

The strong religious convictions of his youth gradually ... crystallised around the fundamental truths of primitive Christian teaching. He appreciated a good sermon; but, even more than attending church services, he loved to sit and meditate in some church or cathedral, communing in solitude and silence.

He had a firm belief in Divine intervention in the affairs of this life; if he had doubts about justice in this world, he had none about matters being evened out in the next! 'The Lord God of recompence [sic] will surely requite' was the thought with which he was wont to comfort himself ... He was convinced that the Day of Judgment would one day come along, and then the men, and the Society ladies who had laboured for their own friends under the cloak of working for the Navy, would get their just reward. Any desire he might have to strike down an enemy in this world was largely satisfied by remembering Dean Page Robert's remark that 'There is no Bankruptcy Act in Heaven, no ten shillings in the pound there; every moral debt had to be paid in full.' ... An ardent admirer of Joshua, David and St Paul, as well as of Nelson, he firmly believed in the prayer, 'O Lord, arise, and let thine enemies be scattered,' being answered; but, at the same time, he believed in his countrymen doing their fair share of the scattering.[1]

Fisher meanwhile had not forgotten the lessons he had learnt at The Hague Conference, and especially the confidence of the German delegation. It was no longer a secret that the United Kingdom and Germany were engaged in a naval arms race. Fisher saw war with Germany as inevitable. It was a case of when, not if, and because he could not be sure just how soon conflict would come, he was all the more impatient for change.

Intolerant of anyone who got in his way, and confident that he, and often he alone, knew the answers, Fisher had a low opinion of most of those occupying the highest positions in the land. He enjoyed being regarded as a 'character', and even a menace to those around him, and having his vanity fed. Doubtless he felt that his status as a 'maverick' allowed him to get away with anything, even upsetting the higher echelons. Some maintain that he was never boastful, but that is debatable, from the evidence of many of his letters, and certainly he did not suffer from self-doubt. He was practically a walking reference volume on the Royal Navy's equipment, and this was the subject to which he always returned. Indeed, although he would have bridled at the suggestion, he was far stronger on equipment than on strategy or tactics, as time would tell.

What was clear was his boundless energy, which at times must have required a determined application of mind over matter as his health fluctuated. He loved to recount how a doctor had once declared that he had such vitality he 'ought to have been twins', which once drew the comment from a commander: 'What a mercy you were not! Just think of two of *you* in the Navy!' Fortunately for the officer concerned, this drew a chuckle from Fisher.

This man had serious defects, and his sometimes unrealistic grasp of strategy and tactics was just one instance. He was obsessed with personalities, surrounding himself with those who took his view and pushing away, often violently and at extreme cost to their careers, those who did not. He retained the childish tendency to throw a tantrum and even throw in the towel if he did not get his own way, and he showed the intolerance of youth in debate, when he would express himself in strong and violent language, suppressing dissension and constructive debate, and often baiting his opponents into over-stating their case. Worst of all, he actually took a pride in his excesses. His taste for religion was of the Old Testament kind, of violent retribution and of grievances nurtured and kept fresh, for he seldom if ever forgave.

THE CHANGING WORLD ORDER

The world was changing, and the Navy had changed so much and yet had to change so much more; and the Army, which started later than the Navy, had farther to go. British troops had spent the last half of the nineteenth century fighting colonial wars against opponents who lacked their discipline, training and most of all, their arms, but had almost failed when faced with a 'European' opponent in the shape of the Boer guerrillas.

The threat from Germany was serious. The 'Two-Power Standard' that had been such a tenet of British policy was coming under threat, and not just from Germany but from the United States and Japan as well. Japan had already displayed the first signs of its colonial ambitions as it sought to conquer Korea and establish itself on the mainland of China. The problem with the Two-Power Standard' was not only that it could not be maintained indefinitely, but that the vast spread of Britain's empire meant that in any one theatre of war, the Royal Navy could be outnumbered and even outclassed even if it were.

Prussia had been a continental power, and had inflicted defeat on France in 1870–71. Unified Germany was determined to be a maritime power. Even before Fisher got to the Admiralty, the German Naval Law, or *Flottenesetz*, of 1898 had authorised the building of no less than nineteen battleships, as well as cruisers, destroyers and other small warships. This was a clear signal that German policy was to rival Britain on the high seas. The German body politic was soon provoked by British actions in searching German merchant vessels for contraband during the Boer War, so that in 1900, the German Navy Minister, *Grossadmiral* Alfred von Tirpitz, was able to get his Naval Act of 1900 approved. The Kaiser, Wilhelm II, stated that he would make his Navy the equal of his Army. Pressure to ensure that a strong German Navy was created extended to the formation of the *Deutscher Flottenverein*, German Navy League, in 1898.

Friction between Japan and Russia then began to produce a marked realignment of British foreign policy. Despite the Tsar's concerns over the cost of armaments, Russia was still a worry for Britain. In 1902 Japan offered to counter Russia in the Far East if the British could woo France away from her long-standing support for Russia. The Anglo-Japanese Alliance of 1902 prepared the ground for the *Entente Cordiale* between the United Kingdom and France that emerged during 1903 and 1904. In the Far East, Japanese warships attacked Russian vessels without a declaration of war, and then in 1905 the Battle of Tsushima saw not one but two Russian fleets destroyed. In fact the first force of Russian ships attacked British trawlers as the former steamed down the North Sea, mistaking the British ships for Japanese torpedo boats, and nearly brought the two countries to war. How small torpedo boats were supposed to have steamed halfway round the world was a question that the Russians, in one of the most incompetent fleet operations ever, never considered.

ENTENTE CORDIALE AND CUTBACKS

The new relationship with France was one that Fisher had long advocated, especially in the light of The Hague Conference. The Anglo-

French Arbitration Treaty of 8 April 1904, drew a line under many long-standing colonial disputes and left the Royal Navy free to prepare to meet the pending challenge from Germany. In July 1905, Fisher ordered the Channel Fleet into the North Sea and then into the Baltic for manoeuvres, stating that: 'Our drill ground should be our battle ground.' This was sabre-rattling pure and simple and it rebounded on Britain as it created uproar in Germany and strengthened the hand of those pressing for ever greater naval expenditure.

The realignment of the Fleet was not without cost. During the long naval peace the Royal Navy had come to be a symbol of power and status, especially the latter, rather than a weapon. It could be used to suppress a local uprising or to show the flag at a social occasion. This became increasingly difficult and the diplomatic and colonial services were not well pleased when they found that they could no longer demand the presence of the Royal Navy.

The number of warships deployed in the Far East started to fall. They did not disappear altogether, but the numbers were cut. All five battleships were withdrawn from the China Station. Admiral Sir Gerard Noel, Commander-in-Chief of the China Station, went over Fisher's head and appealed directly to the First Lord, bringing a stern rebuke from Fisher, who reminded him that in future he had to address the Board directly.

Nevertheless, even the Prince of Wales thought fit to intervene, writing to Fisher on 10 November 1904: 'If you are going to remove the squadron in the Pacific because the ships are obsolete, you ought to send some new ones to take their place.'[2]

Many of the ships deployed overseas were indeed no longer fit for warfare. So Fisher brought them home and scrapped them. As well as the ships being useless for fighting purposes, even worse in Fisher's eyes, their crews were deteriorating. From this time on, the priority was to concentrate naval power in home waters and to a lesser extent the Mediterranean. The standing South Atlantic, North America and Pacific Squadrons were abandoned.

The Mediterranean Fleet's commander-in-chief, Admiral Sir Charles Drury, found that he was to lose his yacht, which, in view of the use made of it by Fisher's family when he held the post, seemed rather unfair. Drury arranged for HMS *Hussar* to be assigned to the Fleet as a dispatch vessel, and when she arrived in Malta almost all of the guns, apart from two retained for saluting purposes, and the torpedo tubes were removed. Extra cabins were built, with the finest fittings, furniture and carpets.

Fisher wrote to the First Lord on 4 October 1906 that meeting the demands of the Colonial Office and Foreign Office would mean that:

> ... we cannot possibly get the Navy Estimates down to the figure which I think the House of Commons will insist upon sooner or later, unless we strictly confine our naval expenditure to *absolutely necessary services* ... it can be proved that any reasonable requirement of the Foreign Office or Colonial Office has never been resisted by the Admiralty.[3]

As an example, the removal of a vessel from Constantinople had saved £15,000 per annum.

Inevitably, such drastic reductions in the overseas presence brought risks. Fisher was attacked in the press after a mutiny amongst military police in Zanzibar after withdrawal and the aftermath of an earthquake in Jamaica cried out for the previously strong naval presence. Unrest in Turkey left British subjects exposed.

'I see the *Globe* has a leading article attacking the Admiralty for not having an ambulance corps of cruisers and gunboats distributed over the earthquake area of the globe! (That's not a joke!),' Fisher wrote in January 1907, to his old friend James Thursfield on *The Times*.

> The Navy Estimates would be a hundred millions if everyone had everything! ... The funny thing is we get a most cordial and unaccustomed official letter from Lord Elgin thanking the Admiralty for sending two cruisers loaded with tents and provisions from Trinidad and Bermuda so very promptly and expeditiously! The *Globe* calmly suppresses the two cruisers, the *Indefatigable* and *Brilliant*! What a surpassing advantage it is to be able to lie freely![4]

Nevertheless, there were difficulties in getting even senior naval officers to comply with the new policies. When Beresford visited Mexico and met the President, he was told that a visit by the Royal Navy would be welcome. The British Minister then proposed that a squadron should visit the country. As it happened, a squadron was visiting the West Indies, but as Fisher pointed out, otherwise it would have involved sending another squadron, steaming an extra 3,500 miles, with attendant wear and tear on the engines and consumption of fuel. In fact, what was happening was that a series of homogenous squadrons was being developed that could operate independently or in a crisis be brought together. These replaced the ships sitting in remote outposts, which may have looked impressive and a symbol of British power to the uninitiated, but which were strategically useless.

Fisher was making other changes at the same time. He decided that the members of the Royal Naval Reserve and the new Royal Naval Volunteer Reserve should train on commissioned warships, whereas previously they had trained on rotting hulks using obsolete, even antique, weapons. His concept of nucleus crews for warships in squadrons unlikely to face the imminent threat of hostilities meant that personnel from shore establishments and from the different categories of reserves could bring these ships up to a fully-manned strength when needed.

NEW FLEET FOR HOME WATERS

These changes enabled the Admiralty to create a new fleet in home waters, aptly enough called the Home Fleet, which consisted of three divisions, Devonport, Portsmouth and the Nore, based on Sheerness. The latter had six battleships, while the other two shared seven battle-ships, manned by nucleus crews that could still take the ships to sea, but which would be expanded in a crisis by the mobilisation of reserves. These three ports were the Royal Navy's 'manning ports' and ratings in particular could expect to spend their careers attached to 'Devonport', 'Portsmouth' or 'Sheerness' (later Chatham) ships, and even when ships were deployed to other fleets or stations, on their return they would go to their home port.

The disputes rumbled on. Fisher felt that he could not commit his thoughts to paper as they were provocative and would alert Germany to his plans. Nevertheless, in turn he had lengthy interviews with Lord Esher and then with the King, who read to him extracts from a letter from the Prince of Wales, and having heard Fisher's explanation, asked him to write to his son. He wrote to the Prince of Wales:

> Our only probable enemy is Germany. Germany keeps her *whole* Fleet always concentrated within a few hours of England. We must therefore keep a Fleet twice as powerful concentrated within a few hours of Germany.

If we kept the Channel and Atlantic Fleets *always* in the English Channel (say in the vicinity of the Nore), this would meet the case, but this is neither feasible nor expedient, and if, when relations with foreign powers are strained, the Admiralty attempt to take the proper fighting precautions and move our Channel and Atlantic Fleets to their proper fighting position, then *at once* the Foreign Office and the Government veto it, and say such a step will precipitate war! This actually happened on the recent occasion of the German Government presenting an ultimatum to acquire a coaling station at Madeira, and the German Minister was ordered to leave Lisbon at 10 pm on a certain Sunday night, and war was imminent, as Lord Lansdowne had told Portugal England would back her. The Board of Admiralty don't intend ever again to subject themselves to this risk, and they have decided to form a new Home Fleet always home, with its Headquarters at the Nore and its cruising ground the North Sea.

'Your battle ground should be your drill ground,' said Nelson.

The politicians and the diplomats will not be the people the Public will hang if the British Navy fails to annihilate the whole German Fleet and gobble up every single one of those 842 German merchant vessels now daily on the ocean! *No* – it will be the Sea Lords! And as one distinguished retrograde Admiral, Sir Gerard Noel (who wants to build sailing men-of-war), told the King, I am to have the proud preeminence of Haman amongst the Sea Lords. I never have been able to ascertain how high Haman was hung, but it couldn't have been higher than Noel wishes me! And yet I patiently enjoy his receiving the high and important command of the Nore! If this isn't charity, I don't know what is. I digress to make this remark to Your Royal Highness, as I am accused of relentless hate towards those who differ from me!

To return to the argument – The only way to obtain this new 'Home Fleet' is by moving six battleships and four armoured cruisers from the Channel, Mediterranean, and Atlantic Fleets (observing that these 3 Fleets are 50 per cent stronger than the present political situation demands) and combining them with the best of the battleships now in commission in Reserve, forming an '*Escadre d'Elite*', backed up by the remainder of the ships in Reserve, as the Reserve or Second Division of this new Home Fleet. The whole of the torpedo craft (some 150 in number) and the whole of the submarines will be incorporated with this '*Escadre d'Elite*' of the Home Fleet, and their crews so increased as to be almost a full strength.

Admiral Bridgeman (about the best Admiral we have) is to be the Commander-in-Chief of this new Home Fleet, with his Headquarters at the Nore and his cruising ground the North Sea, where the fight will be! Perhaps off Heligoland (which was won by the sword and given up by the pen!).

The Board of Admiralty have also decided to adopt a 'sliding scale' of nucleus crews – thus the most important vessels will have the largest nucleus crews, and the least important perhaps not much more than a skeleton crew. For instance, the 'Royal Sovereign' class of battleship, almost obsolete and dangerous for the line of battle owing to their unarmed [probably a slip of the pen and should be 'unarmoured'] ends as against modern high explosive shell, will be relegated to the lowest scale of crew, while those required for the first brunt of war will be almost at concert pitch!

This new 'Home Fleet' thus called into being by Mr Balfour's famous 'stroke of the pen' almost permits of more seagoing work being given to the ships in Reserve, *together with the essential fighting training they do not now get in Battle Practice and other important Fleet Exercises.*

I beg you, Sir, to note especially the following facts: – By this new distribution of the Fleet *not a single ship will be paid off, nor is there the reduction of one single man serving on board ship, and the Fleet, AS A WHOLE, will have more sea work than at present,* but there is also this further advantage, of immense value, that if any ship in the Channel, Mediterranean, or Atlantic Fleets, has to be long absent from her cruising ground, on account of repairs, her place will be AT ONCE temporarily filled from the Home Fleet.

Pure part feeling solely dictates the present *'Press'* agitation. The Board of Admiralty and *no one else whatever* can be responsible for the distribution of the Fleet for War, and the Board is united and determined in their belief that they are acting for the good of the Navy and the safety of the Empire in this and every other step that has been taken. *Reduced Navy Estimates are no sign of reduced naval efficiency.* On the contrary, swollen Estimates engender parasites, both in men and ships, which hamper the fighting qualities of the Fleet. The pruning knife ain't pleasant for fossils and ineffectives, but it has to be used, and the tree is more vigorous for the loss of excrescences.[5]

The letter put the Prince's mind at rest, and Fisher was invited to lunch shortly afterwards, where he was assured that the Prince of Wales was wholly in agreement with all that the Admiralty was doing. Nevertheless, the carping criticism from the Foreign Office continued, and involved the King. Fisher was able to deliver a robust rebuttal:

> The absolute fact is that the Admiralty always knows better than the Foreign Office, and more wisely than the Consuls when vessels are likely to be required, because the Naval officer on the spot is invariably a better and more reliable judge than the frightened or gunboat-desiring Consuls, who one and all pine for the presence of a man-of-war within signalling distance of the consular flagstaff and for the consular salute of seven guns![6]

NAVAL BASES

The concentration of the fleet in home waters was undoubtedly right, Fisher understanding German attitudes and ambitions as he did. But it was equally obvious that the part of home waters most important to curbing Germany would be the northern end of the North Sea and the seas off Denmark and Norway. Unfortunately, these were far from the traditional naval bases in the south of England. Scapa Flow in Orkney provided a fine anchorage, but little was done to protect it during Fisher's time at the Admiralty. Scapa was also unsuitable as a major base because of the difficulty in getting men and supplies there quickly, with the railway line to the north being single track and slow. Further south, work had started on a major naval base at Rosyth, on the north bank of the Firth of Forth.

Rosyth was not liked by many naval officers. It was too far upstream so time would be spent getting the fleet to sea, and the fleet could also be vulnerable to being trapped inside these waters by enemy submarines. The Forth Bridge, carrying the railway line north, was a navigational hazard and as air power developed later in the century, many believed that if bombed, it would lock the fleet in. In addition, there were no suitable gunnery ranges close to Rosyth.

As First Sea Lord, one of Fisher's actions was to insist that not a penny be spent on Rosyth, so work stopped completely between 1904 and 1910. When it restarted, it was too late, and the base was not available for the Grand Fleet until 1916, much to the displeasure of Jellicoe.

This was a major blunder by a man who prided himself on his efficiency and ability to plan and prepare. To some extent, the problem was ameliorated by a decision taken by Jellicoe while at the Admiralty as Second Sea Lord before the outbreak of war, which was to send a floating dock to Invergordon on the Cromarty Firth, part-way between Rosyth and Scapa Flow. This was invaluable until Rosyth was completed in 1916, and even afterwards it was of significant benefit, although the large battleships and battlecruisers still needed to be sent to Rosyth or even to the south for major repairs.

Nevertheless, Fisher made important improvements elsewhere. Scrapping outdated warships was matched by scrapping outdated bureaucracy and working methods. In the Royal Dockyards, he reduced manpower by around 6,000 men, often described as having been 'half-employed'. It was not a case of constantly cutting, for he also set in hand the development of the dockyards at Gibraltar, which were to be an asset in both world wars.

Fisher had by this time passed his 64th birthday. On 4 December 1905, he had been promoted to Admiral of the Fleet, (a rank that no longer exists now that five star ranks have been dropped from the British, American and French armed forces) and had been awarded the Order of Merit. The promotion in theory automatically guaranteed him a further five years service.

Fisher's plans split the press, politicians and the service itself. Many genuinely did feel that the Empire had been abandoned, although clearly there were still ships, in reduced strength, on the overseas stations. Campbell-Bannerman's Liberal government had taken office in December 1905, and was undoubtedly pleased at the way in which the naval estimates had been brought under control. Scrapping the old ships and reducing the presence abroad had saved money. The press did not divide along the party lines one might expect, for the Conservative-supporting *Times* and *Daily Telegraph* were mainly on his side. Despite his high position, Fisher continued to give private briefings and write to those journalists who took his side.

BERESFORD AND THE 'SYNDICATE OF DISCONTENT'

While Fisher dismissed his opponents as the 'Syndicate of Discontent', they included many experienced naval officers, and their self-appointed leader was none other than Lord Charles Beresford. Fisher's tendency to intemperate language had prompted a similar reaction amongst his critics, and in the resulting debate, much heat and very little light resulted. Many were genuinely concerned about the weakening of the Royal Navy away from home waters, while others expressed misgivings over the radical new designs of major warships, and could point out that these were in direct contrast to the Fisher-inspired design of HMS *Renown*.

Vice-Admiral Lord Charles Beresford was Commander-in-Chief of the Atlantic Fleet when the changes started to take effect in early 1905. This force had the staggering complement of eleven battleships and seven cruisers. Many maintain that he was served by officers who in general were inferior to those surrounding Fisher or his old friend Wilson. Some were those who had been rejected by Fisher, such as the former Director of Naval Intelligence, Custance, while others were seen as being of substantially inferior intellect, including Doveton Sturdee, who was to be found wanting in the First World War. Not a few believed that Beresford would replace Fisher as First Sea Lord.

Beresford had been out of sight and out of Fisher's mind for some time, having been on half-pay, during which time he had taken the opportunity to be elected as Member of Parliament for Woolwich. This was not his natural element, despite his upbringing, as he was a poor public speaker and useless in debate, with a mind that failed to be quick enough to refute arguments or fend off slights with charm and wit. His speeches, delivered in a loud booming voice, were inarticulate, repetitive and long, so much so that on one occasion he was interrupted by the Speaker, who reminded him that: 'The noble Lord is not entitled to go into the whole condition of the Fleet in the Mediterranean.' As an opponent in Parliament, Beresford was ineffectual, doing more harm than good as he bored his fellow MPs with his obsessive resistance to the changes that were taking place.

Outside Parliament, however, his popularity was far higher. His speeches had of course been vigorously edited by the anti-Fisher press, and seemed to be hard-hitting and authoritative. In order to keep him quiet, Selborne and Kerr brought him back to active service, promoted him to Vice-Admiral, initially as C-in-C Channel Fleet, on 17 April 1903, which caused him to resign his seat, and hoped for the best. A good sea officer, the ruse worked well at first as he settled down and sought to improve the efficiency of his command.

As Beresford was in so many ways the arch-reactionary it is interesting to note that on some points he and Fisher were in accord. The creation of the Royal Naval Volunteer Reserve in 1903 enjoyed Beresford's whole-hearted support at a time when many believed that citizen volunteers should do more than man the guns, for they could never become sailors. Simply 'manning the guns' had been the role of the Royal Naval Artillery Volunteers, many of whom manned coastal artillery and did not go to sea.

So it happened that both Fisher and Beresford were in key positions on the night of 21/22 October 1904, within a day of Fisher taking up his appointment as First Sea Lord, when the Russian Fleet fired upon British trawlers in the North Sea, as mentioned earlier, believing them to be Japanese torpedo-boats. The Royal Navy prepared for war if necessary, and this included Beresford, who had most of his ships at Gibraltar. Diplomatic efforts defused the situation. Nevertheless, Fisher wished to know what action Beresford would have taken had hostilities commenced:

> Being quite satisfied with the excellence of the gunnery of the Channel Fleet I should only have engaged the Russians at Tangier (in the event of their refusing to proceed into Gibraltar) with four of my battleships, at a distance of from 5,000 to 6,000 yards. It appeared to me that this would only be chivalrous, under the circumstances. If the Russian ships had commenced to knock my ships about I would have engaged them with the whole eight Channel Fleet Battleships.[7]

This reply was received with anger and dismay at the Admiralty, and not just by Fisher. Beresford was reminded that in wartime, such sporting considerations were out of place and that he would have been expected to use his entire fleet. Prince Louis, by this time Director of Naval Intelligence, made the point that: 'If this statement became public property, the taxpayers would probably enquire why they were paying for the other half.' Fisher bluntly, but justifiably, reminded Beresford that: 'Lord Nelson's dictum was "the greater your superiority over the enemy the better" and he was a chivalrous man!'[8]

Fisher demonstrated his disappointment by relieving Beresford of his command early, but it was unfortunate that instead of learning this through official channels, the news reached Beresford through his successor, Rear Admiral Sir William May. Beresford's response was to write to May saying that he would be glad to give him lunch or fight him, but he would not be replaced. He appealed to Lord Selborne, who referred him to Fisher. Fisher confirmed that he was being replaced and would come ashore to serve on a committee. The intention had been that Beresford's next appointment would be as Commander-in-Chief, Mediterranean Fleet, and when Beresford declared that he would not be replaced and would not serve on a committee, Fisher simply told him that he would not be going to the Mediterranean. Beresford used the one threat that was within his power, that if he was denied the Mediterranean, he would resign and seek to return to Parliament. Rather than suffer more of Beresford's anti-Admiralty tirades, Selborne prevailed upon Fisher to let Beresford go to the Mediterranean, a fleet much reduced in size and status since the *Entente Cordiale*. It was probably a sad day for Fisher when in March 1905, Selborne left the Admiralty to take up the post of Governor-General of Cape Colony, now South Africa.

Beresford hoped that his sojourn in the Mediterranean would be brief, as Fisher would be 65 years old in January 1906, when he could be expected to retire, and so he set about a campaign to ensure that he was considered as the next First Sea Lord. All of this became known to Fisher as one of his supporters was the commanding officer of a ship with the Mediterranean Fleet, Captain, later Admiral, Reginald Bacon, of HMS *Irresistible*. In April 1906, with Fisher far from retiring, the King and the Prince of Wales visited the Mediterranean Fleet, with the former complaining that the Navy was becoming full of cliques plotting against each other. Bacon did his best to get the ear of the Prince of Wales, and eventually found himself aboard the Royal Yacht being dined, and with an interview with the King afterwards. He stressed that there was a lack of loyalty to the Admiralty on the part of many of the admirals.

Nevertheless, Fisher recognised that there was a danger that the Prince of Wales might be swayed by the arguments being advanced by so many senior officers against reform and against the Osborne Scheme. He complained that so many of the critics 'won't go to Osborne and Dartmouth to see the actual education going on. They don't want to be converted!' He was also able to state that Beresford had originally come out openly in favour of the scheme. This was not the end of it. Fisher's promotion meant that Beresford would be 64 when Fisher finally retired, and extremely unlikely to be selected as the new First

Sea Lord; so denied the coveted position, he decided to intensify the campaign so that Fisher would be forced to resign. The problem for Fisher was that while he enjoyed the unwavering support of the King, the Prince of Wales was disturbed by the pace of change and the risks being taken by overthrowing tried and tested methods and designs.

Beresford and Fisher could both claim to have the interests of the Royal Navy at heart, but the differences in character and upbringing clouded the issues. Beresford was also showing clear signs of complete insubordination that few superiors would have tolerated. On 24 April 1906, Fisher felt forced to write to the new First Lord, Lord Tweedmouth:

> It is with extreme reluctance that I feel compelled in the interests of the Navy and the maintenance of its hitherto unquestioned discipline and loyalty to bring before the Board the unprecedented conduct of the Commander-in-Chief of the Mediterranean Fleet in publicly reflecting on the conduct of the Admiralty and in discrediting the policy of the Board and inciting those under his command to ridicule the decisions of the Board. I need not enumerate in detail the comparatively minor cases of improperly worded telegrams and letters questioning Admiralty decisions, which in times past would certainly have led to drastic action preventing any repetition of such conduct. Nor do I dwell on the extraordinary conduct of a Commander-in-Chief 'canvassing the captains under his command' as to whether or not they approved the policy of the Board of Admiralty …[9]

If this was intended to bring the matter to a head, other factors intervened. Just seven months later, Beresford, already privately wealthy, was left a fortune when a brother died in South Africa. The money enabled Beresford to mount a more sustained campaign against Fisher. Fisher had his enemies in the service, to which could be added those who regarded him with suspicion because of the colour of his skin – which had led to many asking whether he was a half-caste – his supposed womanising and his aggression against those who opposed him. The radical way in which he rode over tradition and his collaboration with the Liberal Party alienated Conservatives, especially as the Liberals were placing more emphasis on social services than on defence. Against this, Beresford played the part of a generous host whenever he was in London, being able to afford one of the best chefs at his house in Grosvenor Street, and gently began to sway opinions in his favour.

Fisher had by this time made the mistake of bringing Beresford home from the Mediterranean, making him Commander-in-Chief of the Channel Fleet. This was intended to be a temporary measure as the fleet was one that had to disappear as the Royal Navy reorganised itself, although Beresford could possibly end up in command of the merged fleets, with a force of twenty-six battleships and sixteen armoured cruisers, more than double the size of the German Navy at the time. This in itself gave Beresford yet another issue on which to confront Fisher and the Admiralty, and this time he was in home waters, operating out of Portsmouth (with occasional visits to Gibraltar). For most of the time, he was close at hand and within easy reach of those whom he wanted to influence. Short of being Commander-in-Chief Portsmouth or at the Admiralty, he was in the best possible position to cause trouble.

Fisher was grateful for Lambert's intervention, and met Beresford afterwards, but that the meeting was difficult can be judged by his letter to Lord Lambert on 21 January 1907:

> *Your letter splendid!* I had three hours with Beresford yesterday, and all is settled, and the Admiralty didn't give in one inch to his demands, but I had as a preliminary to agree to three things:
>
> Lord C Beresford is a greater man than Nelson.
> No one knows anything about the art of naval war except
> Lord C Beresford.
> The Admiralty haven't done a single d----d thing right!'[10]

If Fisher's account is true, then one must doubt Beresford's sanity, while his sense of proportion had disappeared without trace. Despite this, the battle between the two men developed in earnest during the year, starting in the spring. The Admiralty continued with its plan of enlarging the Nore division so that it was clear that in due course command would move to Sheerness. The Home Fleet would absorb the Channel and Atlantic Fleets, while its importance was stressed by the ships all being fully-manned, and the new Dreadnought pattern battleships and battlecruisers were also assigned to the Nore Division. In the meantime, Beresford could see that his status was being diminished as the Channel Fleet became less important.

ADMIRALTY POLICY CRITICISED

The irony was that after many years of criticising the Admiralty and stirring up his allies in the press and politics, Fisher was now being subjected to the same treatment by one of his own senior officers. This was to be not so much a case of the 'biter bit' as one of the biter being savaged unrelentingly! Beresford used language that was even more intemperate and hostile than Fisher had ever used, while in his internal communications, Fisher had been meticulous in observing the correct service forms of courtesy, had never been insubordinate and had never gone over a superior's head. All these transgressions were committed by the man most likely to be the country's leading commander at sea and in the frontline of a major war! According to Arthur Marder:

> He criticised Admiralty policy, commented on Admiralty orders, and repeatedly addressed the Admiralty on many topics in a decidedly tactless and insubordinate manner quite without parallel in British naval history. His opinions of the Admiralty and Fisher ('our dangerous lunatic') were known to every officer and man in his fleet.[11]

In late April, Beresford wrote to Fisher that there was 'not the slightest chance of any friction between me and you … if a senior and a junior have a row, the junior is wrong … or discipline could not go on … I will do my best to make the Admiralty policy a success.' Yet, on 13 May, he described the planned roles of the Channel and Home Fleets as a 'fraud upon the public and danger to the Empire.'

The wise council and conciliatory tone of Selborne had gone and his successor, Lord Cawdor, had not lasted long. Tweedmouth was an able administrator, but incapable of providing the strong support and clear guidance that the First Sea Lord needed. When faced with trouble, his reaction was to keep it quiet in the hope that it would blow over. While he regretted the tone of Beresford's memoranda, he felt that his past record and his good qualities outweighed the bad, such as his being 'ambitious, self-advertising and gassy in his talk.' He called upon Fisher to listen to officers who could provide ideas and information, but Fisher had always been keen to learn, and Beresford was not providing ideas or information, but simply carping and doing his best to undermine the Admiralty. Beresford was also guilty of the obsession with spit and polish (mentioned in Chapter One) to the detriment of being able 'to fight the ship'. As a young sub-lieutenant serving in Beresford's flagship, HMS *King Edward VII* wrote:

> Everything centred around the person of the Admiral, and ceremonial had become almost an obsession with him. Every time that he showed his head above the coaming of his hatch, the Officer-of-the-Watch was required to call the Quarter Deck to attention, and everyone remained stricken into immobility until the well-known and slightly nasal voice graciously commanded: 'Carry on Mr Officer-of-the-Watch' ... My principal recollection of those days is, accordingly, unending pipings, callings to attention and buglings. Hurried dashes to and fro from the battery ... to my post by the gangway, interspersed with anxious darts from one side of the quarterdeck to the other to see that all was in order with boats at the lower booms, and that their boat-keepers maintained their upright attitude as they sat in them ... Our occupation – whilst I served in her – was principally a professional career around the ports of the British Isles, varied by a few stately and somewhat hackneyed steam tactics ... I do not recollect that any very serious problems of war were either attempted or solved.[12]

Beresford's priorities could be judged by the fact that he kept a bull-dog, Kora, which was obese and allowed to roam around the decks as she pleased, followed by a member of the ship's company who, equipped with broom, dustpan and cloth, had the delightful duty of clearing up the animal's messes as she proceeded. His motorcar, with a Royal Marine driver, was taken everywhere and stowed aboard ship. When Beresford decided to go angling, a lieutenant and two or three midshipmen would be detailed to accompany him to disentangle his lines or get his flies out of the weeds. The coxswain and two members from the ship's galley would follow with rugs and baskets for the picnic lunch. When midshipmen were invited to breakfast on a Sunday morning, their role was not to learn from the great commander, or even to recount what life was like for them, but simply to act as an audience for an endless succession of anecdotes, mainly about life in Ireland, 'which it was best to greet with loud laughter'. The Admiralty yacht *Surprise* had been transferred out of the Mediterranean, and now her role was to trail the Channel Fleet and bring Lady Charles with her.

Whatever the validity of Beresford's criticisms, his fleet was not one being prepared for war, and not one in which the priority was to groom

junior officers for the serious and demanding tasks of command. In
an Admiralty MS, Fisher's memorandum, much toned down doubtless
due to Tweedmouth's intervention, states:

> This Memorandum has become necessary for the information and
> consideration of the Board of Admiralty, in view of the fact that the
> present Commander-in-Chief of the Channel Fleet ... has taken up
> a position of antagonism both to the policy and to the administrative
> arrangements of the Board of Admiralty ... He has forwarded his own
> plan of campaign against Germany, which involves, notwithstanding
> the enormous preponderance of the British Navy, the employment
> of more battleships, cruisers and co and co., than the British Navy
> possesses ...
>
> Further, in official conversation, Lord C Beresford has spoken of
> our naval position being such that 'The Empire is in jeopardy', and
> his Chief-of-Staff (Captain Sturdee) has stated his opinion that we
> are 'living over a live mine'...
>
> The truth is that such language on the part of LCB and CS, besides
> being insubordinate, is perfectly preposterous, and when used, as it
> freely is, in general conversation, it is also most baneful in its effects
> on the personnel of the Fleet in fostering a spirit of disloyalty towards
> the Admiralty. It is certainly a great blow to discipline that such dis-
> loyalty should be overlooked.'[13]

The trouble was that the indiscipline was continuing, and was in fact an
epidemic. An extract from his letter to the Admiralty of 14 June 1907
makes this clear:

> In my opinion, if Germany was to undertake sudden hostilities with
> her naval forces perfectly organised in all details for a definite plan
> of campaign, including a landing party and a raiding party, Germany
> would have a considerable chance of succeeding; or, anyway, inflict-
> ing most crushing reverses at the initial stage of hostilities, in the
> present totally unprepared states of the Home and Channel Fleets in
> regard to the preparation and organisation for war.[14]

Tweedmouth decided to bring the two men for a meeting so that the
three of them could try to resolve the problems, which were in danger
of becoming public knowledge. The meeting took place on 5 July 1907,

and a minute was kept. This was the most Tweedmouth would do, and the least he could do. Perhaps earlier such a meeting would have been beneficial, but too much damage had already been done. Beresford did not perform well at the meeting. Indeed, it is hard to understand how someone so inarticulate and unable to carry an argument or retain facts had risen to such a high rank. He was unable to respond to many of the questions and proposals put to him.

When asked by Fisher if he was satisfied with some proposed reinforcements to his fleet, Beresford replied: 'On those lines. I will let you know that. If I have a Fleet which is a striking force.'

'It is no use haggling over terms and descriptions like this,' replied Fisher. 'It is perfectly ridiculous to think that anything can happen in the shape of a sudden treacherous attack on our Fleet without some preliminary "strained relations."'

'That is a matter of opinion,' retorted Beresford. 'It is most unlikely that this house, in which we now are, is going to be burnt down, but it is possible.'

The two men clearly differed, and Tweedmouth then interjected:

'If you said what were your reasons; but to say, without giving your reasons, that our policy is a fraud and a danger to the Empire, that is pretty hot.'

'You have not got that officially,' replied Beresford. 'You cannot say that.'

'Having yielded to all Lord Charles Beresford's demands so as to bring your squadron up to what you say were Admiral Wilson's component parts,' commented Fisher. 'We do not agree, but we say "This is our Chief Executive officer afloat"; we do not agree, but we will give him the armoured cruisers, the destroyer flotillas and the attendant vessels, as he presses so for them.'

'I cannot see that thing straight off', replied Beresford. 'I will write to you.'

'You must have thought about it,' concluded Fisher. 'You have been writing about it for months.'[15]

The distinct impression arises that Beresford was either being evasive or could not remember what his demands had been. The meeting then took a turn from the sublime to the ridiculous, bearing in mind the tone of previous correspondence:

'Then this thing – Question No 3,' continued Beresford. 'You will allow me to smile for at least ten minutes over Question No 3 ...

Although my views are very drastic, there is not any question of want of cordial relations with the Admiralty. Not privately or publicly have I ever said anything against the Admiralty.'

'If you say, in a letter to me, as First Lord,' responded Tweedmouth. 'That our Home Fleet "is a fraud and a danger to the Empire", that is not very pleasant to the Admiralty, and you have repeated that again and again … I must tell you that to tell the First Lord of the Admiralty that what is a very important part of his Board's policy is absolutely useless and is a fraud and danger to the Empire, I do not think that is very friendly to the Admiralty.'

'It is a private letter,' explained Beresford. 'We have all written much stronger things than that on important questions of that sort … It was only a "term". If we went to war suddenly you would find it is true. If I had said officially that the Admiralty had created that, or if I had pitched into the Admiralty about it, it would be different … That I had any notion of insubordination I absolutely deny. That letter of mine to the First Lord has no right to go before the Board, a private letter like that.'[16]

Tweedmouth responded that the letter had not been marked private, while other letters had been, to which Beresford said that he should have put 'private and confidential' on it. He was told that the letter was so important that Tweedmouth could not simply regard it as a private communication.

'I am quite sure understand we are all equally interested, as you are, in having friendly and cordial relations,' retorted Fisher. 'But it is absolutely impossible if the Chief Executive Officer of the Admiralty afloat is going to be "crabbing" the Admiralty in everything the Admiralty is doing, and writing such letters to the First Lord.'

Tweedmouth, who seems to have become angry, interrupted at this stage, demanding that such serious charges be substantiated and asking how the Home Fleet could be a fraud or a danger to the state.

'It is a "term",' replied Beresford. 'I can write it all out to you in detail. The public think it is ready for instant action. What is your own term? Without an hour's delay: well, it is not.'[17]

Clearly, there was no meeting of minds. Obviously, Beresford's letters must have been drafted by his staff, although no doubt the strong language was his own. While Fisher felt that the meeting had been a waste of time, he thought that it was important that cordial relations should be maintained or, more important, be seen to be maintained by those officers who had supported Beresford. He wrote the following day to '*My dear Beresford*':

> You said yesterday that you heard of my saying things of you, but I hope that you will take my assurance as I took yours on this point – that we have both to complain of liars trying to make mischief. I am most anxious to be as cordial in our relations as in the warmest days of our friendship. I remember Ormonde saying when we were in the Mediterranean – how the mischief makers tried to make out we were not friends. Nor do I forget how you have stood by me against the whole army of fossils in the past.[18]

Beresford also, as the extracts from the meeting implied, got the ships he was demanding. He assured his fellow conspirators that he had brought the Admiralty 'to heel', and wrote a condescending letter to Fisher saying that the Admiralty had obviously taken his point, and that he could now 'make out a plan of campaign'. If he ever did, the Admiralty never saw it! Nevertheless, he sought three more cruisers, over and above what he had asked for.

The scene was set for the antagonism to last throughout the summer, and increasingly other senior officers were being drawn in, often very much against their will. One of these was Vice-Admiral Sir Francis Bridgeman, Commander-in-Chief of the Home Fleet, set to become the most important unit of the Royal Navy. Although Fisher described him as 'about the best Admiral we have', Bridgeman had managed to avoid being involved with the Fishpond and had also steered clear of Beresford. He was not only the 'best admiral' but also professional. Nevertheless, doubtless because of jealousy and pique, Beresford started a campaign of criticism of everything that Bridgeman did. In October 1907, joint exercises between the Atlantic, Channel and Home Fleets under the command of Beresford resulted in strong criticism on the operations of the Home Fleet destroyers, and this, claiming that they were not properly trained, was circulated throughout the three fleets. The Admiralty had to intervene, ordering the withdrawal of the memorandum and any reflection on Bridgeman's abilities.

Rumours started that the Admiralty planned to remove Beresford's key staff officers, including both Captain Doveton Sturdee and Custance. He wrote in his usual uncompromising terms to the Admiralty, which assured him that the rumours were untrue *but* reminded him that he himself had pressed for Sturdee to be promoted. Once again, he was reminded that he continued 'to employ language which has no parallel within their experience as coming from a subordinate addressed to the Board of Admiralty'.[19]

Not all of Beresford's officers were his staunch supporters, indeed many of them backed Fisher. One such was Rear Admiral Percy Scott, who commanded the First Cruiser Squadron, and who shared Fisher's passion for gunnery, innovation and passionate outbursts. He was fanatical about having a unit that was ready for war and at a time when gunnery practice was avoided as far as possible by many naval officers because of the effect on the appearance of their ships, he insisted on frequent gunnery practice, raising the standard of hits from the Channel Fleet's average of just 30 per cent to 80 per cent. These were all characteristics that endeared him to the First Sea Lord. A new post was created for him, Inspector of Target Practice, for which he was ideal.

'A GRAVE INDICTMENT'

Beresford, by contrast, loved holystoning and ceremonial. To his delight, he heard that his Fleet was to be inspected by Kaiser Wilhelm II at Spithead on 8 November 1907, and immediately ordered all ships to Portland at the beginning of November to be freshly painted, and no doubt re-coaled before the work started so as not to spoil the finish. This would have been a good moment for the Germans to launch the sudden attack he claimed to fear. Scott's cruisers were busy at gunnery practice when this signal was received, and the commanding officer, obviously another gunnery enthusiast, of one ship enquired if he could continue, to which Scott replied: 'Paintwork appears to be more in demand than gunnery, so you had better come in, in time to make yourself look pretty by the 8th instant.'

This was the dispute that finally forced the whole Fisher-Beresford affair into the public domain. When he heard about the signal, Scott was ordered to Beresford's flagship to be publicly dressed down before a large audience, many of whom were embarrassed, and then compounded the matter by signalling the entire Channel Fleet, outlining what had happened and describing Scott's original signal as 'contemptuous in tone and insubordinate in character', while the two cruisers concerned had to delete it from their signal logs.

The whole matter was now public, and even journalists who had opposed Fisher in the past turned on Beresford. Scott's attention to gunnery had not gone unnoticed. When Beresford asked the Admiralty to refute the accusations in the press, the Board refused, and also refused to sack Scott, although they did write a letter of 'grave approbation'. Anxious to pour oil on troubled waters, Scott offered his apologies, which Beresford refused to accept, and then banned him from attending his official functions before sending the First Cruiser Squadron to Bantry Bay, in the bleak west of Ireland, for the winter.

Horatio Bottomley, the editor of *John Bull*, a news magazine, wrote an editorial entitled 'A Grave Indictment of Lord Charles Beresford', accusing him of having a 'swelled head' and stating that he was not fit to become the next First Sea Lord. Each and every officer in the Channel Fleet received a copy of the issue concerned in a plain sealed envelope. This was the last straw. Beresford wrote to Sir Edward Carson maintaining that the attack on him, which was 'audacious, treacherous and cowardly' was inspired by the 'gentleman from Ceylon'. Fisher took his argument to the rapidly rising journalist and politician, Winston Churchill and his old friend Esher. King Edward VII intervened, effectively accusing Beresford of undermining discipline and advocating 'serious action'. Fisher met the former Conservative prime minister, Arthur Balfour, only to be told that Beresford was taking his campaign to every drawing room in London and had started a campaign of his own, writing to anyone and everyone who might take his side.

While numbers flocked to Fisher's cause, including many who did so without first being asked, much damage was done. All those who had entertained some doubts about the scale and the pace of Fisher's changes felt free to voice them, and even those who could not do so openly, such as the Prince of Wales, began to change sides. Beresford tried to ingratiate himself with the King, using his Majesty's Assistant Private Secretary as an intermediary, but the effect was spoiled when, despite claiming to be impersonal in his arguments, after a few minutes Beresford forgot and switched to a tirade against Fisher. He then wrote directly to the King, who passed the correspondence via his Private Secretary to Fisher. The House of Commons was urged to call for an inquiry, which would be an implicit criticism of the First Sea Lord.

Beresford then went on sick leave and retired to his home, expecting his supporters to visit him for their briefings. 'Imagine interviewing Beresford in a night cap, with Lady Charles holding his hand on the far side of the bed,' Lord Esher commented to the King's Private Secretary. 'What a picture of naval efficiency and domestic bliss.'[20]

Nevertheless, for the time being, Fisher remained in control and Scott remained with his cruisers. In February 1908, Fisher heard from the Prime Minister that there would be no enquiry, and when Herbert Asquith took over as PM in April, that assurance was repeated. The change of government also meant a new First Lord, Reginald McKenna, who was the sort of inflexible and vigorous minister that Fisher approved of and could work with happily.

Fisher wasted no time in briefing McKenna about the Beresford situation, which continued to be of public interest. The newspapers lost no opportunity to refer to the scandal, and scandal it was. McKenna felt that he needed to consult Asquith about it. The matter was discussed by the Cabinet. Beresford's dismissal was considered, but they shied away from this course of action for fear that it would inflame the situation. There would be no control over Beresford once outside the service, and the resultant row would cause serious harm to the Royal Navy and to the Liberal Party. They also knew that Beresford had many prominent supporters.

The international situation had a bearing on the decision. Relations with Germany were deteriorating and they did not want to have the Admiralty distracted at a time of growing tension.

This showed poor judgement and also cowardice on the part of Herbert Asquith and his colleagues. The popular mood was turning against Beresford; he was no longer a popular hero to be indulged, but an ambitious and badly-behaved elderly man who should have known better. Worse, he had publicly humiliated a subordinate in what many regarded as a cowardly fashion. In fact, he had done even worse, for unknown at the time, he had ruined Scott's career by persuading McKenna not to employ him after February 1909.

Not all of those in the anti-Beresford camp were pro-Fisher. Indeed many regarded both as blameworthy and would happily have got rid of of the pair of them.

PRESS SPECULATION

Press speculation moved on to whether Beresford was to be dismissed, and this was considered again at the Cabinet, but again they could not steel themselves to make the decision. It did, nevertheless, provide Beresford with the excuse to write to McKenna:'I beg to be informed, as I have my private arrangements to consider.' This effectively forced McKenna into reassuring the errant Admiral.

Just when it looked as if the battle would be prolonged and that Beresford would continue to cling to his command like a limpet, he was finally dismissed in December 1908. The excuse used was that the changes in the ships deployed in home waters were to be accelerated by twelve months, with the Channel Fleet absorbed by the Home Fleet in March 1909. Beresford was ordered to haul down his flag on 24 March. In a somewhat unnecessary and even unjustifiable attempt to ease the blow, as a nod to Beresford's hopes of commanding the enlarged Home Fleet, Bridgeman was also stood down as Commander-in-Chief Home Fleet and he was replaced by Admiral Sir William May.

Beresford was far from quiet at this time. He was one of those who created a pressure group called the Imperial Maritime League, although this was scarcely needed by the Royal Navy, which had the Navy League to argue its corner in a way that serving officers often could not. Public meetings were held throughout the country, and prominent citizens, including Fisher, received invitation cards headed 'God and my Country'. Fisher passed his to McKenna with a note, saying: 'This will make you shake in your shoes!' There was even a call for a public demonstration to protest at the end of British naval supremacy and the dismissal of Lord Charles Beresford from the Channel Fleet. This was held in Hampstead, not now an area associated with demonstrations by the common man!

Inevitably, a 'scattergun' approach was taken to sending out invitations to meetings, and many found the wrong target. Lords Redesdale and Esher were two Fisher supporters who let their distaste for the organisation be known.

The delay before his dismissal had been long enough to allow Beresford to return to public favour. Why had he not been dismissed earlier? The Admiralty must have something to hide. Was it really Fisher's fault after all? One biographer of Fisher blamed the Cabinet:

Had the authority of the Board of Admiralty been upheld by the Cabinet when Lord Charles first commenced his unfortunate campaign, and had the proper action been taken of superseding him in his command, the Prime Minister would not have been confronted with a difficult situation ... It seemed to the ordinary person to be obvious that, had the Admiralty been in the right, Lord Charles would have been promptly dealt with; the apparent disinclination of that body to do so interpreted as evidence that the Admiralty feared to take any action that might lead to the exposure of administrative failure.[21]

King Edward agreed, believing that the wrong decision had been taken, and at the wrong time. He had been pressing, inevitably behind the scenes, for Beresford's dismissal from early in the conflict, now he was afraid that he would 'make a disturbance and give trouble and annoyance.'[22] As it was, the long running battle had already begun to take its toll on Fisher's health, who was seen by his friends as being tired and run down. Worse was to come, for in the final year of his being First Sea Lord, he was subjected to almost constant attack. So much so that he threatened: 'When I retire I shall write my reminiscences. I shall call them "Hell. By One Who Has Been There."'

By contrast, when Beresford hauled down his flag at Portsmouth and went ashore, he was greeted by a cheering crowd on the Hard (the area immediately outside the main gate at Portsmouth). The Commander-in-Chief Portsmouth lent him his carriage for the short drive to the railway station, which was probably just a courtesy, but allowing midshipmen to run alongside the carriage was hardly a good idea. Mothers held up their infants to see the great man, and the departure of his train was delayed by people straying onto the tracks. There was another great reception by a vast crowd at Waterloo when his train arrived. All this was balm to Beresford's soul. The *Evening Standard* commented: 'Because he has told the truth, he has been dismissed by Mr McKenna. There is the whole situation in a sentence.'

Free from whatever restrictions he had allowed to intrude while he had been in command of the Channel Fleet, Beresford was encouraged by this massive show of public support to renew his campaign. He had two years in the Royal Navy to run before retirement, and even if he was too old to be appointed as First Sea Lord, he could at least have the satisfaction of ruining Fisher.

In fact, it almost seems surprising that it took Beresford a week before he wrote to Asquith. He wrote on 2 April, attacking the Admiralty for the redeployment of the fleets in home waters, and the absence of any means to prepare war plans scientifically. Perhaps he was missing the literary talents of his staff officers! His aim was an official inquiry into the Board of Admiralty, which granted would have made the position of the existing board members untenable, as even holding such an inquiry would have indicated a lack of confidence in the Board's ability

Beresford on his own could never have managed to force an inquiry, but the continuing naval arms race and pressures on the budget meant that the demands for an inquiry were beginning to gain a momentum of their own. Success for Beresford was failure for Fisher, who did not disguise his contempt in a letter to his ally, Lord Esher:

> Imagine what a state of affairs when a meeting of Naval Officers on the active list in a room in Grosvenor Street is able to coerce the Cabinet and force the strongest Board of Admiralty to totter to its fall! ... The country must indeed be in a bad way if so governed!

There can be no doubt that the blame for this situation lies with Beresford and a succession of weak First Lords, but that is not to absolve Fisher of blame. He was not faultless. He had created a climate, and thrived in it, in which what would today be described as 'lobbying' proved to be an effective means of self-promotion and influencing events. Had not he seen what such methods could achieve, Beresford might have hesitated to adopt them, but he first started to do so when he was in the Mediterranean serving under Fisher, and at that time it suited Fisher to let it pass. (Remember that Beresford had delayed his return from the Mediterranean to England because under Fisher he felt he had 'learnt more in the last week than in the last forty years'.) There were other matters that also contributed to this state of affairs. Fisher kept Beresford at arm's length while they were in the Mediterranean. Beresford could continue with his spit and polish and there was no serious attempt to ensure that he and his subordinate officers adopted Fisher's passion for gunnery, and accurate gunnery at that. The performance of the fleet as a whole improved during Fisher's tenure, but attitudes were not changed.

This was the end of Fisher's first term as First Sea Lord. Fortunately, despite all the infighting and antagonism, events elsewhere had been more successful and it was in his appreciation of technology and his willingness to embrace change that Fisher showed himself at his best and his strongest.

Notes

1 Kilverstone, Admiral of the Fleet Lord, *Records*, London, 1919

2 Ibid

3 Ibid

4 Ibid

5 Ibid

6 Ibid

7 Bacon, Admiral Sir R.H., *The Life of Lord Fisher of Kilverstone*, London, 1929

8 Marder, Arthur J., *The Anatomy of Sea Power: British Naval Policy 1880–1905*, London, 1941

9 Kilverstone, Admiral of the Fleet Lord, *Records*, London, 1919

10 Ibid

11 Marder, Arthur J., *The Anatomy of Sea Power: British Naval Policy 1880–1905*, London, 1941

12 Ibid

13 Kilverstone, Admiral of the Fleet Lord, *Records*, London, 1919

14 Ibid

15 Ibid

16 Ibid

17 Ibid

18 Ibid

19 Lawson, Lionel, *Gone for a Sailor*, London, 1936

20 Marder, Arthur J., *The Anatomy of Sea Power: British Naval Policy 1880–1905*, London, 1941

21 Marder, Arthur J., *The Anatomy of Sea Power: British Naval Policy 1880–1905*, London, 1941

22 Bacon, Admiral Sir R.H., *The Life of Lord Fisher of Kilverstone*, London, 1929

11

Dreadnought – The First Modern Battleship

It's no use one or two knots superiority of speed. A dirty bottom brings that down! It's a d—d big six or seven knots surplus that does the trick! THEN you can fight HOW you like, WHEN you like, and WHERE you like!
Fisher to freelance journalist, Arnold White, 1906.

Fisher's enduring legacy to the world's navies was the battleship, or at least the modern battleship with an all-big gun armament. Although this of necessity had to be augmented by smaller calibre weapons, initially to defend the ship against attack by torpedo-boat, and later with the advent of high angle/low angle weapons, ships had to be defended against air attack. The battleship has had an impact on the consciousness of the maritime nations out of all proportion to its achievements. Today, the unwitting and poorly informed journalist will happily write of 'battleships' rather than 'warships' or 'naval vessels', not realising the specific characteristics of this type of vessel.

The irony was that, while Third Sea Lord, Fisher had laid down the specification for his future flagship, HMS *Renown*, and had famously asked for the lightest big gun and the heaviest small gun, so she entered service with 10-inch guns and 6-inch guns. The specification of *Dreadnought* was to be for the biggest guns available, and as many as possible. Again, there was irony in the fact that the man who so favoured the torpedo, often delivered by fast-moving small naval vessels, and saw attack from the air as having so much potential, did not also specify a substantial lighter, rapid-firing armament to protect the ship from these hazards. Fast-moving surface vessels require guns that can be trained quickly and provide a rapid rate of fire, and must also be capable of being depressed to aim at the threat as it nears the target. Similar needs are required for defence against aircraft, except that the weapons must of course be capable of high angle firing.

It is impossible today to convey the significance of the battleship a hundred years ago. These were the independent deterrent of the day, but they also proved to be a two-edged sword, so expensive and valuable that nations counted them as too much to hazard in a serious naval battle. In warfare, both sides kept a count of the other's battleship numbers, and feared losing one of their own. This was true of both sides in two world wars and especially true of the Germans during the Second World War. The battleship was a weapon that cost so much, needed so many men, and the use of which was circumscribed by fears of losing it.

As metioned, the first big naval battle of the twentieth century was at Tsushima between Russia and Japan. This was between battleships, but not Dreadnought-type battleships. Yet, from the arrival of HMS *Dreadnought* in 1906 to the end of the battleship, actions in which both sides had two or more battleships were very few and far between. During the First World War, armoured cruisers fought at Coronel and battlecruisers at the Falkland Islands, and again at Heligoland Bight and at Dogger Bank. The first real battle between battleships was at Jutland on 31 May 1916. During the Second World War there was the battle at Mers El-Kebir or Oran between the Royal Navy and the French Marine Nationale, then the battle of Punta Stilo or Calabria between two Italian and three British battleships, but at Cape Teulada and again at Matapan, first the British and then the Italians had but one battleship.

On the night of 11/12 November 1940, the true warship of the future made its presence felt when the aircraft carrier HMS *Illustrious* sent just twenty-two obsolete Fairey Swordfish biplanes to attack the Italian fleet in its main forward base at Taranto, leaving three of the six ships out of action, one of them permanently. This performance was repeated at Pearl Harbor in December 1941, except that six aircraft carriers and well over 350 aircraft were used, while at the battles of the Coral Sea and at Midway, the opposing warships never came within sight of each other and the action fell entirely to aircraft. Indeed, the battleship became almost an embarrassment. At Leyte Gulf the Japanese sought to make some use of their battleships when the war was already lost, but failed due to poor planning, appalling intelligence and a failure of nerve by the commander of the battleships.

THE BIG GUNS

To understand the specification of *Dreadnought* and other ships like her, it is necessary to understand the evolution of naval gunnery from the days of sail to the days of steam. The developments in gunnery came almost at the same time as the steam engine began to take over. Indeed, ever larger guns meant that sailing masts soon became a nuisance, an obstacle, as larger guns were no longer ranged along the sides of ships, but placed in barbettes and later turrets fore and aft of the superstructure. Explosive shells meant that wooden planking simply splintered, and it was not a case of damage alone, as the splinters were as big a hazard as the shrapnel from the exploding shell, and, of course, wooden ships caught fire. First ships were iron-plated over the wood, but this resulted in some badly balanced and unwieldy ships, so iron and later steel hulls and superstructure became the accepted standard. The steam turbine was quickly adopted by the Royal Navy after some preliminary hesitation, simply because immediately the engine room height was substantially reduced, so that heavier armament and armour plating over delicate areas, such as machine spaces and magazines, could be introduced without producing a ship that was top heavy.

Another factor that drove the design of the battleship was fear of the torpedo. The threat of attack from torpedoes carried by opposing battleships, with many having fixed tubes below the waterline, meant that the range at which ships would engage each other increased. Larger guns usually had longer ranges, so this was another factor in driving the increase in weapon calibres. Speed also became more important.

Of course, it took some time for the designs to settle and anything like a standard type appear. The early ships had a single calibre armament, like the Italian *Dandalo* and *Duilio*, and the British *Inflexible*. But as it appeared that different calibre guns enabled different targets to be engaged more effectively, some were produced with up to four different calibres of weapon ranging from 3-inch up to 12-inch. This was not easy, as space had to be found for each different calibre of weapon, while magazine space was compromised by having to carry an assortment of shells, and the difficulty in getting these to where they were needed aboard ships was another problem.

Sailors are by nature conservative, preferring to stick with what has been shown to work. The Royal Navy was slow to adopted breech-loading guns, which were quicker to reload than muzzle-loaders and required less space, after unfortunate experiences with the early breech-loaders. It also took time for rifled barrels to become the norm. At first, gunnery practice was over short ranges, little different from those seen at Trafalgar, but whereas in the days of sail the object was to close upon the enemy and board his ships, during the age of the torpedo the best idea was to stay as far away as possible. It was the French who first realised that they could fire almost as accurately from 5,000 yards as from 1,000 yards, and these ranges were soon adopted by the Italians, Germans and the United States Navy. In 1899, Fisher set 6,000 yards as the standard to aim for, by which time, in theory at least, ranges of up to 8,000 yards were possible. During the 1890s, improved explosives and propellants, and then smokeless powder and improved optical equipment for accurate range-finding, all transformed naval gunnery. This is not to suggest that gunnery was conducted in perfect conditions. These were the days before radar, and so visibility was important, which was often compromised by heavy smoke from the coal fires burning furiously down below in the stokehold. In major exercises, not only did the smoke from one's own ship make spotting the other ships difficult, or even spotting the fall of shot, but the smoke from the other ships also helped to blur their outlines. If the wind was in the wrong direction and strong enough, life in the gunnery tower of a major warship was distinctly unpleasant and unproductive.

There were practical lessons to be learnt. The temptation was to fire everything at once, but this only caused confusion when using guns of different calibre. It was hard to see whether shots were falling 'short' of the target, or 'over'. In fact, at longer ranges firing the smaller guns was simply a waste of ammunition – even if they did hit the target, they made little impression on steel armour plate.

DREADNOUGHT – AND BEYOND

As already mentioned in Chapter One, Fisher's appointment as First Sea Lord more or less coincided with a proposal by an Italian engineer, Vittorio Cuniberti, that the ideal battleship for the Royal Navy would be around 17,000 tons displacement and have an armament of twelve 12-inch guns capable of firing salvoes, with armour 12 inches thick over the machinery spaces and magazines, and be capable of 24 knots. Such ideas were shared by Fisher, and the end result was HMS *Dreadnought*, the ship that made all other battleships obsolete and subsequently all such vessels would be divided into 'pre-Dreadnoughts' and 'Dreadnoughts'.

Cuniberti had designed fast and relatively small battleships for the Italian Navy, ideal for service in the Mediterranean. He published his ideas for a British warship in *Jane's Fighting Ships* in 1903, criticising mixed calibre armaments as being wasteful and inefficient. His thinking was radical, as no other warship afloat carried more than four guns of 12-inch calibre:

> Secure in her exuberant protection with her twelve guns ready, she would swiftly descend on her adversary and pour in a terrible converging fire at the belt. Having disposed of her first antagonist, she would at once proceed to attack another, and almost untouched, to despatch yet another ...

Dreadnought was built in a year and a day at the Portsmouth Royal Dockyard and when she sailed for the first time on 3 October 1906, all other battleships were outgunned and could be outrun. *Dreadnought* displaced 17,900 tons, could steam at 21 knots and had an armour belt that was 11 inches thick at its strongest point. Armament consisted of not twelve but ten 12-inch guns, and, showing the importance attached to this particular weapon, she also had five submerged 18-inch torpedo tubes. Nevertheless, with three of the five twin turrets mounted on the centre-line, the ship could fire a devastating broadside, and fore and aft fire was also possible. This was the largest ship of the day to use steam turbines, which hitherto had been the preserve of torpedo boats and other similar smaller warships. This was another innovation, and the reduced height of the machinery made heavier armour plating possible, and practical. There were other advantages to steam turbines, as they required less attention with the absence of reciprocating parts:

> When steaming at full speed in a man-of-war fitted with reciprocating engines, the engine-room was always a glorified snipe marsh: water lay on the floor plates and was splashed about everywhere; the officers were often clad in oilskins to avoid being wetted to the skin. The water was necessary to keep the bearings cool. Further, the noise was deafening; so much so that telephones were useless and even voice-pipes were of doubtful value.[1]

By contrast, Dreadnought's first commanding officer was able to write that 'when steaming at full speed, it was only possible to tell that the engines were working, and not stopped, by looking at certain gauges. The whole engine room was as clean and dry as if the ship was lying at anchor, and not the faintest hum could be heard.'[2]

As we have seen, many at the Admiralty felt that Fisher had introduced too many innovations at once, but Fisher was driven and did not have the time or the budgets to introduce innovation gradually. A good example of Admiralty conservatism was the accommodation aboard warships, with that for officers still aft, a reflection of the importance of their being near the quarterdeck with its steering and navigating positions on a sailing ship, but a long way from the command and control positions on a ship without sail. *Dreadnought* was the first to have the officers' accommodation forward, so that they could be at their posts within minutes.

The view was, expressed by many naval officers that the ship was the wrong type for Britain to build. It was for other nations to experiment, and then for the Royal Navy to improve on the original design and then build in such numbers that supremacy was maintained. In fact, the United States Navy had already started building all-big gun battleships and so *Dreadnought* was not as big a leap forward as many supposed. Indeed, she lacked the super-firing of the latest US warships which would have saved deck space and also enabled 'B' turret to fire straight ahead over 'A' turret through the superimposition of 'B' turret, meaning a 100 per cent increase in firepower if the target was straight ahead. The lack of super-firing suggests some concern over stability; for example, when there have been three turrets forward – as on the later battleships HMS *Rodney* and *Nelson* – 'C' turret was on the same level as 'A' turret.

The initial design of the ship differed considerably from the final version as built. The original design had six turrets each with two guns, but with just two turrets, one fore and the other aft, on the centre line, while the ship would have had three funnels. The final version had ten turrets with two aft and three of them on the centre line, and just two funnels.

Apart from the very high cost, the only real drawback with such a radical departure from the accepted standards for a battleship was that the Royal Navy found itself starting again from scratch, losing its advantage over every other navy. With the commissioning of

Dreadnought, not only the battleships of the potential enemy were obsolete, so were the rest of the British battle fleet and the fleet would have to be rebuilt. This meant that the costly and long-maintained British superiority over other navies no longer existed as the other navies could also introduce their own Dreadnought-type battleships. It would need money and a substantial shipbuilding industry to create the twentieth century's most powerful navy.

The Imperial German Navy received its first Dreadnought, the Nassau-class, the following year, in 1907, and this proved to be the start of the desperate Anglo-German naval race, the Edwardian arms race. Fisher had recognised the danger to Britain's naval supremacy and had ordered construction to be as swift as possible. This was partly because of his experience at Portsmouth, where he had insisted on improving productivity, but also because he realised that the head start on other countries must be maintained for as long as possible. Designed by Philip Watts, *Dreadnought*'s keel plate was laid on 2 October 1905, and she was launched on 10 February 1906 by King Edward VII.

This was an incredible performance by any standard, but all the more so for the ship being the first of her type. The public, politicians and the press, all believed that this had been some kind of superhuman effort, and that it could be achieved again in an emergency. Such a belief was to be a curse for those anxious to develop a strong, modern battle fleet, with so many taking the view that ships really could be built 'just in time'.

The secret of the speed of construction was that Fisher had scoured the shipyard for fittings – and in particular armament – ordered for pre-Dreadnought battleships and these items, which usually set the timescale for warship construction at the time, were ready and waiting. On the other hand, this also meant that the secondary armament was less up-to-date than it might have been, had there been time for 4-inch quick-firing guns to be installed.

There was another problem. The more expensive a ship, the fewer could be built. The more powerful a ship, the greater its loss when away for dockyard work, or if damaged, or even during the all too frequent spells of having to coal every seven to ten days. The implication was that navies could afford fewer of these ships, and were therefore vulnerable when a fleet unit was not available.

Not everyone agreed that 12-inch guns were the answer. Sir Andrew Noble, by this time the chairman of Armstrongs, argued in

favour of the company's new 10-inch gun, writing to Fisher on 21
August 1904:

> Excluding machine guns, there are only two calibres in my type of
> new battleship. The main armament consists of 14 or 16 10-inch guns,
> and the secondary armament of 12 or possibly 16 4-inch guns.
>
> I prefer the armament to be all 10-inch guns. They are nearly as
> powerful as the 12-inch, and you can have far more of them.
>
> Looking at the great use now being made of torpedo vessels I
> think it well to substitute the 4-inch for the smaller gun, 12-pr, they
> now carry. The projectile of the 4-inch gun is much more formidable,
> and its high explosive shell would put a decisive end to any torpedo
> vessel. There ought to be no difficulty in detonating small shell if
> proper means are used, and the Explosive Committee had a most
> successful day at Ridsdale and Silloth a fortnight ago ...[3]

The argument in favour of the 10-inch was valid inasmuch as the lighter
weight of this calibre did indeed allow more guns to be fitted without
compromising the stability of the warship. The flaw in the argument
was that those two inches made a substantial difference both to the
range at which the shell could be fired and the impact on hitting the
target. As an example, the existing 9.2-inch gun in service with the
Royal Navy at the time, although a very satisfactory weapon, fired a
shell less than half the weight of the 12-inch gun. Fisher came near to
being swayed by Noble's argument, but at the Battle of the Yellow Sea
on 10 August 1904, a single Japanese 12-inch shell killed Admiral Vitgeft
and his staff, and Fisher decided that the larger calibre, the heaviest
available at the time, had to be the answer. Where Noble's advice was
sound was in suggesting 4-inch guns as the secondary armament, but
when *Dreadnought* was completed, she was fitted with twenty-seven
12-pounders for defence against torpedo craft. This retrograde step was
almost certainly owing to the need to have the ship ready in time, as
the 4-inch guns would have had to be specially ordered.

Fisher may also have been influenced in this selection of gun calibre by the British Naval Attaché in Berlin, Commander Philip Dumas,
who was able to visit the Schichau Yard at Elbing, where he learnt that
the Germans would be laying down a new battleship in the autumn.
He was remarkably successful in his ability to unearth intelligence, all
of which was reported back to Fisher, and part of which was that the

Germans planned to have a main armament of 11-inch guns on the new ship. In contrast to the Cold War between the Soviet Bloc and the West, the Germans clearly did not restrict the movements of people like Dumas. Far from keeping the specifications secret, Soviet-style, they overloaded him with information, giving him too many details in the hope that he would be bewildered, as their one concession to security was that they did not allow him to take any notes. Nevertheless, there were rumours that new ships were being built 'behind screens', and indeed, on a visit to Kiel, Dumas did discover two Dreadnought-type battleships under construction.

Inevitably, *Dreadnought* was soon to be surpassed by other later ships, especially the so-called 'super-Dreadnoughts', despite her advanced specification. The design was far from perfect, and there were many points at which the haste of her design and construction could be seen. One of the best examples, apart from the primitive arrangement of the turrets that might have been justified on the grounds of stability, was that the foremast was abaft the fore funnel.

Rear Admiral Percy Scott recalled:

On one occasion after the look-out man had gone aloft, the ship steamed at a high speed against a headwind, so that the mast near the top of the funnel got almost red hot. The result was that the look-out man could not come down for his meals, and it was necessary to hoist food up to him by the signal halyards which luckily had not been burnt through.

Nevertheless, Fisher had his radical new ship, which could be improved upon, and was now anxious to extend his thinking down the line. The French had started building a new type of fast armoured cruiser, intended as commerce raiders and too fast to be caught by battleships. The Admiralty Committee on Designs fell to considering this type of ship, for which Fisher again wanted 12-inch guns and anti-torpedo boat weapons, but armour was to be sacrificed for speed. The 9.2-inch gun was considered for these ships, but Fisher argued successfully for the 12-inch, so that these ships would have the armament of a battleship, but with a much higher speed.

The result was the 'I'-class, of which the first were the *Invincible*, *Indomitable* and *Inflexible*, all laid down after *Dreadnought* was completed. Fisher was so taken with these ships that he would have standardised on battlecruisers at the cost of building any further battleships, but he lost by one vote on the committee, which was to prove a blessing when the long expected war with Germany did come. The Committee members termed them 'battleships in disguise', but to Fisher they were the 'greyhounds of the sea' and his 'New Testament ships'. There was certainly some debate over how they might be used. 'A fast light squadron to supplement the battleships in action, and worry the ships in the van and the rear of the enemy's line', suggested Admiral Bacon, 'assist in a general action by engaging some of the enemy's ships that were already fighting our battleships'.[4]

Others saw that their first role would be to hunt down enemy raiders, while the Committee on Design foresaw that they would 'overtake and keep touch with a fleeing battle fleet, and possibly bring it to bay by the wounding which the 12-inch guns are capable of at 7 miles or more'.

Unlike the battleships, on which the *Dreadnought* had a powerful influence across the board, battlecruiser design varied more widely between the navies. The Germans and the Japanese built vessels with more attention to armour protection, which stood the Germans in good stead at Jutland, although they also had the benefit of lessons learnt at the Battle of the Dogger Bank, where the danger of flash penetrating the magazines was discovered in good time for Jutland.

These two great innovations in warship design meant that the Anglo-German naval race was being restarted, with both nations at the same point on the starting line.

Notes

1 Bacon, Admiral Sir R.H., *The Life of Lord Fisher of Kilverstone*, London, 1929
2 Ibid
3 Kemp, Lieutenant-Commander P.K., *The Papers of Admiral Lord Fisher*, London, 1960–1964 (2 vols)
4 Bacon, Admiral Sir R.H., *The Life of Lord Fisher of Kilverstone*, London, 1929

12

The Great Naval Race

England wanted war; not the King – nor perhaps the Government; but influential people like Sir John Fisher.
Kaiser Wilhelm.

The launch of HMS *Dreadnought* and the ordering of the first three battlecruisers was the start. On the one side, there was the desire of the UK to continue as the world's dominant naval power, something made necessary not just by the country's heavy dependence on international trade, but by the need to protect her Empire, the largest ever seen. Not only were assurances freely given to colonial administrations, they were given equally freely to the populations of the dominions, the 'Old Commonwealth', Australia, New Zealand and Canada, and more and more to Cape Colony, which was to become South Africa. The country had also made itself a hostage to fortune by acting as a guarantor of Belgian neutrality, a gesture meant to allow the new state to establish itself, but which was to prove an onerous commitment in 1914.

On the other side, Germany also had trade routes to protect, but the country felt that it had to become a maritime power just as much as a continental power. The Germans wanted colonies, although the great colonial expansion was by this time over as there was nothing much left to annex. Cultural, commercial, political and territorial rivalry meant that Germany sought to be at least the equal of the British.

Neither Britain nor Germany could feed itself without imports, and for the Germans there was the added edge that the poor quality of much of the land meant that fertiliser also needed to be imported. Both countries had abundant fuel in the form of coal, but Germany was short on iron ore and most of that available in Great Britain had too high a sulphur content to be ideal for steelmaking.

In terms of industrial capacity in the early twentieth century, the UK had the edge, especially in shipbuilding. The nation was the world's largest builder of ships of all kinds. Nevertheless, already there were signs that the nation's manufacturers were failing to modernise sufficiently quickly and were losing their edge, while the newer German manufacturing sector was expanding rapidly.

In both countries there were those urging an increase in the armaments budgets, and especially in those for the navies. There were also those on both sides who felt that these policies were of themselves making the slide into open warfare more likely. In between, there were those who wanted strong, but affordable and effective armed forces capable of defending the country. For the mass of both populations, mutual fear meant that the overwhelming need to be defended, to be secure, drove naval expansion.

There was also another problem in both countries, but especially in Great Britain, and that was a growing realisation that social welfare was becoming a real political issue, and that unless treated seriously, social unrest would become a problem. Trade union activity was also fomenting industrial unrest.

BATTLESHIPS OR PENSIONS?

In the United Kingdom, the growing movement for improved social expenditure, removing slums, improving health and education, and introducing old age pensions, was being matched by a similar movement inside Russia, but there of course the game was being played for much higher stakes, with revolution a far more real threat.

Japan had plans of her own. While allying themselves with the British, the Japanese were also anxious to find space for their rapidly growing population on the Asian mainland, first annexing Korea, and then seeking a foothold in China.

Amongst the problems in Europe, there was no guarantee during the 1900s that Italy would later become a wartime ally of Great Britain and France. At times, her interests seemed to be best served through a Triple Alliance with Germany and the Austro-Hungarian Empire. The latter empire was itself crumbling and wary of increasing unrest amongst the peoples in its territories, which were not a homogenous ethnic grouping, but consisted of many racial groups. Indeed, the liberation of the Slav territories from Austria-Hungary was later to become a war aim of Russia during the First World War.

Anglo-German relations had suffered a severe blow with the Boer War. Even after the Boer War ended, instead of relations recovering, they declined even further. Many cite the date of Fisher's arrival as First Sea Lord on 20 October 1904 as coinciding with the start of a prolonged deterioration in Anglo-German relations. Certainly, having recalled all that the German admirals had said to him at The Hague Conference, Fisher believed firmly that German naval expansion was aimed at just one country, the United Kingdom. The First Lord of the Admiralty Lord Selborne was certain that the German Navy 'is designed for conflict with the British fleet'. The rest of the Admiralty shared this view, as did the Foreign Office, leading politicians, and increasingly King Edward VII himself, uncle to the German Kaiser. Indeed, the next year he was recorded as considering that 'the folly of [his] German nephew portended war'.

It could almost be said that a state of 'cold war' existed between the two great powers. The growing concentration of the Royal Navy in the North Sea and the development of the Home Fleet had been noted by the Germans, just as the British intended it to be. Whether this amounted to sabre rattling, or was simply a deterrence, designed to make war unthinkable, usually depended on which side of the Channel you stood. It would have taken little encouragement for Fisher, in his own words, 'to Copenhagen the German Fleet', starting a war without a declaration and hoping to inflict irreparable damage on the potential enemy. The Sovereign discouraged him, saying: 'My God, Fisher, you must be mad!' The Germans never heard of this proposal, but they did hear, and circulate widely, the remark by the Admiralty Board's Civil Lord, Arthur Lee, on 3 February 1905, that Britain should 'get its blow in first, before the other side had time even to read in the papers that war had been declared.'

All of this added to the suspicions harboured by the Kaiser and his ministers that there would be a surprise attack by the Royal Navy. As we will see later, a surprise attack on the Baltic coast at the onset of war was feared by many in the German armed forces. The main culprit was seen not as King Edward VII, but as the First Sea Lord. In fact, Edward VII was seen by his own people as being a peacemaker, and a popular music hall song declared that there would be no war so long as good King Edward lived. It was remarkably prescient.

On both sides of the North Sea the press played up the scares, and fictional works were published, including the famous *The Riddle of the Sands* by Erskine Childers, while the German equivalent was *Der Weltkrieg: Deutsche Traume* (*The World [or Wide] War: Germany Triumphant*). The first book was one of espionage, the second, one in which a Franco-German-Russian alliance defeated the British, with Great Britain invaded after the Royal Navy was defeated. German journalists thought the use of the name 'Home Fleet' for the Royal Navy's main force ironic.

Despite a state visit by the King to Kiel and Berlin in June 1905, and a visit by German warships to Plymouth in July of that year, the unease between the two nations was not dissipated. The British noted the professionalism of the German warships with considerable apprehension. Relations were civil and correct, rather than warm. The *Entente Cordiale* agreed in 1903 was seen, indeed presented by the German leadership, as an alliance against Germany. The Germans also recalled Fisher's belligerent attitude at The Hague Conference in 1899, just as much as he recalled vividly the threats made privately by German admirals.

The Kaiser told Alfred Beit, the South African industrialist:

England wanted war; not the King – nor perhaps the Government; but influential people like Sir John Fisher. He thinks it is the hour for the attack, and I am not blaming him. I quite understand his point of view; but we too are prepared, and if it comes to war the result will depend upon the weight you carry into action – namely a good conscience, and I have that.[1]

WIDENING THE KIEL CANAL

The Kattegat and Skaggerack were difficult and time-consuming to navigate, with much shallow water. To provide easier access between the Baltic and the North Sea, between 1887 and 1895 the Germans had built the Kiel Canal, a ship canal 61 miles in length, through which ships could make the hitherto difficult journey in as little as ten hours, although there were a number of locks to pass through. This meant that the German Navy could move its entire fleet between the two seas, moving the ships to the North Sea for offensive operations, but bringing them back to the Baltic where they would be safer. All very well, but the canal had been built with the existing battleships in mind, and the Dreadnought-types were too wide to use it. Widening the canal, and the locks and their gates, was estimated by the British to cost £12 million at least. It provided a strong clue to German intentions when widening started in 1906. The British consul at Kiel passed the information on to Dumas in Berlin. Not wanting to be caught out again, and finally recognising that warship sizes could only get bigger, the Germans doubled the width of the canal and also eased many of the bends. Oddly, they also placed two new locks at each end, probably to enable large ships to use the canal more easily at all states of the tide.

It says much for Fisher's genius that he was able to use this information not just to calculate the cost of the work, which would be an additional drain on the German economy, but, far more important, also to estimate when the work would be finished. He concluded that it would take eight years to complete the work, taking the most likely date for the start of the First World War to 1914, and he also guessed that the Germans would want to complete harvesting before mobilising their largely conscript Army and going to war. This meant that war would break out in September or October 1914. The logic was impeccable. The work needed to be done, and continental countries had traditionally started fighting after the harvest was completed. Further thought by Fisher resulted in a slight change of mind, and he decided that war would break out during a bank holiday, and in the end, his country declared war on Germany on 4 August 1914, the then date of the August bank holiday.

Earlier, almost as soon as he became First Sea Lord, Fisher had set up a committee presided over by Prince Louis in his role as Director of Naval Intelligence, DNI, to look at the possible threats to the United Kingdom. The 'Two-Power Standard' was still the startying point and taken as the minimum. Now, a new measure had to be calculated, based on the new enemy. The threat looked most likely from an alliance of Germany and Russia, or possibly France and Russia. Realism also dictated that having fought either of these combinations, and having been weakened in the process, the country might be attacked by an opportunistic power. The committee proposed that the Admiralty should plan on creating a fleet that was 'two power plus ten per cent', at least in capital ships. The fact that the new standard was confined to capital ships showed an appreciation that the extra ships would probably mean reductions elsewhere because of financial and manpower constraints. It also reflected the fact that smaller ships were increasingly to play a subservient role and that, with their heavy calibre guns capable of firing accurately over longer ranges, naval warfare would be between battleships, aided by submarines. In February 1905, a second committee reported, and supported the findings of the earlier committee.

Of course, decisions like this did not take place in a vacuum. The problem with defence planning then as now is that the goal posts are forever being moved. In the 1900s, after Tsushima, Japan had become a major naval power and Russia vastly weakened for the foreseeable future. The United States was also beginning to develop a substantial fleet. Germany then suddenly discovered that she had 'great and growing' interests in Morocco, but this had the fortunate benefit of strengthening the *Entente Cordiale* between the United Kingdom and France, so that war with France seemed much less likely. It also showed that Germany was no longer content with simply continuing as a continental power.

The problem for the leaders of the armed forces was, of course, that politicians saw things differently. The social reforms promised by the new Liberal administration that came to power in December 1905 meant that defence expenditure was given a lower priority. The Cabinet was encouraged in this attitude by the new alliance with Japan and the growing closeness with France. This meant that the possibility of the country fighting a major war on its own was much reduced, and this became the excuse for limiting the demands of the Admiralty.

The weak new First Lord was also not one to take on the rest of the Cabinet in battle. Even so, he inherited a commitment from his Conservative predecessor, Lord Cawdor, for a rolling annual programme of four capital ships, although this included battlecruisers as well as battleships. This was designed to compensate for the loss of numerical superiority consequent upon the creation of the Dreadnought-type battleship and battlecruiser. At first the new government agreed to continue the plan, with provision made in the budget laid before Parliament in March 1906. It took just four months for the mood to change as the cost of introducing pensions became clear, and on 12 July, the new First Lord, Lord Tweedmouth agreed to cut the number of capital ships in the 1907–1908 programme to two ships instead of four, with the promise that the number could be increased to three if the second Hague Peace Conference, scheduled for 1907, failed to reach an agreement on the reduction of armaments.

The cuts were announced on 27 July 1906, creating an immediate uproar on the opposition benches and in the press. Accusations of cowardice were bandied about. The *Globe* in its issue of 21 September was especially bitter about the role of the naval officers in this:

> Lord Tweedmouth and Mr Robertson, having tasted blood in their reduction of this year's estimates are about to strike a blow at the vital efficiency of the Navy. But what are we to think of the naval officers on the Admiralty Board, men who cannot plead the blindness and ignorance of their civilian colleagues? No one knows better than Sir John Fisher the real nature and the inevitable consequences of those acts to which he is a consenting party. And we are not speaking at random when we assert that more than any one man, the responsibility and the guilt for those reductions lies at this door.

Poor Fisher – by this time being attacked by Beresford on the one hand and by the press and the opposition on the other! He could have resigned in protest, but that would have meant leaving his plans – still being implemented – to fate, and quite probably, the unsympathetic attentions of Beresford. The trouble for service chiefs is that politicians can always find another one.

GERMANY STOKES THE FIRES

In fact, in Fisher's view the situation was not as bad as the press seemed to think. Nevertheless, the Germans were keen to stoke the fires of unease. While the stories about Germany taking the opportunity to increase her shipbuilding programme were based on rumours, the claim that the German Dreadnoughts would be bigger and more heavily armed than those of the Royal Navy were deliberately planted by the Germans. The press criticism also went beyond concerns over warship building and extended to maintenance, with Fisher warning Tweedmouth in a letter while on holiday in Levico that the press were maintaining that the 'Repairs of ships are so in arrear [sic] that the fighting efficiency of the Fleet is being sacrificed.'

In one sense, this was unfair, because no one was a greater advocate of a strong and modern navy than Fisher, and his supporters were known as the 'Blue Water School', which led the freelance journalist, Arthur White, to describe those opposed to them as the 'Blue Funk School'.★

But it was also unfair in another way. The situation genuinely was not as black as it was painted. Fisher's letter to Tweedmouth continued with a summary of what was in fact happening. There was one Dreadnought built, with three to be laid down that year and three the following year because, with his experience both of the last conference and of human nature, he knew that The Hague Conference in 1907 would be 'futile'. There were also three Invincible-class battlecruisers being built, which he regarded as superior to the existing *Dreadnought*. On the last point he was to be proved wrong, but that is with the benefit of hindsight. Meanwhile, by the end of 1908, the Royal Navy would have ten Dreadnought battleships and battlecruisers, while the Germans were likely to have just two.

The problem was that many naval officers were bypassing Fisher and writing to the First Lord, while others were bypassing both and writing to the King! Fisher himself felt bound to write directly to His Majesty, but this was because King Edward has asked for his views on a book, *Germany's Swelled Head* by Dr Emil Reich, critical of Admiralty policy. Fisher pointed out that in preparing the Kiel Canal and the entrances to their ports and harbours to take the planned German Dreadnoughts, they were also making it easier for attacking British Dreadnoughts to get closer. It was not only the large capital ships in which the Royal Navy had supremacy. 'We have 123 destroyers and 40 submarines,' Fisher assured the King. 'The Germans have 48 destroyers and *one submarine*.'

In November 1907, Fisher was asked to speak at the Lord Mayor's Banquet, and promised those present that they could sleep soundly in their beds. Nevertheless, in little more than a month, he had reason to regret his bold words. With just two significant political parties at the time, it was perhaps inevitable that both were of necessity broad churches, but the Liberals in particular had become home for elements that were radical and anti-military, although outright pacifism might be

---

* Naval forces can be divided into the blue water and brown water categories. A blue water navy has true oceanic capability, and ideally, worldwide reach. A brown water navy is largely a coastal defence force. In Europe today, the UK, France and the Netherlands all have blue water navies, the Belgians and the Danes are definitely brown water. The Germans could only operate as a blue water force with the aid of their allies.

too strong a word. For these, who included amongst their ranks Lloyd George, Herbert Asquith and Winston Churchill, defence expenditure had to be cut to pay for their programme of welfare provision. They also had part of the press on their side, including the *Manchester Guardian*. If all was as well, as Fisher maintained, they could stop building battleships and start clearing the slums.

Hard on the heels of Fisher's Mansion House speech followed the news on 18 November 1907 that Germany was increasing her warship construction programme. The programme called for extra battleships that would increase the fleet by 25 per cent over five years, and in addition five battlecruisers would also be ordered. This would give the German Navy almost sixty capital ships, although not all would be Dreadnoughts. Such a programme was unprecedented and should have set the alarm bells ringing. After all, Germany's international trade was far less than that of Great Britain, and much of it came overland. It was clear that Germany wanted to be both the major continental power *and* the major maritime power.

These developments did not go unnoticed, with the Navy League demanding an emergency programme of warship construction, but the complacent attitude of the Liberal elite was that one really couldn't expect anything else of this particular pressure group. The Navy League was not without allies in the press and the Conservative Party, and even some Liberals were alarmed. Bowing to government pressure, the Admiralty Board proposed a shipbuilding programme for 1908 of a battleship and a battlecruiser, six light cruisers, sixteen destroyers and a small number of submarines, holding back its demands for a larger programme until 1909. The Cabinet, led by Prime Minister Campbell-Bannerman, rejected it and cut the estimates by £1.34 million, which meant that the battleship had to go.

This was more than just a missing ship, it meant that the armour plate industry would have to close down and mothball its plant, which would make restarting the programme in 1909–10, let alone achieving a substantial increase, so much more difficult. On 2 December, the Admiralty Board reported to Tweedmouth on the revised naval estimates:

With the full knowledge and absolute certainty (now afforded by the German programme just issued) of having to commence a larger battleship programme in 1909–1910, it would be most unbusinesslike, and indeed disastrous to close down the armour plate industry of this country by the entire cessation of battleship building. It would be similarly disastrous to abruptly stop the manufacture of heavy gun mountings, which the omission of the battleships would also involve … it would be on all grounds quite inadmissible to omit the one battleship in next year's programme, and indeed severe criticism must be expected at our not commencing two battleships.[2]

The hapless Tweedmouth had to go back to the Cabinet to fight the Navy's corner. Starting in January 1908, the discussion was dragged out over a series of meeting over a period of around three weeks. Fisher intervened, and finally threatened not only his own resignation but that of the entire Board if the estimates were not changed. He even hinted that it might, for once, be difficult to find other officers prepared to take their place.

This did not have the impact that it should have had: Lewis Harcourt, an ally of Beresford, declared that he knew one officer who would happily take over as First Sea Lord. He went further, and advised Lloyd George that Beresford would cut £2 million from the naval estimates if he was given Fisher's post. When he heard this, Fisher declared that the Beresford would 'sell' the government within three months.

Amidst this rising storm, Lloyd George attended a meeting of the Admiralty Board, and the estimates were re-examined with the sea lords maintaining their stand. Fisher then asked Lloyd George if he could see Campbell-Bannerman and carefully explain the minutiae of the estimates and the difficulties that would follow further cuts. The Prime Minister accepted the arguments and the original Admiralty Board proposals were kept.

HOSTILE PRESS

The Admiralty Board were right in expecting severe criticism for not ordering two battleships, and they got it! The *Daily Mail* asked: 'Is Britain going to surrender her maritime supremacy to provide old-age pensions?'

This criticism was to continue for some time. On 20 March 1909, after four Dreadnoughts had been ordered and four more likely to be ordered, a leader in the *Daily Express* attacked Fisher:

The sole responsibility for the fact that in a few months Great Britain will be in a more vulnerable position than she has been since the battle of Trafalgar belongs to the First Sea Lord ... Above all, he is responsible for the starving of the Navy for the past three years ... his notorious 'sleep safely in your beds' speech was a direct justification of Radical policy. We arraign Sir John Fisher at the bar of public opinion, and with the imminent possibility of national disaster before the country we say again to him, Thou art the man!

Lord Esher also challenged the decision, but defended Fisher against an attack by Beresford and rejected an invitation to join his Imperial Maritime League. He had his reply to the League published in *The Times* on 6 February 1908:

You say the general position is that by economies introduced for the purposes of securing money for social reform the efficiency of the Navy as a fighting force has been most dangerously reduced. I suppose you honestly think Sir John Fisher and the Sea Lords have lent themselves to so indefensible an enterprise.

If I could believe this, I should be glad to see Sir John Fisher and his colleagues meet the fate of Admiral Byng ... there is not a man in Germany, from the Emperor downwards, who would not welcome the fall of Sir John Fisher.

Rarely can a letter published even in *The Times* have had so much impact. None other than the Kaiser himself sat down and wrote to Tweedmouth a letter of nine pages, in his own hand. He argued that the German naval expansion programme was purely defensive. Naturally enough, Tweedmouth was amazed at this personal response, and he was sufficiently flattered to show it to his friends. While indiscreet, that much could be understood and even accepted, but he then went a step too far, not simply writing a private reply but also giving the head of state of a potentially hostile power advance information on the Navy Estimates, information that was not available to Parliament as these had still to be published. He then let the Foreign Secretary know!

'If there was any doubt before about the meaning of German naval expansion,' thundered an editorial in *The Times*, 'none can remain after an attempt of this kind to influence the Minister responsible for our

Navy in a direction favourable for the German interest.' Tweedmouth's lack of discretion was attacked from all sides, and he was forced to justify himself on 9 March in the House of Lords, but was sacked shortly afterwards. Possibly his lack of judgement was due to the fact that he was ill, and died of a cerebral haemorrhage in spring 1909.

There was now no hope of Beresford replacing Fisher, and instead Fisher was soon to gain a strong First Lord with whom he could work. Lord Esher was soon able to note that Asquith, while deputising for Campbell-Bannerman, was forced to pledge that sufficient warships would be laid down over the next three years to maintain British superiority. He noted drily that this would 'never have been obtained but for the Kaiser's letter'. Nevertheless, Esher's letter to *The Times* regarding the Imperial Maritime League had also done him harm and upset his relations with the King because of his remarks about the Kaiser. This was a time when monarchs tended to stick together. When Fisher next had the opportunity of a meeting with King Edward, after his Sovereign had unburdened himself of his anger with Esher, Fisher pleaded his case, and at the end, the King agreed that it was a good letter, 'because he [Esher] is a most able man!'

The paradox was that Fisher had created a powerful Home Fleet and was actively pursuing a naval building programme that would see the continued dominance of the Royal Navy in terms of both numbers and the technology used. The Home Fleet was intended to secure the North Sea and prevent any surprise attack or attempt at an invasion, viewed as most probably coming from Germany. Yet, with his old friend Arthur Wilson, he now decided that the North Sea was becoming too dangerous for the main battle fleet because of the threat from torpedoes and mines. He was still forcing through plans for the first of the so-called super-Dreadnought battleships, displacing 20,000 tons and with new calibre 13.5-inch guns. He foresaw the super-Dreadnoughts and the ships that followed making the Dreadnoughts scrap, even while explaining that by '1910 Dreadnoughts may be out of date' thanks to the growing capability of the submarine.

THE ZEPPELIN THREAT

Fisher always maintained that one should 'build few and build fast'. Today, the idea of building few would be anathema to anyone interested in shipbuilding. The general rule is to build as few different designs as possible, and the argument is made that the sixth ship of a standard class, if all are built in the same shipyard, takes half as long to build as the first. During both world wars, but especially during the Second, shipyards achieved miracles of production by building in quantity.

Fisher was remarkably prescient in appreciating the threat and potential of the submarine, and the danger of the torpedo and the mine. There was still at this stage no defence against submarines and no means of detecting them, unless they were caught on the surface. He was also quick to appreciate the danger from the air, but at this time that meant airships, dirigibles, not aeroplanes. Although the Wright brothers had made their first flight on 17 December 1903, it was not until 1908 that the world finally recognised their achievements, and lighter-than-air flight showed the most potential. It was not until 1912–1914 that the aeroplane began to show its offensive and reconnaissance potential and multi-engined aircraft began to appear.

Once again, the indefatigable Dumas, working hard in Germany, was a source of vital information. He wrote that while out playing golf: 'A German dirigible balloon came over our heads (one of the first journeys it has made) and I took copious notes.' It was to be another few years before the Zeppelin became more widely regarded as a threat. In October 1912, the Zeppelin L1, under the command of Count Ferdinand von Zeppelin himself, made a record 1,000-mile flight, leaving its base at Friedrichshafen at 8.35 a.m. on Sunday 13 October and returning to Johannisthal, near Berlin, the following day at 3.43 p.m. The near round-trip caused a considerable outcry in England following a claim that it had been heard over Sheerness during the night, although no one had actually seen it. Questions were asked in Parliament, and the government proved unable to provide any answers. The German response that the airship had not approached the English coastline at any time did not convince anyone.

Before this, in 1910, the Royal Navy had ordered its first airship, the dirigible named, probably most unfortunately, *Mayfly*. It didn't! The specification was altered to lighten the craft and thus help to extend its range and the load that could be lifted. The centre of the envelope collapsed soon afterwards as a result. In the event, during the First World War, the Royal Navy preferred to use semi-rigid blimps, which were good as convoy escorts, but lacked any effective offensive and reconnaissance potential.

Meanwhile, the question of budgets arose again. Fisher firmly believed that any invasion must be preceded by a period of 'strained relations', and not only were relations insufficiently tense at this time, 1908, but he had also satisfied himself that the German Fleet was neither large enough nor able to get its new ships through the Kiel Canal to pose a threat. He also took the view that while a raid might be possible, a successful invasion was impossible while the Royal Navy remained strong and placed its largest concentration in home waters. Nevertheless, there were those in the Army who believed that an unexpected invasion was possible, and these included Field Marshal Lord Roberts, 'Bobs' to his men, who had resigned from the Army in 1905 to campaign for a stronger army, based on conscription and supported by strong reserves, all very much continental-style. In the meantime, Roberts had started establishing village firing ranges and providing voluntary part-time military training, although the results were dismissed by Fisher as the work of the 'bows-and-arrows' brigade. Sir Frederick Ponsonby, Assistant Private Secretary to the King wrote to Fisher:

> My point is, if we are not safe from invasion, then make us so. Spend money on submarines, destroyers, etc, but don't waste money on an armed mob. You might as well arm all the caretakers in London houses instead of supplying them with a police force. Why wait until the enemy has landed?[3]

The primary reason for Fisher objecting to conscription was that the cost of a far larger Army was bound to adversely affect funding for the Navy. While these were the days before a unified Ministry of Defence and defence estimates, nevertheless, it was clear that a large Army and a large Navy would be beyond the country's means, even without the planned expenditure on welfare programmes.

Almost as bad, however, was the fact that a large standing Army was, in his view, almost certain to be drawn into a conflict on the mainland of Europe. He had visions of the cream of the country's manpower being bogged down in a major European land war, or alternatively, the Army embarking on Imperial campaigns, with the Royal Navy dispersed in its support.

The two preceding centuries had shown how a nation could have its manpower resources squandered in a costly and bloody conflict. Once again, history was to prove him right.

It is important to place the Liberal Government's desire for higher expenditure on welfare, and for higher taxes to pay for matters such as pensions rather than improving the nation's defences, into context. This was period of social unrest, not just in the United Kingdom but in other countries as well. The rumblings that preceded outright revolution in Russia had been going on for some years, and indeed had been behind the Tsar's enthusiasm for The Hague Conference in 1899. Winston Churchill feared revolution in his own country more than he feared war with Germany. If the rich continued to become richer and the poor remaining helpless, 'I think there is nothing before us but savage strife between class and class,' Churchill warned in a speech. The paradox was, of course, that the cut in naval shipbuilding had precisely the effect that Churchill and Lloyd George, the two most radical members of the Liberal Cabinet, wished to avoid. In the towns dependent on shipbuilding and armaments production, the reduced orders led to unemployment, poverty and misery.

Nevertheless, Fisher was nothing other than thorough when it came to mastering his arguments. He was meticulous in research and in using the intelligence resources available to him. Once again, he was fortunate in the person who was the naval attaché in Berlin. He wrote on 8 January 1908:

Colonel Repington [military correspondent of *The Times*] ... who is assisting Lord Roberts on the National Defence League and frightening the country out of its wits by an imminent German invasion of England, has placed before the Defence Committee ... that a Naval Surprise is not only possible but likely ... without any period of strained relations and without any warning whatsoever or any information leaking out, that 70,000 to 100,000 German troops could be embarked and leave in thirty-six hours from the German Emperor's order being given ... The question I ask you is whether you think it conceivable that no sort of rumours or indication of this great embarkation of German troops should not reach us for, say, twenty-four hours. Haag, the Vice-Consul at Bremerhaven, says it is absolutely impossible. The daily commercial interchange of communications if stopped or tampered with would at once indicate something amiss. Thirteen thousand telegrams a day come to London from Hamburg alone. Let us fully admit the tonnage is available and always sufficient but the mere fact of stopping steamers

sailing on their ordinary dates and the absolute dead stoppage of all
commercial and passenger traffic would, it seems to me, be instantly
reflected across all frontiers and thus become known to us at once
… Please think it over and send me a letter which could be placed
before the Defence Committee.[4]

Dumas duly did so, but no less a person than the German Navy
Minister, von Tirpitz, confirmed Fisher's arguments in a meeting with
Dumas early in February. He referred to the 'nonsense about invasion
lately written in England', and went on to say that 'Of the 30,000 or so
military officers in Germany one might expect that one or two sheep-
headed lieutenants might write such rubbish.' Tirpitz found it incredible
that someone with Roberts' reputation could advance such arguments.
Napoleon had found an invasion of England impossible across the distance of twenty miles. It would be impossible for Germany to embark
100,000 men, and, what was more, maintain their lines of communication. In short, landing an army would be difficult enough, but it ran the
risk of being cut off. He concluded by mentioning that the figure of
100,000 men would be 'wholly useless in England even if we had no
Army there to oppose them,' as it would be certain that a million semi-
trained soldiers would volunteer immediately 'like magic'. He even
drew the attention of Dumas to the Germans halt before Paris in 1870.
    This was good enough for Dumas and for Fisher, but not for the
'invasion scare' lobby. This had worked itself and everyone else up to
such a fever pitch that on 27 November 1907, there was the first meeting of a sub-committee of the Committee of Imperial Defence, chaired
by Asquith, to consider the risk of invasion. The debate dragged on
and many who had been on Fisher's side, such as Lord Esher, began to
have doubts. The Under-Secretary of State for the Colonies, the young
Winston Churchill, became involved. Although part of the anti-mili-
tarist wing of the Liberal Government at the time, he was interested
in defence matters and this was the beginning of a friendship with
Fisher that would last, despite pitfalls and difficulties, to the end of the
Admiral's life. Churchill's contribution to the debate was not inspir-
ing. He started in January 1908 by asking if there was a third option,
between a raid and an invasion, arguing that it would be worthwhile
for Germany to sacrifice a force of 60,000 men 'for the pleasure of
burning London to the ground' as this would be a staggering blow at
the beginning of a long (or even a short) war.

Fisher enlisted the aid of the distinguished naval historian, Sir Julian Corbett, who acted as the voice of reason during the long and often ill-tempered meetings of the CID sub-committee. This was heated debate rather than informed discussion. Nevertheless, when the sub-committee finally published a report in October 1908, the Admiralty view was broadly supported, although with the caveat that the Home Defence Army should be large enough to deter not only raids, but an invasion of up to 70,000 troops. If logic had been applied, a government anxious to curb defence expenditure would not have been convinced, as the report continued: 'So long as our naval supremacy is assured against any reasonably probable combination of Powers, invasion is impracticable … If we permanently lose command of the sea, whatever may be the strength and organisation of the Home force, the subjection of the country to the enemy is inevitable.'[5]

Notes

1 Bacon, Admiral Sir R.H., *The Life of Lord Fisher of Kilverstone*, London, 1929
2 Report to the First Lord on the Navy Estimates, 1908-1909, by the Sea Lords, 2 December 1907.
3 Kilverstone, Admiral of the Fleet Baron, *Records*, London, 1919
4 Ibid
5 Marder, Arthur J, *The Anatomy of Sea Power: British Naval Policy 1880-1905*, London, 1941

13

Treachery!

We are going to win all right, as I don't think they will face the consequences of the Board of Admiralty resigning.
There is black treachery besides unspeakable weakness.
Fisher to Viscount Knollys, Private Secretary to King Edward VII.

One of Fisher's innovations was a Naval War College, established at Portsmouth, and one of his last before resigning was the creation of a Naval War Council at the Admiralty. Once again we find Fisher to be a man of sometimes quite starting contradictions. He recalled in his autobiographical *Memories* that:

A Naval War Staff at the Admiralty is a very excellent organisation for cutting out and arranging foreign newspaper clippings ... the mischief of a Naval War Staff is peculiar to the Navy. I understand it is quite different in the Army – I don't know. The mischief to the Navy is that the very ablest of our Officers, both young and old, get attracted by the brainy work and the shore-going appointment.[1]

In fact, his belief was that the First Sea Lord and the First Sea Lord alone should prepare the war plans in secrecy and only on the outbreak of war divulge these to the Army! This was to be one of the criticisms made of him and played a part in his downfall. The Secretary of State for War, Lord Haldane, was one of those pressing for a naval staff and at one stage made the suggestion that there should be a combined Ministry of Defence. His interference was not appreciated by Fisher, and no more so than when Haldane backed Beresford. Both Corbett, the naval historian, and Fisher's old friend and constant supporter, Lord Esher, pressed Fisher to reconsider and establish a naval staff. Esher argued, in a letter dated 4 February 1907, that Fisher had 'shown mistrust and dislike of the Defence Committee instead of converting it to your uses ...

the forces ranged against each other have been Fisher versus Beresford. They should have been Fisher plus Defence Committee'.[2]

The explanation was, of course, that Fisher had become less disciplined and more inflexible as he grew older. The younger Fisher had often found a way of gaining the approval of his superiors. It is possible that as he got older Fisher felt that he had no need of this, or that he had no superiors!

Of course, the Navy was different from the Army in so many ways, as Fisher recognised:

> The Navy is always at war because it is fighting winds and waves and fog. The Navy is ready for an absolute instant blow; it has nothing to do with strategic railways, lines of communication, or bridging rivers, or crossing mountains, or the time of year ... No! the ocean is limitless and unobstructed; and the Fleet, each ship manned, gunned, provisioned and fuelled, ready to fight within five minutes.[3]

On 24 August, Esher again wrote to Fisher after the First Sea Lord had expressed his fury over Balfour's recommendation that the Committee for Imperial Defence should investigate the risk of an invasion:

> What on earth do you mean by maintaining that a paper written by Mr Balfour for the *Defence Committee* is purely an 'Admiralty business'? and talking of an 'irresponsible sub-committee'? [sic]
>
> (a) Mr Balfour's original memorandum was a Defence Committee paper, and his speech in the House of Lords was *based upon* it, and not upon any Admiralty decision.
>
> (b) The Committee for Imperial Defence, of which the *Prime Minister* is the Chief, and its sub-committees, *if appointed by the Prime Minister*, are every bit as 'responsible' as the Board of Admiralty, of which the *First Sea Lord* is the Chief ...
>
> The Admiralty will have to recognise, as the War Office has recognised, that the Defence Committee is a new factor in our administrative system ...[4]

Fisher, on holiday in Carlsbad, replied on 8 September, saying that he had expected to get 'slated' by Esher, and had also expected that Esher would get his 'wicked way', and that he had.

Immersed in the technicalities of his profession – the great reforms, his redistribution of the fleet, the creation of a new ship and weapons – he literally had no time to devote himself to a profound study as to how the Navy could best be used as an instrument of war. No war plan that existed in his brain had ever been considered in all its aspects or worked out. It was repugnant to him to delegate powers to others, and that comparatively junior officers, in a considered staff opinion, should voice their opinions as to the conduct of the war. He preferred to do his own thinking. Therefore no War Staff worthy of the name existed.[5]

So wrote one of his contemporaries some ten years after Fisher's death. This was wrong. Fisher did delegate and had a reputation for listening to junior officers, provided that they knew what they were talking about. Indeed, he was more inclined to listen to them, fresh to the service and often specialising in a relatively new field, such as submarines or torpedoes, than the traditionalists. He also believed that the only man that could execute a war plan was the man who had formulated it. That meant that his successor would have to prepare his own war plan. While not having a plan at the time of the handover from one First Sea Lord to another was certainly a problem, and could have been disastrous, it is the case that circumstances change and Fisher's approach had the merit that it forced each new First Sea Lord to prepare a plan that reflected the needs of the day. This, of course, assumes that the successor had Fisher's genius. He did not. There was one other drawback that left this overall approach open to doubt. One advantage of having a 'transferable' plan was that its implications could be considered and the necessary naval assets made available for deployment in the event of hostilities. Fisher's ideas for hostilities often lacked realism, as would be seen when he returned to the Admiralty in 1914.

Not only did Fisher work long hours as First Sea Lord, and indeed in every position he had held before that, his annual holidays were not work free. Despite telling his friends that it was 'not good for the cure to have a busy mind', he received papers and correspondence while on his spa holidays and dealt with these promptly. Marienbad remained his favourite resort, with his daily walk along the *Kreuzbrunnen* where he could be sure of 'bumping into' prominent politicians and even royalty, and would create unease amongst those Germans who also went for the waters, but he would go elsewhere, including Carlsbad. He was even on good terms with the Emperor Franz Joseph of Austro-Hungary, whom he would reproach for not repressing the Kaiser's maritime ambitions.

Of course, the person Fisher most desired to meet was his own Sovereign, and he did this often until late 1908, when it seemed politic not to be seen having long lunches with His Majesty or being a guest at the many dances and other functions. Before this, however, he had been invited to join the Royal party on a state visit to Reval in June 1908 to meet the Tsar of Russia. This was the most enjoyable visit as far as Fisher was concerned, spending plenty of time with his beloved King. The trip started badly, however, the Royal Yacht *Victoria & Albert* encountering bad storms and everyone from the King downwards suffering from sea sickness. Even Fisher suffered from a sick headache. It gave the Royal Party a chance to view the Kiel Canal, which Fisher described in a letter to his wife as being 'quite lovely', although no doubt after the 'horrible knocking about' they had all suffered in the North Sea, anything flat and calm would doubtless have been sweet balm to the senses.

The grand banquet and ball at Reval was very much to Fisher's taste, with him being able to renew his acquaintance with the Tsar's young sister, the Grand Duchess Olga, whom he had first met at Carlsbad. He would later write:

> At the banquet preceding the dance the Grand Duchess and I, I regret to say, made such a disturbance in our mutual jokes that King Edward called out to me that I must try to remember that it was not the Midshipmen's Mess; and my dear Duchess thought that I should be sent to Siberia or somewhere.[6]

The fun and frolics apart – and there were many, including Fisher dancing a hornpipe to the delight of everyone at the ball – there was a serious purpose to the visit. King Edward VII had to ensure, or attempt to ensure, that the Tsar would not ally his country with Germany in the event of hostilities.

FAMILY LIFE

While Fisher was often away on visits, short or long, while at the Admiralty, he did his best to maintain family life. The Admiralty and the family were, for the most part, kept in separate compartments. Gone were the days on the North American Station and in the Mediterranean when his family could follow him. He rarely spoke about his work with his family, although he did cover it in some of his letters. He regarded his work as of being of no interest to his family. He spoke to his son and his daughters at meal times, or when walking, although he was a man of few words. When he did talk, it was about people whom he had met, or a sermon that he might have heard. He did take a keen interest in the lives of his children, and in their health. It seems that as the years advanced, health matters, and not just his own, preoccupied him considerably.

Two of his daughters, Pamela and Dorothy, remained unmarried until they were thirty and thirty-five respectively (astonishingly old) and their weddings coincided with his period at the Admiralty. Pamela married Commander Henry Blackett in 1906, and was followed by Dorothy's marriage to Lieutenant Eric Fullerton in 1908.

That same year, Josiah Vavasseur died and Kilverstone Hall passed to Cecil, who had retired from the Indian Civil Service to manage the estate in Norfolk.

Kilverstone was close to Sandringham and while there Fisher was able to visit the King, and it was a mark of His Majesty's regard for Fisher that he repaid the visit on at least one occasion.

On 26 October, the Prime Minister, Asquith, wrote to Fisher:

I have the pleasure of formally proposing to you that, on the occasion of His Majesty's approaching birthday – November 9th – you should be raised to the peerage ... I desire, at the same time, to express to you the sincere and grateful acknowledgements of His Majesty's Government for the great work – unique in our time – which you have accomplished in developing and strengthening the Navy, and assuring the maritime supremacy of Great Britain.[7]

For most men, this would have been wonderful. A peerage and a letter acknowledging the nation's debt to him, and it came at a time when the dispute with Beresford was reaching its climax, a shaft of light amidst dark days.

This was Fisher, of course, and he was not most men. For him the news was tainted by the fact that he was being offered a barony, when he thought that he deserved a viscountcy!

'WE WANT EIGHT, AND WE WON'T WAIT'

Meanwhile, the news from Germany was getting worse, even though many tried to present German intentions in a good light, and some presented Fisher as a warmonger. As early as 1908, it had become clear that the fleet Germany was building was far larger than that announced to the world, and it seemed, according to Admiralty calculations, that by 1912 Germany would have thirteen Dreadnought battleships and battlecruisers in commission. By contrast, just two had been authorised for the Royal Navy in 1908, and even if six were ordered in 1909, the service could expect to have eighteen Dreadnought battleships and battlecruisers by 1912. This was not the two-to-one standard that the nation had become accustomed to. The problem was that with worldwide responsibilities, the fleet was always vulnerable to being overwhelmed in any one region. Worse, if more ships were not laid down, there was the all too real possibility that Germany could have three more ships than Britain by 1912. Later, the Sea Lords advised the First Lord, McKenna, that Germany would definitely have seventeen Dreadnoughts by 1912, and that even if the United Kingdom did manage to have eighteen, that was:

> ... not considered in any way adequate to maintain the command of the sea in a war with Germany without running undue risk ... We therefore consider it of the utmost importance that power should be taken to lay down two more armoured ships in 1909–1910 – making eight in all.

It was not just in shipbuilding that Germany was making vast strides and catching up on the United Kingdom. The major armaments firm of Krupps was improving its production of guns and gun mountings. Lloyd George in particular chose to treat these reports as propaganda, stating that 'the Admirals are procuring false information to frighten us', something with which Admiral Jellicoe was to tax him during the First World War. Early in 1909, Fisher wrote to the King:

> The outlook is very ominous. Herculean efforts of which we know secretly and *certainly*, are being made by Germany to push on their Dreadnoughts – so much so that McKenna, who was when he came here an extreme 'Little Navy' man, is now an ultra 'Big Navy' man,

and Your Majesty would be astonished by his memorandum to Grey and to the Prime Minister as to building more Dreadnoughts next year than intended, and we shall certainly get them![8]

Cabinet unity soon came under strain, with the members early in 1909 pressing for four, six or eight Dreadnoughts, while Churchill tried to maintain that the British Dreadnoughts were in fact superior, doubtless implying that the Royal Navy could manage with a lower figure. The tussle within the Cabinet continued for some months, until July, and news soon leaked out. Pacifism became the subject of scorn, and the cry went up, apparently originating with a Conservative MP: 'We want eight, and we won't wait.' The slogan was taken up in a way that would be hard to believe today, with protest marches and demonstrations. 'Insist on "the Eight, the whole Eight, and nothing but the Eight",' ran an editorial in *The Observer*. 'With more to follow, and break any man or faction that now stands in the way.' In desperation, Asquith proposed ordering four Dreadnoughts immediately, and four more before April 1910 if the news from Germany warranted it. The second batch of four became known as the 'contingent ships', and McKenna showed considerable skill in getting authority to order equipment for these ships when the first batch was ordered so that completion would be as quick as possible. In an attempt to stop McKenna's ploy from succeeding, Churchill and Lloyd George offered to agree to six ships instead of the four they had been advocating, but McKenna and Fisher rejected this offer. Fisher at one stage facetiously suggested calling the 'contingent ships' *Winston, Churchill, Lloyd* and *George*.

The preoccupation with Germany and that country's intentions was soon disturbed by news that several other countries were building or planning to build Dreadnoughts. The first of these were Italy and the Austro-Hungarian Empire, which were laying down four each. Not only were the other great powers, France, Japan, Russia and the United States building such ships, Turkey and even some South American countries were also planning Dreadnoughts, albeit that these countries would have to buy them from elsewhere. On 29 July 1909, McKenna was able to tell the House of Commons that the four 'contingent ships' would indeed be built.

While this was going on, the Committee for Imperial Defence subcommittee was meeting. There were fifteen meetings in all, starting on 27 April and ending on 13 July. The sub-committee consisted of

Haldane, Grey, the radical Lord Morley and the Earl of Crewe, who supported a big navy. The Admiralty view was advanced by McKenna, while the contrary view was put by Beresford, with the aid of Custance. There were many who believed that given enough rope, Beresford would hang himself, and that Fisher had much to gain by not going on to the attack. Nevertheless, on 5 May 1909, Ponsonby wrote to Fisher saying that His Majesty did not take that view. Others discussed Fisher's resignation, but under attack and under investigation, Fisher shared the opinion of his friend, Lord Esher, that this was not the time to go. Nevertheless, a valuable ally in the form of the Prince of Wales changed sides, something for which, inevitably, he was never forgiven by Fisher.

When the sub-committee finally reported on 12 August 1909, it generally supported the Admiralty Board: 'During the time in question no danger to the country resulted from the Admiralty's arrangements for war, whether considered from the standpoint of the organisation and distribution of the fleets, the number of ships, or the preparation of War Plans.' But it also noted that these plans were 'seriously hampered' by the 'absence of cordial relations' between Beresford and the Admiralty. They did not support Beresford's complaint about the lack of war plans, but the Admiralty Board was criticised for not taking him into their confidence. The report looked forward 'with much confidence to the further development of a Naval War Staff, from which the Naval members of the Board and Flag Officers and their staffs at sea may be expected to derive common benefit.'[9]

Beresford's claim about the shortage of destroyers and other small craft in home waters was rejected with 'There is no such deficiency as to constitute a risk to the safety of the country.' As for the lack of War Plans, the Committee were 'satisfied that he had no substantial grounds for complaint'.

VINDICATION?

The result was in fact a qualified vindication of Fisher, but Beresford's insubordination was not criticised as severely as Fisher had hoped. The careful language used, intended not to offend either side, left it possible for either to greet the report as a victory. If Fisher and his supporters had welcomed the report as a vindication of his stand, the reaction of press, politicians and public could have been favourable, but they did not and instead fostered the First Sea Lord's growing resentment, with Fisher, ever quick to take offence, attacking the 'cowardliness' of those who had prepared it. Had he received letters of congratulation, his attitude might have been different, but instead he received letters in which his correspondents commiserated with him.

By contrast, Beresford and his supporters treated the findings as a great victory. He issued a circular letter to the press announcing his 'great satisfaction'. The press took this up with enthusiasm and Fisher became the target of many harshly-worded editorials.

Still, it was the wrong time for Fisher to resign, for that would imply that Beresford was right as were those who read that the Report was unfavourable towards him. Nevertheless, once again, as on the eve of Fisher's arrival as First Sea Lord, the Board of Admiralty found itself in a difficult position, lacking any authority and even less credibility. The letter from Asquith offering the peerage was some comfort, but not enough (had it been a viscountcy, it might have been a different matter) and it was decided that while he would have the peerage on the King's birthday, he would retire the following January on his own 69th birthday. He had sent the King the letter from the Prime Minister, and received a reply that he regarded as the 'very best letter I ever received in my life'.

Many thanks for sending me the Prime Minister's letter to you of 26th inst. to read, which I return. It is a charming letter in every respect and one which I know you would wish to keep. I endorse every word in it and nobody deserves the thanks of your Sovereign and your Country more warmly than you do. Time will show what admirable Reforms you have created in the Royal Navy, and you can afford to treat with the contempt that it deserves 'those back biters' who have endeavoured to calumniate you! When you leave the high and important post which you now occupy in the Admiralty, I hope you will still render the best services that lie in your power for the good of the noble profession to which you belong, and I hope continue a member of the 'Defence Committee'! You possess too much vitality to 'lie fallow'![10]

His elevation to the peerage, followed by the announcement on 2 December of his impending retirement, caused a flood of correspondence containing tributes and praise. His supporters provided a mass of praise and acclamation that, had it followed the publication of the Report, would have changed his mood and could have changed that of the country. He also received a silver model of a submarine as a Christmas present from King Edward, and Queen Alexandra sent him a model of a Dutch ship in full sail.

When he actually left office, the press took the opportunity to assess his career and his achievements. Some of his critics remained silent for they had already had their say. *The Times*, that had supported him so often in the past, by this time had a naval correspondent who was firmly in the Beresford camp, so its response was muted after having earlier published many anti-Fisher articles in which Custance had had a hand. Perhaps, given the inclination of the paper, its summary on 25 January 1910, was generous:

> During these five strenuous years which have seen the consumma-
> tion and crown of a long career equally strenuous, Lord Fisher has
> for good or for evil – and in our judgement largely for good – left an
> indelible mark, a mark deeper than that made by any of his immedi-
> ate predecessors, on the administration, organisation, disposition and
> equipment of the Royal Navy ... it is probable that some things may
> have been done amiss, that some reforms ... necessary in themselves
> may have been introduced somewhat brusquely, and that the manner
> of effecting them may not always have been unimpeachable from the
> point of view of official conventions and service traditions. It is cer-
> tain, at any rate, that they have aroused much bitter antagonism and
> much painful controversy.[11]

On the other hand, Fisher's old friend, W.T. Stead, by this time editor of the *Review of Reviews*, listed his achievements and reforms, dockyard reorganisation, establishing a school of navigation, developing subma-rines and minesweepers, the launch of a Fleet reserve and arrangements for mobilisation, as well as the redistribution of the fleets and the crea-tion of the Dreadnoughts. It was a sad day for Fisher and his friends when Stead went down with the *Titanic*. McKenna, the First Lord, was convinced that Fisher would be back in Whitehall within a year – his timing was amiss!

In his book, *The World Crisis*, Winston Churchill was generous in his appraisal of Fisher:

There is no doubt whatever that Fisher was right in nine-tenths of what he fought for. His great reforms sustained the power of the Royal Navy at the most critical period in its history. He gave the Navy the kind of shock which the British Army received at the time of the South African War. After a long period of serene and unchallenged complacency, the mutter of distant thunder could be heard. It was Fisher who hoisted the storm-signal and beat all hands to quarters. He forced every department of the Naval Service to review its position and question its own existence. He shook them and beat them and cajoled them out of slumber into intense activity. But the Navy was not a pleasant place while this was going on.[12]

Fisher's choice as successor was his final victory, but it was a mistake. He briefed the First Lord, McKenna, to attend upon the King and urge him to press for Fisher's old friend, Sir Arthur Wilson, to become the First Sea Lord. The King summoned Wilson to Sandringham, and when told of his new appointment, accepted with reluctance, after telling His Majesty that he had been the 'worst Controller [Third Sea Lord] the Navy had ever had'.

Notes

1 Kilverstone, Admiral of the Fleet Baron, *Memories*, London, 1919
2 Brett, Maurice V., and Esher, Viscount Oliver, *Journal and Letters of Reginald, Viscount Esher*, London, 1934–1938 (4 vols)
3 Kilverstone, Admiral of the Fleet Baron, *Memories*, London, 1919
4 Brett, Maurice V., and Esher, Viscount Oliver, *Journal and Letters of Reginald, Viscount Esher*, London, 1934–1938 (4 vols)
5 Dorling, Captain Taprell 'Taffrail', RN, *Men o' War*, London, 1929
6 Kilverstone, Admiral of the Fleet Baron, *Memories*, London, 1919
7 Kilverstone, Admiral of the Fleet Baron, *Records*, London, 1919
8 Ibid
9 Ibid
10 Ibid
11 *The Times*, 25 January 1910
12 Churchill, Winston, *The World Crisis*, London

14

Always Ready

It's not invasion, it's starvation that has to be contemplated. A British Army of four millions led by Moltkes instead of Asses is no use if we have not command of the sea! ... Give the Navy every d—d thing they want!
Fisher on compulsory military service.

As arranged, Fisher left the Royal Navy on 25 January 1910. As a half pay Admiral of the Fleet, he was on a pension of £2,000 pa, while he and Lady Fisher by this time had acquired a private income of £300 pa. Despite being on half-pay, they no longer had children to consider or the upkeep of a First Sea Lord's lifestyle, and it seems that their income was sufficient.

It also seemed to the casual observer that after a lifetime of hard work and in later years constant struggle and planning, that at first he was content simply to relax and tend the roses at Kilverstone Hall, his son's home. He took up golf, learning from a professional on a neighbour's private links.

In fact, those who knew him realised that his life was slightly different from this. He did spend some time with the roses, and did take up golf with his usual thoroughness, but he also maintained a late night, or in reality early morning, correspondence with people like Lord Esher and Reginald McKenna's wife. Moreover, he remained an active member of the Committee for Imperial Defence. The strange hours at which he handled his correspondence was due to his fondness for dancing – if there were young and energetic women available, he would still dance until three in the morning, be they visitors to Kilverstone or perhaps acquaintances met while he was abroad on a spa holiday.

PRESSING FOR REFORM

He was at last free from the burden of responsibility, or at least direct and compelling daily duties. This is not to suggest that he did little or took no further interest in the service. Everything suggests that he spent his time preparing for his return. He also pressed for further reform of the Royal Navy, and at the time his great project was to make it easier for both 'Bluejackets and Marines to attain commissioned rank'.

In the Victorian Navy, it had been virtually impossible for ratings to become officers. In theory, warrant officers could be promoted to the rank of lieutenant for gallantry in action, but it was not until the golden jubilee honours of Queen Victoria in 1887 that two warrant officers received this promotion. The result was that warrant officers could spend as much as thirty years in the rank, and, as mentioned earlier, pressure for reform built up in the service and this eventually took the form of the monthly *Naval Warrant Officers' Journal* to press their case. It was not until 1912 that Churchill resolved the issue by introducing the Mate Scheme, under which petty officers and above could attain commissions, and this option was extended to engineers in 1914. Churchill had been guided in this by Fisher, who had pointed out that the service had to be open to all classes, writing: 'Our officers are restricted now to less than 1/40th of the population. *We want the brains of the other 39/40ths!*' By this time, the rank of 'mate' equated to a lieutenant, while in Fisher's early career it had been equivalent to the twentieth-century rank of sub-lieutenant.

AN AUTHORITARIAN RADICAL

Fisher continued to maintain his links with the press and certain politicians. He could still be indiscreet, writing letters to editors in which he would warn them 'This is a deadly secret, so burn and don't talk in your sleep.' Fisher actually warned one journalist off coming to Kilverstone in case people thought that he influenced the series of articles he was writing. He continued to show a complete lack of modesty, writing to the editor of the *Daily News*: 'Secret – I am more powerful now in the Committee of Defence than when I was First Sea Lord. I had masters then, now I have none and I have a platform.'

His disdain for politicians as a breed remained undiminished. Indeed, it sometimes appeared as if he would have supported a dictatorship. He advocated a mild authoritarianism led by a chastened Bismarck. In writing to McKenna he mentioned a conversation with John Jellicoe:

> ...it didn't signify what d—d fools we had to govern us – we got on! The Tories gave up Heligoland, the key to the Baltic, and the Liberals gave up Corfu, the key of the German Mediterranean ... and some other ass gave up Curaçao, the key of the Panama Canal, and Ceuta, more precious than them all.[1]

It mattered little to this flow of vituperation that Heligoland would have been difficult to hold in an all-out war with Germany, and during the Second World War, it would have been unlikely that Corfu could have been held either.

He also ranted that he did more for the Conservatives than for the 'Radicals', by which he meant Liberals, but the former had given him abuse and calumny while the latter had given him £2,000 a year and a peerage. He later wrote:

> I increased the Radical estimates nearly 10 millions. I decreased the Estimates 9 millions and reduced prospective charges by nineteen millions sterling for the Conservatives, and they never lifted even a little finger to help me, *but on the contrary* have heaped dunghill abuse on me![2]

He was in fact a radical by inclination, albeit an authoritarian, although that was not so unusual, and remains so. His own struggle to make his way in the world made him resentful of inherited privilege, including titles, and despite his close friendship with Edward VII, he was no monarchist. Perhaps his view of the monarchy, which had been so helpful to him in two reigns, was coloured by the defection of George, Prince of Wales, to the Beresford camp. He exchanged messages of commiseration with his old friend Esher when Edward VII died shortly into his retirement:

> What an *inexpressible* sorrow! How we both know the loss! What a great National Calamity! And *personally what can I say? What a splendid*

and steadfast friend! No use saying any more to each other – is it? *I really feel heart broken.*

A fortnight later:

I really can't get over the irreparable loss. *I think of nothing else!*[3]

Some of this really was euphuistic and overstating the case. Nevertheless, this was his manner of writing. He would write to people that he loved them, and loved their husbands too! In warmth and friendship, Fisher was as extreme in his use of language as he was in anger and enmity. Reginald McKenna's wife was addressed in correspondence as 'My Beloved Angel'.

He was sent a telegram by Queen Alexandria inviting him to see his old friend in 'his last beautiful sleep'. This was not simply form, but an acknowledgement of the close ties with the Royal Family. He spent 'an affectionate half-hour with the Queen – too sacred to talk of', he wrote to McKenna. 'No one knows what I have lost. I've burnt his letters ... But he has gone at his zenith like Elijah, Nelson and Moses ... It's the best way to go.'[4]

At the funeral, attended by eight kings and the Kaiser, as First and Principal Aide-de-Camp, Fisher walked alone, and was described by the *Illustrated London News* as being 'a striking figure, to whom the attention of all was drawn irresistibly'. Indeed he was, in full dress uniform, complete with decorations and orders, and with his head bowed low in genuine grief.

There was some comfort. His three daughters had all married, albeit two of them did so late in life. Cecil had thus far avoided marriage, but on 22 November 1910 he married the American heiress Jane Morgan. Fortunately, Fisher approved heartily of his son's bride, 'and all is most suitable in all ways in her! Looks, age, character, and means.' Young Cecil Fisher seemed to have a fine touch in the securing of wealth and good fortune.

Fisher sailed in the liner *Baltic* for the wedding in New York, and was most impressed with the United States. Here he felt was an ally, and he wasted no time in writing to his friends to say so.

DIESEL DREAMS

In fact, he continued to bombard people with his thoughts and ideas. He ignored the poor relations between his successor, Wilson, and McKenna, and brooded on the fact that the submarine was being neglected. He hated the English winter, and on 18 February 1911 he took his wife across the Channel, intending to spend some time there, living cheaply, until Wilson was due to retire in March 1912, when he fully expected to be invited back – at the age of 71 years!

Meanwhile, there were other causes that attracted him, although being away from the service soon showed his lack of in-depth technical knowledge. He continued to champion the submarine, and he extrapolated its technical features, becoming an early advocate of the diesel engine for major warships. The submarine had introduced the diesel or heavy oil engine to the Royal Navy, being much safer and more economical than the petrol engine, with its spark plugs and explosive fuel. Fisher was not wrong, just very far ahead of his time in advocating a diesel-powered battleship.

> Motor battleships. No funnels – no boilers – no smoke – no engineers – no stokers – only a d—d chauffeur and prodigious economy! '*Colossal billig*'! As the Germans would say! And imagine the fighting effects of all this! [*billig* – cheap, reasonable]

In fact, it was not until the late 1930s that the Germans realised the potential of the diesel engine for their so-called 'pocket battleships',★ actually *Panzerschiff*, armoured ships and later reclassified as armoured cruisers. The genuine German battleships, the sisters *Bismarck* and *Tirpitz*, used steam turbines. He was also far off the mark in believing that such large diesel engines would not need funnels, and they would have to be extremely well designed, well built and well maintained to be completely smoke free. As for no engineers or stokers, well, the former remained vital and the latter still controlled the flow of fuel. The

★ The term 'pocket battleship' was coined by the British media. They actually replaced the coastal battleships Germany was allowed to retain by the Treaty of Versailles.

problem with the large marine diesel engine was that it gave range, but not speed, and was far less reliable and smooth than the steam turbine.

While he was away on his grand tour of Europe, he continued to write, mainly to McKenna, Esher, Jellicoe and the journalist Arnold White. They all replied and he felt that he remained in touch with developments, and by letting them know what his other correspondents wrote, ensured that they did so too. He remained convinced that McKenna would have him back at the Admiralty, but that hope was dashed when, in October, the First Lord was sacked. Asquith and other senior members in his Cabinet were now taking the German naval threat very seriously, but nothing was happening at the Admiralty. Modernisation of the Royal Navy had all but stopped, and the Naval War Staff remained a hope for the future. Few would have expected Arthur Wilson to be an innovative First Sea Lord, but none had expected him to be a complete failure, unable to inspire, let alone implement developments, lacking imagination and drive. Only he had predicted how bad he would be. This was Fisher's greatest mistake as First Sea Lord, for it was Fisher, and none other, who had pressed for his old friend to be his successor, as his last act in office.

MEETINGS WITH CHURCHILL

McKenna had to take the blame for not goading Wilson into action or not dismissing him. On 24 October 1911, he was replaced by Winston Churchill, who had made no secret of his desire to be First Lord, so much so that many believed that he had plotted and schemed, or at least lobbied behind the scenes, to get this prize post. McKenna was shunted into the Home Office, at that time a lesser department of state, and went, according to some accounts, unwillingly, although not so unwillingly that he sought to return to the back benches.

Churchill wasted no time and was in at the front door of the Admiralty with almost indecent haste.

'I want to see you vy [sic] much,' he telegrammed Fisher, who was in Lucerne at the time. 'When am I to have that pleasure? You have but to indicate your convenience & I will await you at the Admiralty.'

This put Fisher in a difficult position. He had hoped that McKenna would have him back, and indeed McKenna had indicated his desire for his return. He wanted to be back and realised that without McKenna it could be difficult. But Churchill! No mean manager of his own ambitions, he suspected that Churchill had manipulated behind the scenes to replace his friend McKenna. Just as bad, he could not forget or forgive Churchill's fight to cut the 1910 naval estimates, which to Fisher was simply treasonable. That Churchill had undergone a conversion and wanted Fisher back, and most probably for the right reasons, was probably not immediately obvious to Fisher. After all, in all probability, given the pace that news was diffused at the time, the telegram from Churchill was the first communication he had received about the changes in the government.

Nevertheless, completely unabashed and driven by his enthusiasm, Churchill sent a second telegram, and this time made it clear that he had McKenna's support. Fisher agreed with considerable reluctance, and only on condition that his visit was kept secret. This was all done in a hurry, for on 28 October Fisher arrived, having travelled incognito from Switzerland. He dined with McKenna on his arrival before being taken by Churchill by car to Reigate Priory, where most of the other Cabinet members were present.

Just three days had passed since Churchill had become First Lord of the Admiralty. On 25 October, he had apparently wanted nothing more than to have Fisher as his First Sea Lord, but by 28 October, he had changed his mind. Possibly this was because he had confided his plans in Asquith and other senior members of the Cabinet, and been warned off. It was too soon to forget the problems and the arguments that had threatened to split the Royal Navy. There were far too many people with axes to grind and who could not forgive the behaviour of the First Sea Lord. Perhaps there were even some who knew enough to blame him for foisting Wilson on them.

Nevertheless, the Cabinet and its new First Lord were also dangerously near to getting out of their depth. They needed a new First Sea Lord chosen as Arthur Wilson would be retiring within six months. They also needed advice on the other naval posts on the Board. Churchill in addition needed Fisher's advice on the estimates for 1912, and help with his speech.

This was not the only meeting. Fisher helped and then left, but another telegram from Churchill brought him back on 17 November to a second secret meeting. This time it was held aboard the Admiralty yacht *Enchantress*, moored in Plymouth Harbour. The problem was that competition and lobbying for the post of First Sea Lord seemed to have become accepted as par for the course at the time, and in addition, Churchill, impatient as always, wanted to retire Wilson early. Several senior officers were being proposed, including Sir John Durnford, whom the new King George V (known as the 'sailor-king') favoured, and against him there was Sir William May. Fisher was having none of it. He had while at the Admiralty praised Bridgeman as the 'best admiral' in the Royal Navy, and Sir Francis Bridgeman it was to be. Once again, he had his own man in charge. He also ensured that it was his own man who became Second Sea Lord, Prince Louis of Battenberg, although he came with the added benefit that it would please the King and to some extent act as a consolation prize.

Wilson's early retirement was mishandled by Churchill, who, with his customary impatience, was upsetting senior officers at a rate that Fisher might have envied. Wilson was basically called upon to retire, and as a throwaway line told that he could have a peerage if he wished. Wilson in turn bluntly refused the peerage, but had to go anyway.

Other appointments were also decided at the same time. On 21 October 1914, John Jellicoe was to find himself in the role of *Admiralissimo*, the term coined earlier for the most senior naval officer actually at sea. Once again, the anniversary of Trafalgar became the date for an appointment.

Fisher treated Churchill with considerable disdain. When the First Lord asked for a third meeting, Fisher refused, so Churchill went to see him in Naples at the New Year. This was the beginning of a friendship that would soon replace the enmity that had existed between the two men, but further storms were never to be far away.

Bridgeman, like Wilson before him, had had his moments of greatness, and like Wilson before him, he was another bad choice as First Sea Lord. At first, he seemed to be pliable enough to work with the impatient and impetuous Churchill, but while Wilson had been obstinate and immoveable, Bridgeman was weak, but also truculent. Perhaps the only real step forward at this time was that at last, indeed almost too late, the Naval War Staff came into existence.

A tremendous correspondence started between Churchill and Fisher, at its heaviest during the first four months of 1912, with frequent letters occasionally interspersed by telegrams. Churchill was eager to learn, Fisher was eager to teach, and preach. He was also anxious to state that war at sea had moved on in the short time since he had retired.

The most damnable person for you to have any dealing with is a Naval Expert! Sea fighting is pure common sense. The first of all its necessities is SPEED, so as to be able to fight –
When you like
Where you like
And *How* you like

Therefore the super-*Lion*, the super-*Swift*★ and the super-Submarine are the only three types for fighting (*speed* being THE characteristic of each of these types). AVIATION has wiped out the intermediate types …

It was at this time that he urged Churchill to improve the opportunities for men to be commissioned from the ranks.

Fisher also prompted Churchill to take action about the poor standards of gunnery, advising him to have Jellicoe call on some other pretext before having a private conversation with him, because of his strong loyalty towards the First Sea Lord.

So you have to draw him carefully, but I counsel this because I want you to assure yourself by the testimony of the best officer the Navy has ever had since Nelson that I am correct in warning you of the vital danger hovering around …

THE KING'S INFLUENCE

The 'on-off-on' nature of the relationship between Fisher and Churchill soon manifested itself yet again. King George V began to exert his influence in the absence of McKenna and Wilson and started to press for the Admiralty to elevate officers who had impressed him. Fisher's influence with the new monarch was non-existent, in woeful contrast to his relationship with the late King Edward VII. While he was young, the future King George V had been favourably impressed by Fisher, but he was one of those whose support ebbed away during the years of the conflict with Beresford. Not content with Battenberg's appointment

---

★ New 'super-Dreadnought' designs.

as Second Sea Lord, the King was pressing hard for his other friends to be promoted. Amongst those who benefited was Beresford's close supporter Custance, while others included Lambton, who for some reason had changed his name to Meux, and Milne, an officer of considerable incompetence, as was proved early in the war during the chase across the Mediterranean after the German battleship *Goeben*, which he allowed to slip through with the cruiser *Breslau* to join the Turkish Navy at Constantinople.

Churchill did not have a good relationship with His Majesty at this time, and this was partly because of his relationship with Fisher and his refusal to accept his candidates for the Board of Admiralty. At a time when the Sovereign wielded considerable influence, even Churchill had begun to feel vulnerable, hence his appointment of some officers for promotion who were favoured by King George, but not, of course, by Fisher. He regarded Churchill as having 'betrayed the Navy in these three appointments ... *I can't believe that you foresee all the consequences!*' And to his old friend Lord Esher, he wrote: 'Winston has sacrificed the Country to the Court.' He even went on to suggest that a weathercock should be the Royal crest.

Churchill was so eager to have Fisher on his side and to regain his support and advice, that he did all he could to explain his actions. It was to no avail, at least not immediately. As further evidence that they did things differently in those far off days before the First World War, Asquith, senior members of his Cabinet, including Churchill, and senior naval officers such as Bridgeman and Battenberg, took the Admiralty yacht *Enchantress* cruising in the Mediterranean, investigating 'strategical [sic] problems, to visit the Fleet, and to inspect Naval Establishments.' Fisher was invited to travel to Naples, embark for a few days, and 'talk of things that can't be written about!' He agreed. The excuse was put out that the yacht had put into Naples because of bad weather, to Fisher's amusement: 'How every one is always so afraid of its being known that I have anything to do with them!'

Of course, afterwards, on his return to Lucerne, Fisher in his usual indiscreet way almost immediately wrote to a journalist friend, in this case Gerard Fiennes, about his 'cruise' aboard *Enchantress*. The letter was headed '*Burn*' and sub-headed '*Secret and Private*'.

I was nearly kidnapped and carried off in the Admiralty Yacht! They were very sweet about it! My old cabin as First Sea Lord all arranged for me! I had a good time and came out on top! The Prime Minister is 'dead on' for my coming back, and he has put things so forcibly to me that, with great reluctance to re-enter the battlefield, I shall probably do so! *But not a word of this*, except perhaps in *the very deepest confidence* to dear Gavin. I had great talks with the Prime Minister upon every sort of subject ('China to Peru'!). No doubt I am *'all there'* with him! (This sounds rather egotistical, I fear!) Don't breathe a word. I just sent you this line to say all went well and I am here at Lucerne. They pressed me for three days to go with them, but I had very good public reasons for not doing so. Winston came ashore with me at 2 am the last night to have last words with me! I thought what a story dear old Stead would have made out of that episode of the early morning hours! I grieve very much for him. He was a great wonder and very attractive![5]

The Naval Secretary to the First Lord at the time was the arch-playboy, the then Rear Admiral David Beatty, who wrote about the 'cruise' to his American heiress wife:

That old rascal Fisher arrived on board directly we got here looking very well and young, never stopped talking, and has been cosseted with Winston ever since, wasn't that something to come to Naples for? Do not mention to *anyone* that Fisher is in close confidence with Winston. It would be injurious to the Service, if it ever got out, and the Navy would hate it …[6]

Beatty, being Beatty, actually meant that it would be injurious to *his* future career! Here was another maverick, not quite as undisciplined or blunt as Fisher, far smoother and much more subtle, but he too was to play games later with a superior, letting Jellicoe take the blame for the failure of the Grand Fleet to destroy the German High Seas Fleet at Jutland in 1916.

This was no pleasure cruise, and even Fisher complained that he suffered four nights without sleep as Churchill tried to drain him of all information. 'When I wasn't talking I was writing,' complained Fisher to Fiennes.

With Fisher's own nominee Bridgeman in place as First Sea Lord, it would have been difficult, but not *that* difficult, to have Fisher back as First Sea Lord. Nevertheless, memories of how difficult a man he could be had not been completely eclipsed by the growing panic over

German intentions and her growing strength on the seas, and nor had they been dissipated by the earlier reluctance to maintain Britain's position as master of the seas. Indeed, over and above other objections to his return was the growing certainty that he had, for the most part, been right, and the radical politicians wrong.

RETURN TO LONDON

The cover for his return to London, where he would be on hand to offer advice whenever Churchill and the rest of Asquith's Cabinet could have it, was to head a commission on oil and the available resources of oil, especially in wartime, with particular reference to their importance 'to this country and the Royal Navy'. This was acknowledgement that the age of coal was nearing its end. Fisher needed no persuading that coal was the fuel of the past, and described himself as an 'oil maniac'. He also knew the importance of the fuel and the difficulty of guaranteeing sufficient quantities should war with Germany come to pass, which he had already calculated was a little over two years away. Yet, he also saw a poisoned chalice of responsibility without power, and himself back into the old battlefield of Westminster politics. Everything he did would be viewed with suspicion by his old enemies.

On 16 June, still at Lucerne, he went to the Anglican Church and heard the priest give a sermon. 'No man still in the possession of all his powers has any right to say, *"Now I'm going to rest, for I've had a hard life,"'* declared the priest. 'For he owes a duty to his country and his fellow-men.' After making such a challenging statement, and at the time having fixed his eyes 'steadfast' on Fisher, it was not perhaps too surprising that when Fisher met him later in the day, the chaplain was in Fisher's words, 'very meek and nervous'.

Fisher had things to do other than frighten nervous clerics. He sent a letter to Sir Francis Hopwood, the Additional Civil Lord of the Admiralty, that was eight pages long, and another of nine pages to Churchill, all long hand, and all on the same day. With due modesty, writing to his wife the following day, he admitted that they were right when they all said that 'no one else can do it'. Self doubt was never a Fisher weakness.

On 19 June, Fisher returned to London. Churchill was forgiven, at least for the foreseeable future. Photographs of the two men together at this time show the younger Churchill wrapt in admiration and hanging on to every word of his mentor. Fisher was to miss the warmth and the sun of Switzerland, not to mention the local peaches and strawberries, but he was also enthusiastic about chairing the Royal Commission on Fuel Oil and once again he was present at meetings of the Committee for Defence. The Commission worked fast, and was one of the few to have its findings noted and recommendations implemented as a matter of national urgency. The Government encouraged the building of oil refineries and the construction of tankers, while additional oilfields were acquired in the Middle East, mainly in Persia, by the Anglo-Persian Oil Company, the predecessor of British Petroleum, BP, in which the Government took a 51 per cent interest in return for which the company gained the rights to provide fuel for the Royal Navy. Even so, the Admiralty, concerned about the security of fuel supplies, still built a number of warships that were coal-burning, as did most commercial ship-owners, especially in the coasting trades.

The final report was signed on 10 February 1914, by which date Fisher's restless imagination and power of foresight had been exercising itself elsewhere.

ABOVE AND BELOW THE WAVES

One of the most important matters for consideration was aviation, for Fisher had foreseen that aerial warfare would be all important in the future. The Royal Navy needed its own aircraft. This was at a time when the Royal Flying Corps had absorbed all British service aviation, but this was no true autonomous air force as it was part of the Army, even though it had an Army Wing and a Navy Wing. Fisher wanted the naval element back under Admiralty control. He got his way, with the Royal Naval Air Service formed before the outbreak of the First World War, although formal handover from the Army did not follow until 1915. He pressed for merchant vessels to be armed, recognising what many people did not want to see, that once war broke out, peacetime promises would be broken. He also pressed for more submarines and larger ones, including semi-submersibles with telescopic masts that could circumnavigate the globe without refuelling, and for large diesel-engined battleships capable of 25 knots. The irony was that, in its quest for larger submarines capable of keeping up with the fleet, the Royal

Navy produced a class of steam-powered submarines, which proved to be disastrous and more of a threat to those serving in them than to any enemy. He also wanted a dozen large underwater pipelines beneath the English Channel to ensure security of oil supplies in wartime.

Progress following Churchill's arrival at the Admiralty had been rapid. While Bridgeman continued as First Sea Lord, he was a cipher, a front man there for appearances as the real decisions were taken and implemented by the First Lord with characteristic ruthlessness and at all times with completely single-minded tenacity. It may have been these qualities that won him renewed favour in Fisher's eyes. In addition to taking on Fisher's recommendations over commissioning officers from the ranks, and improving the conditions and pay of the ratings, he had also listened to his guide and mentor on other matters. One of the most significant with the coming war was the laying down of a new class of battleships more powerful than anything else being built, with eight 15-inch guns in four turrets mounted fore and aft on the centreline, and a speed of 24 knots, the Queen Elizabeth class.

On their return from Europe, the Fishers found a house at Ham Common, Langham House, just west of London but within easy reach of the capital, which was the main reason for not settling at Kilverstone. This was a relatively quiet time of life for Fisher, perhaps the calm before the storm, but many of the changes which he had pressed so hard for were in hand. He could find little to grumble about in the large fleet that was being assembled, the renewed interest in the submarine, or the development of the Royal Naval Air Service. He would, of course, have liked larger submarines with a greater endurance, but the Royal Navy was developing almost as he would have it, but if only he was at the Admiralty with Churchill!

Notes

1 Kilverstone, Admiral of the Fleet Baron, *Memories*, London, 1919
2 Ibid
3 Ibid
4 Ibid
5 Ibid
6 Chalmers, Rear Admiral W.S., *The Life and Letters of David, Earl Beatty*, Hodder & Stoughton, London, 1951

15

Return to Admiralty

Strong nowhere, weak everywhere! Never such rot as perpetrated by Sturdee in his world-wide dispersal of weak units.
Fisher.

The British public entered the First World War on a surge of optimism and enthusiasm. The belief that it would be 'all over by Christmas' was widespread. Central to this belief was the idea of an early clash between the two opposing fleets, a modern day Trafalgar, but instead of being fought off the south-west point of the Iberian peninsula, it would be fought somewhere off Denmark or Heligoland. Both sides, however, decided to harbour their fleets, figuratively and literally. Capital ships were too precious to risk, and neither felt that it could afford to lose any. The British wanted to retain their numerical superiority in home waters; the Germans did not want to see the gap widen.

On 4 August 1914, Germany had sixteen battleships and three battle-cruisers, while in home waters the Royal Navy had twenty battleships and five battlecruisers. These were the backbone of the fleet. In all, the Royal Navy had 68 capital ships, most of them pre-Dreadnoughts, scattered around the world, mainly in the Mediterranean, as well as 103 cruisers and 319 torpedo craft. Despite this, and despite the growing threat of war that should have stimulated naval shipbuilding even more, the service had a surplus of manpower once the reserves were mobilised. Thus it happened that the surplus was assembled into the Royal Naval Division, with battalions named after famous admirals,* and instead of fighting at sea, went to war ashore. They were later absorbed by the Army, but in the meantime the Admiralty even advertised for

* Battalions in the Royal Naval Division were named Drake, Benbow, Hawke, Collingwood, Hood, Anson, Nelson and Howe.

recruits, describing the personnel of the division as 'Handy men to fight afloat or on shore'. The surplus manpower in 1914 amounted to between 20,000 and 30,000, enough to form two naval brigades and one of Royal Marines. On 4 October, almost four weeks before Fisher returned to the Admiralty, Churchill threw one of the brigades into a hopeless last-ditch defence of the Belgian port of Antwerp.

The British hastened to destroy German links with the world outside Europe. Just five hours after the UK and Germany found themselves at war, a British cable ship, the *Teleconia*, dropped grappling irons into the mud of the sea bed off the German port of Emden, and one by one broke five German overseas telegraph cables, running to Brest in France, Vigo in Spain, to Tangier in North Africa, and two running to New York.

That same day, 5 August, also saw the first German ship sunk, when the steamer *Konigin Louise* was caught disguised as a Great Eastern Railway ferry dropping mines near the Thames estuary. She was promptly sunk by gunfire from the light cruiser *Amphion*, which then rescued 56 from her crew of 130. Half the prisoners were cast into a compartment in the bows of the cruiser, so that if she hit a mine, they would be the first to go, and shortly afterwards, when she did, they were. There was just one survivor. An idea of how intensive the mine laying must have been can be judged from the ship striking a second mine, which exploded as she settled in the water. In the end, in addition to 27 German prisoners, 132 members of *Amphion*'s ship's company were killed or seriously wounded.

Like the mine, Fisher's predictions about the significance of the submarine in any future conflict were also soon to be proved correct.

MAJOR MOVES

At the outbreak of war, two major moves had to be implemented, transporting British troops to France and moving the Grand Fleet★ to a secure anchorage. Of these, priority had to be given to moving

★ Grand Fleet replaced the Home Fleet on the outbreak of war. It included the First Fleet of fully manned warships; the Second Fleet of warships that were partially manned and expected to be 'topped up' by reservists; and the Third Fleet of ships that would be manned from personnel from shore establishments and reservists.

the British Expeditionary Force to France. Between 9 August and 22 August, 80,000 British infantrymen and 12,000 cavalrymen with their horses were transported to France, reaching ports between Le Havre and Dunkirk. The busiest days were 15–17 August. During this period a major German assault was expected, although no one knew whether it would be by U-boats, destroyers or the entire German High Seas Fleet, in which case the major sea battle so long expected might have materialised. British submarines maintained a watch off the German coast in the Heligoland Bight, supported by destroyers, but the Germans remained in port and the BEF reached France without being challenged and without losing a single soldier or horse.

At the same time, with the start of hostilities, Fisher's protégé Vice-Admiral John Jellicoe was promoted, slightly ahead of the planned date, to admiral and sent to take command of the Grand Fleet from Admiral Callaghan. The provisional wartime anchorage of Scapa Flow, just south of the mainland of Orkney, was judged in need of stronger defences; while Rosyth, on the north banks of the Firth of Forth, was considered inadequate, was in any case incomplete, and also too far from the open sea, and any British warships using the port could be penned in by submarines.

It was not until 28 August that the two navies made contact, with the Germans losing three cruisers and a destroyer in the Heligoland Bight. The action stemmed from a plan to attack German cruisers and destroyers that had been disrupting mine-laying in the Heligoland Bight. The Royal Navy was to use destroyers and three submarines, hoping to lure the German destroyers towards a further line of British submarines. Commodore Tyrwhitt had taken the light cruiser *Arethusa*, in which he flew his pennant, and the Harwich-based Third Flotilla of destroyers into the Heligoland Bight, followed by the light cruiser *Fearless* and the First Flotilla of destroyers. The operation was against Jellicoe's better judgement, who felt that such a risky venture into enemy waters should be supported by the entire Grand Fleet, but the Admiralty insisted it was none of his business, although they allowed him to send Beatty's battlecruisers to provide covering fire.

The Germans had guessed what was happening and engaged the Harwich flotillas in a running battle that lured the British ships into a trap comprising a strong force of cruisers. Tyrwhitt soon called for assistance, not realising that Beatty's battlecruisers were nearby, and sped into the Bight, and it was their 13.5-inch guns that accounted for the

German losses. The Germans lost 1,200 men killed, wounded or taken prisoner against just 75 British casualties; but Tyrwhitt's ship, *Arethusa*, was so badly battered that she had to be towed back to port.

Meanwhile, all was not going to plan elsewhere. So poor were anti-submarine detection methods at this stage of the war, that a seal accounted for the first big scare of the war at dusk on 1 September, when the lookouts on a light cruiser spotted a periscope in the fading light. The alarm was raised, with some ships shooting at the 'submarine' and others racing around to avoid torpedoes. This was the incident that persuaded Jellicoe to take the Grand Fleet to Lough Swilly on the north coast of Ireland, judged to be far from the risk of surprise German attack.

U-BOAT DEPREDATIONS BEGIN

Five days later, on 6 September, the armoured cruiser *Pathfinder* was sunk by *U-21*, with heavy loss of life. This was the first major warship to be lost by either side. Further grim reality was not long in coming. On 22 September 1914, three elderly British armoured cruisers, *Aboukir*, *Cressy* and *Hogue*, were on patrol when they were spotted by Otto Weddigen, commander of *U-9*. Weddigen fired his first torpedo at the middle ship of the three, *Aboukir*, at 06.20, at a distance of 550 yards, before taking his submarine down to fifty feet. Exactly 31 seconds later he and his crew heard an explosion and a crashing sound. The torpedo had penetrated the cruiser amidships on her starboard side, below the waterline, and water started to flood into the engine and boiler rooms and she began to list. No one had seen the submarine's periscope or the torpedo, so aboard the assumption was that she had struck a mine. Her commanding officer hoisted a mine warning and called for the other two ships to come alongside so that the wounded could be transferred.

Attempts were made to save the stricken ship by flooding compartments to correct the list, but it soon became clear that she was sinking. Only one lifeboat was available, the others being destroyed by the explosion or they could not be swung out as there was insufficient steam to power the derricks.

It was aboard *Hogue* that it was first realised that there was a submarine in the area, and her commanding officer signalled *Crecy* to look out for a periscope. At 06.55, as *Aboukir* rolled over and slid beneath the waves, leaving the sea dotted with the heads of the members of her ship's company, *Hogue* was struck by two torpedoes, about five seconds apart. Despite closing all watertight doors immediately, within five minutes the quarterdeck was awash, while there was an explosion from below, and the order was given to abandon ship. At 07.15, *Hogue* too rolled over and sank.

By this time, *U-9*'s batteries were running low, but Weddigen still had one torpedo left for his bow tubes, and two more in his stern tubes. Immediately after *Hogue* had been hit, *Crecy*'s commanding officer heard that a periscope had been spotted and ordered his engines to full speed intending to ram, but he saw nothing and decided to return to pick up survivors. *Crecy* was stopped in the water, picking up survivors from her two sister ships when, at 07.20, *U-9* fired both stern torpedoes, and those aboard heard one explosion. The cruiser was struck on the starboard side, quickly heeled over to starboard and then briefly righted herself. The other torpedo had passed under the ship without doing any damage. At 07.30, another torpedo struck the ship on her port side, rupturing the tanks in the boiler room and scalding the men on watch below. *Cressy* followed her sisters, rolling over, but then remained afloat upside down for twenty minutes before, at 07.55, she finally sank.

For the ship's company of *Cressy*, the awful truth was that all of her boats were away rescuing those from the other two ships when she went down. They had to make do with whatever came to hand. Dutch trawlers nearby were reluctant to approach having seen three large ships sunk in less than ninety minutes. It was not until 08.30 that the first trawler approached and eventually picked up 286 exhausted men from the water. Another small Dutch vessel rescued 147 men. British trawlers then began to help, followed later by Tyrwhitt's destroyers from Harwich. Just 837 men were disembarked at Harwich, shoeless and many had also lost their clothes and were wrapped in blankets, while 62 officers and 1,397 men had been lost. It was little comfort that a month earlier, the outspoken Commodore Roger Keyes, the commanding officer of the Harwich-based submarines, had called for the ships to be removed, and Churchill had only days earlier also called for their removal from an area that was clearly dangerous and where they served little strategic purpose.

Meanwhile, those ashore at the Admiralty were casting around for culprits. Fisher, in retirement, criticised the decision to send the ships on patrol so close to waters in which the Germans were likely to be present. It was clear that the southern North Sea was no place for large warships.

GRAND FLEET WEAKENED

Nor was the Atlantic any safer, for on 27 October, the Second Squadron, a powerful force comprising eight of the new 'super-Dreadnoughts', was taken to sea early from their base at Lough Swilly for gunnery practice. They were steaming line ahead off Tory Island when an explosion occurred on the port side of the new super-Dreadnought *Audacious*. She had struck a German mine. Attempts were immediately made to tow her to safety, providing much entertainment for American passengers aboard the White Star liner *Olympic*, on passage from Liverpool to New York; but that evening she suffered an internal explosion, blew up and sank. The Grand Fleet had already had some of its strength taken and deployed elsewhere, and was down to twenty Dreadnought and super-Dreadnought battleships, now it was just nineteen to sixteen German ships.

Promoted to the rank of full admiral on the eve of taking over command of the Grand Fleet, Jellicoe wasted little time. As early as October, 1914, he established his strategy for a major fleet engagement. His aim, set out in a letter to the Admiralty on 30 October, was to confront the Germans in the northern North Sea rather than the southern end because the latter would favour the Germans, who would be able to deploy minelayers and submarines. Even so, for fear of finding a chain of submarines waiting for his forces when in pursuit of a retreating German force, he might hesitate to follow in the desired direction. He wrote: 'The situation is a difficult one: it is quite possible that half our battle fleet might be disabled by underwater attack before the guns opened fire at all.'

This was realistic and should have appealed to Fisher, who had claimed for some years that the submarine could make the battleship obsolete. Jellicoe's plan was to move the battle fleet at high speed to a position on the enemy's flanks before engaging them. Jellicoe saw his duty as retaining control of the seas and he placed this as a far higher priority than engaging the enemy. The loss of significant fleet units was a factor in this as he needed to keep the Royal Navy's overwhelming dominance intact, but he also knew that being able to maintain the blockade of German ports was the key to winning the war on land as well as at sea.

Churchill had sacked two First Sea Lords in his short time as First Lord of the Admiralty. He had got rid of the dogged and unimaginative Wilson, and then the weak Bridgeman, both of whom had been complete disasters and both of whom had been Fisher nominees. Next, he appointed Admiral Prince Louis of Battenberg, whom Fisher was to describe as 'Churchill's dupe', although he had earlier recommended him for the Board. An excellent administrator, at a time of anti-German feeling he was in the wrong place, or at least the right place to be blamed for the Royal Navy's early failings. His other drawback, apart from poor health, was his Chief of the War Staff, COS, a new appointment, who was none other than Beresford's former Chief-of-Staff, Vice-Admiral Doveton Sturdee. Sturdee's limitations had long been known to senior officers, including Fisher, although the man himself seemed to believe that he was 'the only man who knew anything about war'. Nevertheless, by October anti-German feeling ran so high that the personal attacks on Battenberg reached such a pitch that he had to go because the attacks had become a distraction from the war. When Churchill broached the subject, the Prince promptly gave him his resignation.

Churchill was in no doubt as to who the next First Sea Lord should be. This was his last chance to make a decision that would be accepted as the misfortunes of the Royal Navy early in the war were being laid at his door. There was no consensus. King George V was furious, declaring to Churchill that Fisher 'was not trusted by the Navy' and also noting in his diary that it was 'a great mistake & he is 74'. He gave in reluctantly. The King's preferred list of First Sea Lords included several who had been close to Beresford, and included Sturdee. Perhaps the most perceptive opinion of the appointment was that of David Beatty, who wrote to his wife: 'I cannot see Winston and Jackie Fisher working very long together in harmony. They will quarrel before long.'[1]

The King was being unfair to Fisher, who by all accounts, including, needless to say, his own, was in excellent health at this time. Indeed, his time away from the Admiralty seems to have done him good. Churchill had also paid close attention to the condition of Fisher whenever they had met, including on one occasion when Fisher threw one of his infamous fits of extreme temper: 'He left me with the impression of a terrific engine of mental and physical power burning and throbbing in that aged frame.'

This was fine, and probably Fisher was in good health for peace-time, but his ability to work for fourteen hours a day had gone, and his performance faded during the evening so that he was often in bed before 9 p.m.

He had suffered a bout of pleurisy, and been advised by none other than the King's doctor, Sir Bertrand Dawson, to husband his resources. The sixteen hour days of which he had once boasted were definitely a thing of the past. The problem was that in wartime, no one was in complete control of their workload or the demands that might be placed upon them. This was especially true of the Admiralty, an operational headquarters which could send orders and intelligence to ships at sea, and in an age of wireless communication, might be expected to do so at any hour of the day or night. Could any First Sea Lord sleep peacefully knowing that his ships were closing with the enemy? Nevertheless, Churchill was desperate for a like mind.

Lord Beaverbrook wrote of Churchill at this critical stage of the war:

> A cold wind was blowing on him in October 1914, and he has since recognised the fact. He therefore pressed hard for Fisher's appoint-ment as a support to his own position – which was really another mistake.
>
> Churchill co-opted Fisher to relieve the pressure against himself, but he had no intention of letting anyone else rule the roost. Here, then, were two strong men of incompatible tempers both bent on an autocracy. It only required a difference of opinion on policy to produce a clash ...

The problem was that, after a run of unsuitable First Sea Lords, the choice was narrowing down. Sturdee was definitely unsuitable, but as necessity forced a rethink in some eight months, it was clear that other talent was available if those in charge looked hard enough. It has to be said that the King's intervention was unhelpful and did little other than muddy the waters.

AMPHIBIOUS DREAMS; FALKLANDS REVENGE

Fisher had never fought in a conventional naval battle, but then hardly anyone else serving in the Royal Navy at that time had. His strengths were technology and organisation, and when he arrived at the Admiralty, he naturally enough found that it was in a mess. His concept of technology had also outrun the technical standards of the day, with the diesel-powered battleships being just one of those items on his 'wish list' that were beyond the capabilities of the shipyards or the engine designers and builders. In terms of strategy, his idea of the Royal Navy shooting the Army into position and the latter causing mayhem and disruption behind enemy lines ignored the strategic realities of the war that was being fought. The British had no choice but to send increasingly large numbers of troops to France, unless they were prepared to accept French collapse. Fisher, on the other hand, looked at ways of shortening the war. He saw amphibious warfare with surprise attacks as shortening the war, but it was not until the Second World War had been waged for some time that practical landing craft appeared and no such suitable craft existed in the First World War, although Fisher pressed for such to be built, each carrying 500 men and diesel-powered. It was also true that many of the successful amphibious campaigns of the later conflict were supported by airborne assaults, as in Sicily, with heavy losses, and at Normandy. No such technology existed in Fisher's day. He was on the right lines when he wanted aircraft to be mass produced like Ford motor cars, but still slightly ahead of his time. A strategist of real genius would have appreciated some of these facts and returned to reality from their pipe dreams. Most of all, Fisher could not accept that his country had become embroiled in a continental war, draining its reserves of manpower, and had strongly opposed the despatch of the British Expeditionary Force to France. His solution was different and would have required fewer men, if only because of the difficulty of moving huge numbers at any one time. 'He was a strong advocate of keeping the Expeditionary Force ready till the psychological moment, and then throwing it ashore at some point where it would place the enemy at a disadvantage.'[2]

Fisher had always found fault with his new commands and had striven to cure them of it. The Admiralty on 30 October 1915 was no different. As far as he was concerned, the ships were in the wrong places and in the wrong numbers, manpower was not being used effectively, and he found making progress against the bureaucracy slow and frustrating: 'I have to lose my temper everyday to push things.'

He was also under other pressures. The outbreak of war in 1914 had caught many by surprise. British merchant ships were caught in German or Austro-Hungarian ports and seized, their crews interned for the duration. British subjects were also caught; amongst them his eldest daughter Beatrix and her husband, Captain Reginald Neeld, RN, who were at first to be kept by the Germans until the end of the war, but in December came the good news that they were to be returned. Fisher was overjoyed and described the homecoming as a 'resurrection'.

From the start, Fisher tolerated no opposition. Finding Sturdee as Chief-of-Staff, he demanded that he resign, and told Churchill that if Sturdee did not go, then he would. Even when Churchill appealed to Sturdee directly, the officer refused to go. The unfortunate First Lord was faced with losing his new First Sea Lord within days of his coming aboard. Events soon proved otherwise. Sturdee had been blamed for the poor disposition of the Royal Navy outside home waters, with too few ships scattered across the world. Despite the new tonnage built in the run-up to the war, there were also many older ships that would be vulnerable to a powerful modern German vessel. In any event, the German surface raiders were creating havoc amongst British merchant shipping.

On the night of 8/9 November, off Coronel in Chile, Vice-Admiral Maximilian von Spee took his force of cruisers and destroyed Rear Admiral Sir Christopher Cradock's armoured cruisers. Of more than 1,600 officers and men, there was not a single British survivor. Fisher immediately ordered two battlecruisers to the South Atlantic and a third to the North Atlantic in case the Germans tried to return home through the Panama Canal. Churchill had a moment of inspiration, and proposed that Sturdee command the battlecruiser squadron. Fisher immediately agreed, accepting Sturdee's quality as a commander at sea, and also because he blamed Sturdee for the fiasco.

This was a case of good fortune following ill. Sturdee's ships hastened to the Falkland Islands, arriving secretly, and the following morning, when by sheer chance von Spee's inferior forces appeared, raced off to catch them accompanied by their screening cruisers and sunk four out of five of the German ships. 'This was your show and your luck,' Churchill minuted Fisher. 'Your flair was quite true. Let us have some more victories together and confound all our foes abroad – and (don't forget) – at home.'

BEATTY PROVED RIGHT

Beatty had got it right, however, for these were two incompatible individuals, both of whom wanted to run the Admiralty. His only mistake was in believing that 'Fisher would rule the Admiralty and Churchill with a heavy hand.'[13] Fisher only brooked First Lords for as long as they were useful at fighting battles in the Cabinet and kept the hum drum of politics, that is the politics not initiated by his lobbying, away from him. Churchill would happily have done without the Sea Lords at all. He wanted to run everything, but so did Fisher. While both had a tremendous appetite for work, their working day was different. Fisher was the early bird sine qua non, while Churchill was a night owl. These differences were over and above the clash of one who was old and wise, and the other who was young, perhaps with a more varied experience, but inexperienced in naval matters, or even in running a major department amidst a crisis.

On 20 December Fisher to his 'beloved Jellicoe':

> I find much difficulty in snatching a few moments in which to write to you. Winston has monopolised all initiative in the Admiralty and fires off such a multitude of purely departmental memos (*His power of work is absolutely amazing!*) that my colleagues are no longer '*superintending Lords*', but only '*the First Lord's Registry!*' I told Winston this yesterday and he did not like it at all, but *it is true!* And the consequence is that the Sea Lords are atrophied and their departments run really by the Private Office,★ and I find it a Herculean task to get back to the right procedure, and quite possibly I may have to clear out, and I've warned Winston of this. But please do not mention this to a soul. I only wanted to explain to you that I have so little time to write.

Not the most reassuring letter to send even such a well-balanced and senior officer as Jellicoe, the most senior admiral at sea, especially

★ Private Office means the office of a government minister, in this case the First Lord.

when he is contemplating a major fleet engagement that could happen at any time.

THE BALTIC PROJECT

The turn of the year was a frustrating time for Fisher. His beloved Royal Navy had seen little action, and nothing on the scale for which he had worked so hard to prepare it. Meanwhile, the original BEF, the 'old contemptibles', had suffered a tremendous mauling in a form of mass warfare for which their commanders had no experience and the men little training. In 1915 it would be the turn of the reservists, and then of the conscripts after that. Fisher wished to avoid this at all costs, and now started to push a scheme that he had first considered when visiting the Tsar with King Edward in 1908. He had first revealed this concept in 1909. He wished the Royal Navy to enter the Baltic and land a substantial force of troops on the coast of Pomerania, just over eighty miles from Berlin (just a little more than the distance from Dover to London). He enlarged upon his theme by having a large Russian army also participate in the plan:

> The Baltic project meant victory by land and sea. It was simply history repeating itself. Frederick the great, for the only time in his life (on hearing that the Russians had landed), was frightened and sent for poison.
>
> Geography has not altered since his time. The Pomeranian coast has not shifted, and a million Russian soldiers could have been landed within eighty-two miles of Berlin.[4]

The idea was that such an invasion would pull a million German soldiers away from the front, although it was more likely that this would mean the Eastern rather than the Western Front. There were two major problems. The first was getting the Royal Navy in sufficient strength into the Baltic in wartime, and the second was the fighting cohesiveness of Russian troops, with the country descending into anarchy and revolution.

In plans such as these, Fisher and Churchill were soul mates. Both loved the idea of bold, decisive strokes, and both were wont to overlook the realities. Even before Fisher returned as First Sea Lord, Churchill was pressing for this project to be accepted, even raising it with the Russians. The First Lord's contribution to the plan was that an island such as Borkum should be seized first, to provide a secure base for operations on the mainland. Borkum, off the German North Sea coast west of Emden, was a strange choice as it was inconvenient for the Skaggerak and it was scarcely conceivable that the Germans would stand back and allow the Kiel Canal to be used. The 'Battle for Berlin', would have to start with the seizure of Schleswig-Holstein, after which the Germans could begin to guess the Allied plan in advance. Nevertheless, the Chancellor of the Exchequer, David Lloyd George, also supported the plan.

The plan would require no less than 612 vessels to be built, and quickly, but it says much for the credibility of the project that many of these were already started by the end of 1914, despite the other demands on the war economy, which was also soon to see skilled labour siphoned off by conscription. Fisher had his say in the design of the vessels, which included 'light battlecruisers', almost an oxymoron, with shallow draught and big guns, four 15-inch in two turrets for the first two, and two massive 18-inch guns for the third ship, HMS *Furious*. These ships were to be disastrous failures, only rescued by conversion to aircraft carriers.

The construction effort required was massive, but Fisher's great passion in life, probably more than any other, was shipbuilding. The country was at war after all, but then that also meant that there were other demands. Fisher was furious when he discovered that the army had been recruiting in the shipyards. He went to see Lord Kitchener, Minister for War, and demanded that he put a stop to recruiting shipyard workers, otherwise he would resign. Kitchener wrote the order immediately. At this time, Fisher was justified in threatening resignation, and it worked, but later he was to use this threat far too often. He knew that for someone in his position to resign in the middle of a major war would be at the very least an unacceptable embarrassment to the government.

For the first time in the country's history, as the war progressed Britain's shipbuilding industry could not keep up with the demands made by the Royal Navy. When additional minelayers were required, they were ordered from the United States.

Fisher began to interfere with every detail of the operation, including much that would be best handled by an experienced and imaginative senior army officer.

… prepared by own self with my own hands alone, to preserve secrecy, all the arrangements for landing three great armies at different places – two of them feints that could be turned into a reality. Also I made all the preparations, shortly before these expeditions were to start, to practise them embarking at Southampton and disembarking at Stokes Bay [on the Hampshire coast at Gosport, a few miles west of Portsmouth], so that those who were going to work with the Russian Armies would be practised in the art.[5]

Then Churchill joined in, writing to Fisher on 22 December 1914:

I am wholly with you about the Baltic. But you must close up this side first. You must take an island and block them in, *a la Wilson*; or you must break the Canal or the locks, or you must cripple their Fleet in a general action. No scattering of mines would be any substitute for these alternatives.

The Baltic is the only theatre in which naval action can appreciably shorten the war. Denmark must come in, and the Russians can be let loose on Berlin.

There are 4 good Russian Dreadnoughts.

A week later, Asquith noted in his diary that Churchill and an army officer, Colonel Maurice Hankey, were pressing for new theatres to be opened with the Allied armies. Churchill wanted to go to the Baltic, while Hankey favoured Turkey, where they could align themselves with the Balkan states and sweep the Turks out of Europe.

What is most interesting about the debate over where to launch an attack that would shorten the war and ease the pressure on Russia was that, in considering these wonderful schemes, Fisher and Churchill were neglecting one of the main duties of the Royal Navy in wartime, the protection of trade. The U-boat menace, which Fisher had so successfully predicted, had yet to evolve into a major threat to Britain's supply lines, but it had already started. In 1914, 866 tons of merchant shipping had been sunk in the Atlantic and the North Sea by German U-boats in October, rising to 2,084 tons the following month and then falling to 419 tons in December. In 1915, the tonnage would rise to 155,637 tons in August out of a total of 700,782 tons for the year. The worst month of the war was to be April 1917, when 447,913 tons were sunk out of a total for the year of 2,895,983 tons. These figures did not include losses to U-boats in the Mediterranean.

What was needed, and not introduced until late in the war after Jellicoe became First Sea Lord, was a convoy system. The concept of convoy dated from Roman times and it was not new to the Royal Navy, which had used convoys to protect shipping during war with France. The argument against using the convoys to protect shipping from submarines was that the convoys would attract submarines, but unless submarines were attracted to a target, they could rarely be found. Jellicoe cannot take the full credit for belatedly introducing the convoys, he did so under intense political pressure, including a visit to the Admiralty by David Lloyd George, by this time Prime Minister.

THE DARDANELLES

Whatever the merits of the Baltic plan, the War Council was quickly diverted by a plan to aid Russia by an offensive in the south, and thus was the decision to take the Dardanelles born. This plan had been considered earlier, but shelved.

On 3 January 1915, Fisher sent Churchill a plan prepared with the assistance of Hankey for a joint naval and army attack on Turkey. Old pre-Dreadnought battleships would be sacrificed to bombard the forts in the Dardanelles, while an expeditionary force would be landed south of the entrance to the straits. The whole plan demanded the involvement of allies, with the Greeks heading for Gallipoli, the British heading for Besika, the Bulgarians advancing on Constantinople, and finally, a combined force of Russians, Servians (Serbians) and Romanians attacking Austria. There was a major flaw in this scheme, as neither Greece nor Bulgaria were belligerent nations, although Greece did indicate a desire to help.

Unfortunately, most plans need to be considered and implemented in their entirety, or at least consist of elements that can work together. Churchill decided to persuade the Cabinet to bombard the Dardanelles forts, against Fisher's urging him that this should only be done if accompanied by landings. Fisher was right. Bombarding the forts simply alerted the Turks and their German allies to the danger of landings, and they strengthened the forts, re-equipped them and also moved troops to the area. Churchill ignored Fisher's advice and his arguments carried the day. For some reason, Fisher then supported the First Lord, and even went so far as to propose sending the first of the super-Dreadnoughts, with the 15-inch guns, to join the bombardment. What amounted to a flight from reason then occurred as the War Council proposed that the Royal Navy, *on its own*, should bombard Gallipoli, take the peninsula and then advance on Constantinople! No one explained how the Navy could take Gallipoli, when all the service could do would be to land some of its small force of Royal Marines.

It could be that Fisher had not thought about the idea in sufficient detail at first, but certainly he had changed his mind by 19 January, when he wrote to Jellicoe claiming that he did not agree with 'one single step taken' and indicated that his only course was to resign. Then on 28 January, Fisher objected, going over Churchill's head to Asquith, to sending the first super-Dreadnought, HMS *Queen Elizabeth*, to the Dardanelles. He had a point, as she was the only ship in commission with 15-inch guns. He offered his resignation. Asquith decided to arbitrate between the First Lord and the First Sea Lord, an unheard of intervention, and then told them that the operation would go ahead. When the War Council discussed the plan, Fisher sat and listened to men who knew nothing about military or naval matters talk enthusiastically about its success, then stood up to go, but was dissuaded by Lord Kitchener and returned to the table. Fisher's own experience in Egypt earlier in his career had taught him that simply bombarding forts from the sea usually ended in failure unless accompanied by landings. Warships were more vulnerable than forts ashore, especially the old pre-Dreadnoughts proposed. The Dardanelles, the straits that separated Gallipoli from the mainland of Asian Turkey, or Anatolia, were known to be difficult to navigate, with little room for a large ship to manoeuvre, having strong currents and treacherous shallows, and being extremely narrow in places. The proposed force would pass the forts like ducks in a shooting gallery.

Fisher was actually now making a series of three mistakes. His first was the plan for the attack on Turkey; the second was to change his mind; and then the third was to object to the plan to bombard the forts on the grounds that any attack would be better in the Baltic than in the Dardanelles, when he should have stressed, with his naval experience, the difficulty of successfully bombarding forts from the sea.

This line of talk in January 1915 gave the Dardanelles advocates a beautiful chance to spread the word that the old Admiral's formal objections were based on his preference for an attack elsewhere, and not in any inherent unsoundness in the naval plan.[6]

Whether the Dardanelles operation allied to the Gallipoli landings could ever have succeeded is a moot point. Had the two been combined as early as possible in the war, and been driven with enthusiasm and given the strong leadership at the front that the operation so badly lacked, it might have succeeded, even without Greek assistance. It is a matter of record that it did not and that it was a costly and bloody failure. The operation took too long to mount and should have accompanied the first bombardment of the forts, which simply alerted the defenders. There was colossal ignorance at the War Office and contempt for the Turks, who, it was believed would surrender if a British submarine surfaced in the Sea of Marmara and ran up the Union Flag. The officer sent to command the landings was unwell and untried. In the end, this simply became another example of trench warfare with opposing armies facing each other in appalling conditions. When the Greeks offered to enter the war and attack into Thrace, they were ignored.

The disillusionment that soon set in over the Gallipoli landings blinded the War Council and the Cabinet to possibilities elsewhere, and the Baltic operation died in the process.

It is impossible to say, now, whether the scheme could have survived the detailed and critical examination essential before such an operation could be justifiably undertaken; but it is unjust to dismiss the project offhand as impracticable, and with a shrug of the shoulders to say that it was madness on Lord Fisher's part to propose it. Scientific and thorough preparation would certainly have caused many of the objections which have been hastily advanced to fall into insignificance. The German Battle Fleet would have been placed in a difficult situation, for they would have been forced by public opinion to take some action, and this would have had to be carried out in the Baltic, in the face of a large fleet of submarines and of extensive and unknown minefields.[7]

On the other hand, would not the capture of Schleswig-Holtsein and the Kiel Canal have been enough? The Germans would have lost a major naval base and their best route between the Baltic and the North

Sea, while a third front would have been opened, no doubt to be called the Northern Front, drawing troops and war materiel away from elsewhere. If completely successful, then perhaps the landings in Pomerania could have followed, but only if the Russians could spare the manpower and this would have been unlikely. The landing craft would also have had to face the German High Seas Fleet in the confined waters of the Baltic.

SUBMARINERS' ACHIEVEMENTS

The one achievement that is so often forgotten in the history of the First World War was that of the Royal Navy's submariners who managed the difficult feat of getting their small and still primitive craft into both the Baltic and the Sea of Marmara, and wreaked havoc on the enemy's shipping and, especially in Turkish waters, on land communications as well. The speed of the German advance into Russia and then the Bolshevik Revolution cut short the Baltic operations, while the evacuation of British forces from Gallipoli reduced the appeal of operations in the sea of Marmara, as these then became too far from a convenient base, such as that on the island of Mudros.

Of course, the strength of the submarine arm and the fact that it was led by officers with spirit, such as Commodore Roger Keyes, and had so many young and able commanders, including people like Max Horton, later Commander-in-Chief Western Approaches during the critical days of the Second World War – a fine case of 'poacher turned gamekeeper' – protecting the Atlantic convoys, was to the credit of one man, Fisher. The Dardanelles also had many of the Royal Naval Air Service's finest airmen, including the piratical Lt Col., later Air Commodore Charles Rumney Samson. Again who can take the credit for the Royal Navy's involvement with aviation? Fisher, of course; and it should be remembered that the Navy was in many respects more forward-thinking in this than the Army, notably in the development of the heavy bomber.

Men who are bold enough to achieve big successes can also be bold enough and even foolhardy enough to suffer significant failures. This was Fisher's involvement in a nutshell.

Perhaps when one looks at this period of his career, his biggest mistake was that he kept his detailed plans for the Baltic operation to himself, and these were never divulged. This was in line with his attitude to war planning, that the First Sea Lord must have a plan, but divulge it to no one until the time came. Had he set up even a small staff – and he better than anyone could have chosen the right kind of officers to run it, with, ideally, a number of equally talented army officers on it as well – to plan the detail and work out what would be required and the best means of forcing the operation through to success, the operation could have gained sufficient momentum to have become the preferred course of action. Many senior German army and navy officers viewed the Baltic as their weakest border.

'If the British fleet had attacked in the first week of war, we should have been beaten,' Admiral Reinhard Sheer, Commander-in-Chief of the High Seas Fleet, told Cyril Brown of the *New York World* on 30 June 1919. 'Under cover of the British navy, the Russian armies, then available in great numbers, could have been landed on the coast of Pomerania and could have easily marched to Berlin.'

The sequence of events in the Dardanelles, from the ineffectual first bombardment on 19 February 1915 and the landings at Gallipoli in March, placed a massive strain on Fisher. He foresaw disaster, and he was right, but was by now powerless to stop it. By 18 March, six major warships were out of action, including the modern battlecruiser *Inflexible*, halfway towards Fisher's prediction that the campaign would cost a dozen battleships. This would have been wearing for a fit and active younger man, but for Fisher, it was too much.

This bleak period also marked a further deterioration in the relationship between the First Sea Lord and his political master. Between January and May, Fisher threatened to resign nine times. Not only was the Royal Navy unable to destroy the Turkish forts, it lost the pre-Dreadnought battleship HMS *Triumph* when it was torpedoed on 12 May, with the loss of 570 men. As German submarines were known to be heading for the area, and possibly Austrian submarines as well, Fisher insisted that the most modern battleship in the area be called home where she was desperately needed by the Home Fleet. Nevertheless, while this was the right decision in the circumstances, he had to agree to send two old battleships as well as two 14-inch monitors, a new class of shallow-draft ship intended for heavy coastal bombardment and built for the Baltic landings. When Kitchener complained that the withdrawal of a large battleship would affect army morale, Fisher had to threaten to resign before he was able to issue the order. The army

was by this time stuck in the very trench warfare that the operation had
been designed to avoid. The operation was going nowhere.

On Friday 14 May, *The Times* carried a story exposing the lack of
shells for the heavy guns on the Western Front. The situation was in
fact even worse than stated, as many of the shells were duds, almost
certainly the result of skilled manpower being conscripted out of the
armaments factories. That same day, the War Council demanded additional warships for the Dardanelles, and Fisher finally saw that his Baltic
dream had no future, and that the War Council, the Cabinet, and indeed
everyone else, saw the Dardanelles as being the only operation that
mattered. Worst of all, every additional warship sent undermined the
strength that Fisher and Jellicoe had created in the Home Fleet. There
was a growing danger that when the German High Seas Fleet did venture out, the Grand Fleet would not be strong enough to counter it.

FISHER WITHDRAWS

Fisher was by this time deeply depressed. He left the War Council meeting and returned to the Admiralty, telling his Naval Assistant, Captain T.E.
Crease, that he would not stay long. Before he left, Churchill popped
in to his office and assured Fisher that the naval reinforcements for the
Dardanelles would be no more than those agreed at the morning meeting. Churchill then settled down to his night's work, staying until 1 a.m.
on the Saturday morning. His work included writing four minutes to
Fisher, but none of these confirmed the reinforcements agreed at the War
Council meeting. What was to be sent included nine monitors, as soon as
they were ready, a fifth 15-inch howitzer with fifty rounds of ammunition,
which was to go across France by special train, as well as two 9.2-inch
guns, either independently or aboard the monitors. Four Edgar-class
cruisers, dating from the early 1890s and retired in 1914 as structurally
and operationally unfit, fitted with bulges as protection against mines and
torpedoes, were also to be sent. Additional E-class submarines were to be
sent immediately. The hope was expressed that the arrival of the monitors
might permit more battleships to be released, but this depended on the
view of the naval commander on how the monitors worked. As most of
them only had 9.2-inch guns, this was a vain hope.

At some time between 4 and 5 a.m., Fisher returned to his office to
find the offending documents waiting for him. Fisher did not wait for

Churchill to return to his office, which would in any case have been much later, around 10 or 11 a.m. On waking at his home, he found that Fisher's note of resignation had been delivered by messenger. His initial reaction was that the old admiral was crying wolf once more. The most relevant part read:

> I find it increasingly difficult to adjust myself to the increasing daily requirements of the Dardanelles to meet your views – as you said yesterday I am in the position of continually veto-ing your proposals.
>
> This is not fair to you besides being extremely distasteful to me.
>
> I am off to Scotland at once so as to avoid all questionings.

Churchill fully expected to find the First Sea Lord waiting for him when he eventually arrived at his office, but there was no trace of him. His staff told him that they did not known where he was, but that 'he was going to Scotland at once'.

Fisher had gone, but via the Treasury, where he confronted David Lloyd-George, who recalled:

> … a combative grimness had taken the place of his usually genial greeting; the lower lip of his set mouth a thrust forward, and the droop at the corner was more marked than usual.
>
> His curiously Oriental features were more than ever those of a graven image in an Eastern temple.[8]

Lloyd George immediately contacted the Prime Minister, Asquith, who simply shrugged it off with: 'Fisher is always resigning.' Lloyd George did not agree.

Far from going to Scotland immediately, Fisher had gone to the Charing Cross Hotel, one of the closest to the Admiralty, possibly after going to pray at Westminster Abbey. He was soon traced, and a messenger sent by Asquith ordering him to remain at his post in the name of the King. Fisher called on Asquith at No 10 Downing Street that afternoon, where the Prime Minister pleaded with him to remain, but Fisher emphasised that this time his resignation was final, but did agree to postpone his trip to Scotland.

In the meantime, Churchill also sent him an urgent plea, writing:

The only thing to think of now is what is best for the country and for the brave men who are fighting. Anything that does injury to those interests will be very harshly judged by history, on whose stage we now are.

I do not understand what is the specific cause which has led you to resign. If I did, I might cure it. When we parted last night, I thought we were in agreement. The proposals I made to you by minute were, I thought, in general accord with your views, and in any case were for discussion between us. Our personal friendship is and I trust will remain unimpaired.

It is true the moment is anxious and our difficulties grave. But I am sure that with loyalty and courage we shall come through safely and successfully. You could not let it be said that you had thrown me over because things were for the time being going badly at the Dardanelles.

In every way I have tried to work in the closest sympathy with you. The men you wanted in the places you wanted them, the ships you designed, every proposal you have formally made for naval action, I have agreed to. My own responsibilities are great, and also I am the one who gets the blame for anything that goes wrong. But I have scrupulously adhered to our original agreement that we should do nothing important without consulting each other. If this is not so, surely you should tell me in what respect.

In order to bring you back to the Admiralty I took my political life in my hands with the King and the Prime Minister, as you know well. You then promised to stand by me and see me through. If you go now at this bad moment and thereby let loose upon me the spite and malice of those who are your enemies even more than they are mine, it will be a melancholy ending to our six months of successful war and administration. The discussions that will arise will strike a cruel blow at the fortunes of the Army now struggling on the Gallipoli Peninsula, and cannot fail to invest with an air of disaster a mighty enterprise, which, with patience, can and will certainly be carried to success.

Many of the anxieties of the winter are past – the harbours are protected, the great flow of new construction is arriving. We are far stronger at home than we have ever been, and the great reinforcement is now at hand.

I hope that you will come to see me to-morrow [sic] afternoon. I have a proposition to make to you, with the assent of the Prime

Minister, which may resolve some of the anxieties and difficulties which you feel about the measures necessary to support the Army at the Dardanelles.

Although I shall stand to my post until relieved, it will be a very great grief to me to part from you; and our rupture will be profoundly injurious to every public interest.[9]

Fisher sent his reply, undated, the following day:

The Prime Minister put the case in a nutshell when he stated to me yesterday afternoon the actual fact that I had been dead set against the Dardanelles operation from the beginning! How could it be otherwise when previously as First Sea Lord I had been responsible for the Defence Committee Memorandum stating the forcing of the Dardanelles to be impossible! You *must* remember my extreme reluctance in the Prime Minister's room in January to accept his decision in regard to the Dardanelles, and at the War Council held immediately afterwards I stated, in reply to a question from the Chancellor of the Exchequer, that the Prime Minister knew my views and I left the matter to him to explain.

Ever since (as, I fear, to your great annoyance!) I have been, as you truly said the other day, in the unpleasant position of being antagonistic to your proposals, until the series of fresh naval engagements for the Dardanelles you sent me yesterday morning convinced me that the time had come for me to take a final decision, there being much more in those proposals than had occurred to me the previous evening when you suggested some of them.

YOU ARE BENT ON FORCING THE DARDANELLES AND NOTHING WILL TURN YOU FROM IT – *NOTHING*. I know you so well! I could give no better proof of my desire to stand by you than my having remained by you in this Dardanelles business up to this last moment against the strongest conviction of my life, as stated in the Dardanelles Defence Committee Memorandum.

You will remain. I SHALL GO. It is better so. Your splendid stand on my behalf with the King and the Prime Minister I can NEVER forget, when you took your political life in your hands and I really have worked very hard for you in return – *my utmost* – but here is a question beyond all personal obligations. I assure you it is only painful having further conversations. I have told the Prime Minister

I will not remain. I have absolutely decided to stick to that decision. NOTHING WILL TURN ME FROM IT. You say with much
feeling that '*it will be a very great grief to you to part from me*'. I am certain you know in your heart no one has ever been more faithful to
you than I have since I joined you last October. *I have worked my very
hardest!*[10]

Most men would have taken this as a clear and final indication that the
game was up, but Churchill was not most men, and he was desperate.
In fact, looking at the correspondence, one has to doubt Churchill's
judgement. He had indeed gambled much to bring Fisher back, he had
coped with all the difficulties of working with the outspoken First Sea
Lord, including disagreements in the face of his political colleagues,
and now he knew that if Fisher went, they would abandon him. He
sent one last plea that Sunday:

I am touched by the kindness of your letter. Our friendship has been
a long one. I remember how in 1908 you tried to bring me to the
Admiralty as First Lord. When I eventually came in 1911, I proposed
to the Prime Minister that you should return to your old position,
and only the difficulties which your enemies were likely to make at
that time prevented the accomplishment of my first wish. As it was I
followed your guidance in the important decisions which have given
us the 15-in gun and Jellicoe today.

Six months ago in the crisis of this great war you came to my aid;
since then we have worked together in the very closest intimacy. One
difficulty after another has been surmounted; vast new schemes of
new construction have been carried through; and tremendous reinforcements are now approaching the Fleet. Over the whole range of
war-policy and Naval administration there is nothing that I know
of on which we are disagreed – except the series of events which
have led us into the 'Dardanelles'. Even then we are agreed upon the
immediate steps, for I shall not press my wish about reinforcements
beyond the point to which you were willing to go – namely the 6
earliest monitors. We are now fully agreed that the Fleet is not to
attempt to rush the Narrows but is to support the Army in its gradual
advance on the forts by land. Orders in this sense have been given
with which you were in complete accord ...

The announcement of your resignation at this juncture will be accepted everywhere as proof that the military operations as well as the naval at the Dardanelles have failed ... The admission of failure at the Dardanelles, for so your resignation would be exploited all over the world, might prove the deciding factor in the case of Italy, now trembling on the brink. The knowledge of these facts forces me, not for my own sake (for the fortunes of individuals do not matter now), to appeal to you not to make your resignation operative until at least Italy has declared herself, for which the latest date is the 26th. Meanwhile, Sir Arthur Wilson could, if you desire it, do your work.

There ought to be no reproaches between us, and you, my friend, must at this moment in your long career so act that no one can say you were unmindful of the public interests and of the lives of the soldiers and sailors.

In any case, whatever you decide, I claim, in the name of friendship and in the name of duty, a personal interview – if only for the purpose of settling what explanation is to be offered to Parliament.[11]

But Churchill was refused even an interview:

As usual, your letter is most persuasive, but I really have considered everything and I have definitely told the Prime Minister that I leave tomorrow (Monday).

Please don't wish to see me. I could say nothing, as I have determined not to. *I know am doing right.*[12]

What Fisher did do on the Monday, was write to his old friend Andrew Bonar Law, Leader of the Opposition, with the stricture that the letter must not be shown 'now or ever to any living soul.'

In reply to your letter, after repeated refusals by him I have written to the P.M. this morning to say that now my *definite decision* is I am absolutely unable to remain with W.C. (HE'S A REAL DANGER!) *But he is going to be kept* (so I ho! *at once*, TODAY), only they are 'forking' me till Parliament rises for 3 weeks or more. I regret to say your *A.J.B.* has been backing W.C. all through and I have refused to have anything to do with him (A.J.B.) in consequence! *Keep this private.* I must not see you, BUT PARLIAMENT SHOULD NOT

RISE UNTIL THE FACT OF MY GOING IS EXTRACTED.
Lots of people must know – for instance see enclosed from Lord
Esher. You might see him at 2 Tilney Street, Park Lane, and let his
informant be your source of information. *I could not see you – I have
seen no one. I have written to no one.*[13]

Throughout this time, the pressure on Fisher to remain continued,
although given the contents of the letters, how anyone could believe
that Fisher and Churchill could work together, or that Fisher could
even work with Asquith, beggars belief. Relationships and trust had
completely evaporated. In fact, the government needed him as a
face-saving exercise because this war on an unprecedented scale had
overwhelmed them. They had lost their senses of proportion and judgement, and their moral compass was defective. Keeping a show of unity
was more important than overseeing a war. Fisher was even offered the
elevation of First Sea Lord to a Cabinet post. A friend advised him that
his departure would bring down the government, but Fisher doubted
this. A note of sanity and hope, as always, came from Lord Esher, who
wrote to '*My dear, dear Jackie,*' that:

> You will never *permanently* paper up these quarrels. The only thing
> to be done is to revive the office of Lord High Admiral and take it
> yourself. Otherwise we are beaten presently at sea; and useless Lord K
> takes the war in his own hands.

Proposing that Fisher could be Lord High Admiral was the one
thing that would have kept him at the Admiralty. The entire Board of
Admiralty existed to conduct the functions of the Lord High Admiral,
the 'one man chief' of the Royal Navy. Everyone would be subservient to him, and there would be no need to seek a consensus, still less
have a First Lord. He began to prepare a list of demands for his return.
He refused to serve under Churchill or Balfour and his old friend,
Arthur Wilson would have to leave. The last condition was perfectly
understandable, for the elderly admiral lacked Fisher's powers and had
been working unpaid at the Admiralty, but his judgement was doubtful. He had in any case been a failure in his two Board posts, first as
Controller, or Third Sea Lord, and then as First Sea Lord. Fisher also
sought to have men who would do his will rather than offer advice
and opinions, or, still less, have ideas of their own.

Fisher sent a memorandum to Asquith, who was outraged. He remarked to King George that Fisher 'indicated signs of mental aberration'. Lord Selborne and other friends took a similar view when they heard about the document. How Asquith must have regretted trying to dissuade Fisher from leaving, and how he and the King must have regretted allowing Churchill to have brought him back in the first place. If Fisher's abrupt departure had not been Churchill's undoing, his demands certainly were.

His friends rallied to him, with Queen Alexandra urging him to 'Stick to your post like Nelson!' McKenna wrote that he was dismayed, while far away from the maelstrom that was the War Council, Jellicoe wrote that he would rather lose some of his ships than see Fisher leave the Admiralty, and assured him that the Fleet was 'numbed with the thought of the possibility'. Even King George V, not a friend or supporter of Fisher, wanted him to stay.

Queen Alexandra had in fact hit the nail on the head. Fisher's behaviour was unacceptable. Given his age, it would have been understandable if he had asked to be relieved of his duties and given his political masters time to find a successor and an orderly handover of responsibilities. As it was, he had deserted his post, and was guilty of dereliction of duty. He was fast losing the regard of his supporters and earning the contempt of his enemies who had never doubted his ability to remain at his post, no matter what they felt about his reforms or the manner of their introduction. Given this it was not surprising that the newspapers had the story on 18 May.

Before the story hit the newspapers, on 17 May Asquith did the only thing he could do to divert the political storm that the Conservative opposition was to unleash upon him. He sought a coalition. Fisher had not brought the government down, but he had come as close as possible to it.

Meanwhile, the war continued. In complete ignorance of the chaos and uproar at the Admiralty, and indeed within the heart of government in London, the Germans ordered the High Seas Fleet to sea on 17 May. The Admiralty intercepted the signals and decoded them, passing the news to Jellicoe and Beatty, and to Fisher, who had returned to his private accommodation at the Admiralty. He refused to go to the Admiralty War Room where, if a battle seemed imminent, he could be in contact with Jellicoe and Beatty. This was the last straw as far as the other Sea Lords were concerned. It was not just the Sea Lords. The King was livid over his behaviour, and radical Liberal or not, Asquith, the Prime Minister, wanted him shot for desertion.

It was not until 22 May, a full week after his original declaration of going to Scotland 'at once', that Fisher finally left Euston Station and headed north. That was the day that the Admiralty finally telegraphed its acceptance of his resignation, which he had passed to him when the train stopped at Crewe.

He was finally free of the Admiralty, and the Royal Navy, the service that he professed to love, was free of him!

Notes

1 Chalmers, Rear Admiral W.S., *The Life and Letters of David, Earl Beatty*, Hodder & Stoughton, London, 1951
2 Ibid
3 Bacon, Admiral Sir R.H., *The Life of Lord Fisher of Kilverstone*, London, 1929
4 Ibid
5 Kilverstone, Admiral of the Fleet Baron, *Memories*, London, 1919
6 Marder, Arthur J., *The Anatomy of Sea Power: British Naval Policy 1880–1905*, London, 1941
7 Bacon, Admiral Sir R.H., *The Life of Lord Fisher of Kilverstone*, London, 1929
8 *War Memoirs of David Lloyd George*, London, 1933–1936 (6 vols)
9 Kilverstone, Admiral of the Fleet Baron, *Memories*, London, 1919
10 Ibid
11 Ibid
12 Ibid
13 Ibid

16

A Stormy Petrel!

'Nothing will ever induce me to go to London again till the war is over!'
Fisher to his wife, 1915.

'Scotland' actually meant Strathaven (pronounced Straven), a small town in Lanarkshire. Close by was Dungavel, home of the Duke and Duchess of Hamilton. For Fisher this meant he was out of reach of journalists and photographers, but this was due more to his being accommodated on a private estate than on any distance from civilisation, being within twenty miles of Glasgow.

Fisher and the Hamiltons were old friends and he had visited in the past. The Duke had been a midshipman in 1879 aboard the cruiser *Northampton* in which Fisher had been flag captain on the North America and West Indies Station. Despite the difference in rank, Alfred Douglas Douglas-Hamilton had been admired by Fisher and he had been upset when this athletic young man, renowned for his courage and quick thinking, had suffered a tropical disease that left him partially paralysed and a semi-invalid. Douglas-Hamilton married Nina Poore and in 1895, he succeeded to the title of the Duke of Hamilton, the premier Scottish peer, and inherited vast estates (and debts).

It was two years after the Hamiltons married that Fisher came to know the Duchess. She was the sort of woman that Fisher always admired, being beautiful, intelligent, energetic, and well-informed as well as an excellent conversationalist. Rare at the time, she was an ardent anti-vivisectionist and campaigner for animal welfare, while she was also a social reformer with strong religious convictions. The Duke and Duchess had four sons and three daughters. By 1908, Fisher was sufficiently close to the Duchess to ask her to send a *'large* photo' of herself in return for his sending a portrait of Nelson, which he entreated her to keep private. Even amidst the problems of late 1914, he was able to invite her to drop in for lunch at the First Sea Lord's House at the Admiralty, 'any day *without notice*'. Many believe that she was Fisher's mistress, but his correspondence with her proves nothing, as he was as effusive in his endearments to those whom he liked and admired as he was scathing and contemptuous of those whom he found lacking, or who simply did not view the world and the Royal Navy in the way that he did. It was also the case that photographs were exchanged between friends more often than happens today, partly because it is far easier and cheaper to visit now than it once was. When she visited London, they not only had lunch, but they also visited Westminster Abbey and prayed together, and throughout, their relationship contained a strong spiritual dimension.

CAST OFF

The kindness of the Duke and Duchess in 'taking in' Fisher should not be under-estimated. The war had gone badly on the ground and at sea, and here was the man in overall charge of the Royal Navy leaving his post. He had thrown away the respect and regard of his professional colleagues and of the politicians and journalists who had supported him, sometimes through difficult periods and contentious decisions, over many years. He was adrift, all but friendless.

The question does arise as to why he did not spend this time at home with his wife. Kitty Fisher was sympathetic and loyal, and unstintingly supportive, having vowed when they were wed that she would 'never rest till I see Jack First Naval Lord of the Admiralty. Never will I stand in his way, even if it means separation for years.' Nevertheless, she never listened as attentively as Lady Hamilton or others such as Pamela McKenna, and could not respond with humour and flattery, both of which he needed desperately. A family photograph shows her gazing downwards, and away from the camera, lost in thought. Fisher's outward show of confidence and aggression was as thin as an eggshell, and his ego needed regular polishing. She was first and foremost a nest builder and homemaker, never happier than when she had the children around her. It could also be that she was a 'navy wife', accustomed to making decisions on her own, standing on her own two feet and coping with whatever crisis might be thrown at her. His letters to her were always loving, but somehow lacked the enthusiasm of those to some of his other correspondents, (but not necessarily co-respondents!). After all, some of his letters to other men would make most men today cringe with embarrassment.

It is almost certain at this time that Fisher had had, if only briefly, his fill of politics and bureaucracy. Shortly after he arrived in Scotland, he wrote: 'I shall probably stay on here as the Duke and Duchess are both very dear friends, and it is like home being here with them.' He also wrote to his wife within a day or two of arriving at Dungavel: '*Nothing will ever induce me to go to London again till the war is over!*', and this in red ink. Being away from London slowly brought him back down to earth and reality began to dawn, at least as far as his domestic arrangements were concerned. He owned to feeling ashamed at having left his wife to sort out the domestic arrangements alone, in a letter to her. This was probably no more than she had become used to over the years, moving between London and Portsmouth, or the West Indies, or Canada, or Malta; the life of a naval wife. Indeed, at the time, many naval officers' wives would have welcomed the opportunity, if the alternative was spending many years parted from their husbands.

It would not have helped that, with his customary lack of tact, Fisher wrote to Kitty that he was 'in extreme luxury, *with a suite of apartments fit for a King!*' Perhaps it was not surprising that she chose to move to Kilverstone. The Duke and Duchess made it clear that she was perfectly welcome to join them, but it was equally clear that Kitty was hurt by his sudden departure to the Hamiltons. There is some evidence that she made several appeals to him to join her at Kilverstone, and indeed Fisher did visit Kilverstone on at least one occasion, but with the Hamiltons as company. According to Countess Jellicoe, who was present at the time, the atmosphere during the visit was tense and unhappy. Not surprisingly, this created a rift in the family, with the three daughters feeling that their mother, in her declining years, had been abandoned.

To be charitable, there were other reasons why Fisher found his time at Dungavel so appealing. He was well looked after and enjoyed country pursuits, most especially the excellent trout fishing. Nevertheless, all was not well with the Duke's affairs. Mismanagement and some of the provisions of the previous Duke's will meant that the estates were not in robust financial health, and the family's generosity to Fisher at this time was all the more laudable as a result. The Duke was himself not well enough to take on the demanding task of managing the estates, and Fisher threw himself into the task with his usual unbounded enthusiasm. Later, he was to get a private bill into Parliament and establish a trust for the Duke's children.

In fact, his spell of relaxing in glorious isolation was short. He was back in London on 5 July, much restored in health and outlook, and hooked by letters from Asquith and Balfour, both of whom dangled the bait of the chairmanship of a Board of Invention and Research. He took the opportunity to grant the editor of *The Times* an interview, which lasted two hours. Afterwards, he maintained that the editor told him that the whole country wanted him back. But, he then went on to say: 'But so long as "Wait and See" and the "*Philosophic Doubter*" are where they are, I am out of it!' These were his nicknames for Asquith and Balfour, yet these were the very men whose appeal he was answering by visiting London.

The new position was one that he anticipated holding great responsibilities, and an early decision was to rename the Board's headquarters *Victory House*. This was somewhat premature. He headed a committee consisting of himself and three eminent scientists, including Charles Parsons, the inventor of the steam turbine, the chemist George Beilby, and J.J. Thomson, President of the Royal Society.

For Fisher, it was a sad disappointment to find that any findings or recommendations were simply advisory, and as so often happens with advice from a committee, it was more often than not ignored. This, hardly surpisingly, made him angry once again. By November, many were calling for his return to the Admiralty, but after Churchill criticised Fisher for his part in the Dardanelles fiasco, he made his first speech in the House of Lords:

I have been sixty-one years in the service of my country and I leave my record in the hands of my countrymen … It is unfitting to make personal explanations affecting national interests when my country is in the midst of a great war.

This was a brief and dignified statement that was widely and favourably reported in the press. If only he had adopted a similar tone whilst at the Admiralty. Nevertheless, while pressure for his return continued, Asquith and Lloyd George refused to countenance it, and not surprisingly. It was not so much the disagreement as the manner in which Fisher had conducted it.

DOING NOTHING AT ALL

His family began to believe that the Duchess was beginning to convince Fisher that he might once again return to the Admiralty. This was unwelcome as they wished him to enjoy a quiet retirement, and no doubt did not wish to be exposed to the whole sorry business yet again if he did not get his way. It does seem to be the case that the Duchess of Hamilton believed that Fisher could win the war, and began to lobby on his behalf, writing to Lord Rosebery and others, and then also seeking the support of several newspaper editors, most of whom ignored her. She did get some support from C.P. Scott, editor of the *Manchester Guardian*.

It remained a surprise to many who knew the details of what had happened that there was still a sizeable pro-Fisher lobby. Many of those who had not been privy to the full state of events in May 1915 thought that only his return to the Admiralty could remedy the problems of the war. These were the same people who had soon forgotten his feud with Beresford. They also remembered that the victories at Dogger Bank and the Falklands occurred while he was First Sea Lord, and even his opposition to the Dardanelles was seen as being right. What was surprising was that Reginald McKenna soon joined this group. Indeed, by late summer 1915, just a little more than three months after leaving the Admiralty in such an unprofessional manner, he was writing to members of the Cabinet giving advice and offering his services. On 28 October, he wrote briefly to Asquith:

> At this juncture and amidst such great anxieties, I am trusting to be made some use of, as probably few (or I might say no one) can know as much of Navy work, and I am doing nothing at all.[1]

Clearly, he was not doing much, if any, work at the Board of Invention and Research by this time. This left him free to return to his old ways, that of an untiring and unsympathetic critic of the Admiralty, and indeed of the entire running of the war. No one could get it right except Fisher. Each successive failure justified his outlook. Not even members of the Fishpond were spared criticism. Jellicoe was accused of being timid at Jutland. Fisher was not to know that the Admiralty had failed to keep him in the picture, even though its own intelligence showed the High Seas Fleet to be at sea, partly due to a misunderstanding, and some bloody-mindedness, between two individuals. (For the full story, see '*Blinker' Hall: Spymaster* by David Ramsay.) Nor was he to know that Beatty had also failed to keep his own commander-in-chief fully in the picture, and had not handled his forces well, not even performing the usual courtesies when a battleship squadron was attached to his battlecruiser force (to replace ships away on gunnery practice). Being what might be described as a 'gung ho' leader, Fisher probably refused to understand the pressures on Jellicoe to keep his fleet intact. This was the problem with the battleship, it was too expensive and took too long to build to be put at hazard. It was the same for both sides. In any event, as early as October 1914, Jellicoe had highlighted his fears of the fleet being drawn over a waiting line of U-boats that could have destroyed his ships.

It was small consolation to Fisher that he was right about the effectiveness of the submarine. The British had made good use of small numbers in both the Baltic and the Sea of Marmara, but the German U-boats were a menace that threatened to force the United Kingdom into starvation. Part of the problem was that the Admiralty turned its back on tradition and did not introduce a convoy system until late in the war. The argument was that a convoy would only attract submarines, but unless they were 'attracted', there was little hope of finding them. In desperation, 'Q-ships' had been introduced, with these masquerading as merchant vessels and hoping to encourage U-boats to surface so that they could be destroyed. The crews of these ships went to considerable lengths to convince U-boat skippers that they were real merchantmen, even having 'panic parties' who would race for the ship's lifeboat and 'abandon ship', leaving the gunners with their concealed weapons behind. A variation was for the ships to tow a submerged submarine, and on 23 June 1915, the submarine *C24*, being towed by the trawler *Taranaki*, sunk *U-40*, the first German submarine to be sunk by a decoy ship.

FISHER OFFERS JELLICOE HIS SERVICES

Fisher had been replaced as First Sea Lord by Admiral, later Admiral of the Fleet, Sir Henry Jackson, whom King George V would have preferred as First Sea Lord instead of Fisher in 1914. Now, after Jutland, Jellicoe was brought to the Admiralty as First Sea Lord on 29 November

1916, being replaced as commander of the Grand Fleet by Beatty. Fisher objected to this, despite Jellicoe being a friend and a member of the Fishpond, on the grounds that he was an able commander at sea, but not an administrator. Fisher met Jellicoe on 31 January 1917, offering Jellicoe his services as Controller of the Navy, or Third Sea Lord, a post he had vacated in 1897.

This was folly, as it would have made Jellicoe's position untenable, and no one who knew Fisher even remotely could believe that he would confine himself to the job description. In short, even as Third Sea Lord, or 3SL in modern parlance, Fisher would try to run the Admiralty, the Royal Navy, and even the entire war!

Jellicoe did not reply immediately, although he must have been shocked and even appalled at the suggestion as soon as he heard it. He wrote to Fisher on 13 February.

> I have thought a great deal over the suggestion which you made to me during your visit, but I have come to the conclusion that it would not be practical for such a scheme to be adopted.
>
> There are only two posts which, in my opinion, you could hold here – those of First Lord or First Sea Lord. In any other position, I cannot help feeling that difficulties are bound to arise.[2]

This shows Jellicoe's sound judgement. He knew his old chief very well, but even if he did not, it would be a difficult relationship serving with a subordinate who had done your job not once, but twice. Some have written that Fisher found Jellicoe's reply 'deeply wounding', but what else did he expect? First Lord or First Sea Lord were indeed the only two posts that Fisher could occupy, and as Third Sea Lord he would be unable to help himself and not interfere. During the Second World War, many very senior retired naval officers took a drop in rank to return as convoy commodores, but this was different. They had an independent command at sea, Fisher wanted to be at the heart of matters.

Naturally enough, Fisher took offence:

> A *soliloquy!* When you have done your very utmost for your country, then sit down under the Juniper Tree [sic] with Elijah and ask of God that you may die! And exclaim with the deepest humility and unutterable self-degradation and self-effacement: 'I am an unprofitable servant!'[3]

Hardly unprofitable. Back at Dungavel he continued his work on the estate and this, combined with the understanding of the Duchess, he claimed to have helped him survive the war years. He even wrote to her that: 'No one else understands me as you do!' This was not the old story of a man saying to his paramour, 'My wife doesn't understand me!' It seems like it, but by all accounts she was not his mistress and there was a spiritual element to their relationship above all else. In his *Memories*, he later wrote: 'No woman will ever appear against me at the Day of Judgement.'[4] Nevertheless, he soon became aware that his continued presence was in danger of compromising his hostess's reputation for he was not only with her at Dungavel, but at other places that the Duke and Duchess leased in the south of England. It is hard to accept that the relationship was innocent when they wrote to each other as frequently as three times a day, yet there was a religious theme throughout their correspondence, and Fisher was reluctant to use the telephone, even if an internal system existed at Hamilton Palace, which it almost certainly did not.

Typical of these letters was one in which Fisher stated: 'We don't make enough of the Lord's Prayer! "Give us THIS DAY our daily bread" – not for tomorrow even, *let alone the future.*' This was not the only reference to the Lord's Prayer in a letter that was centred around this one theme and concluded with a prayer. Like many of an evangelical frame of mind, the Duchess wanted to reprint the Holy Bible, or 'Great Bible' as Fisher put it, in modern prose, and he supported her in her quest that it should have 'spelling that won't spoil her children.'[5]

FAMILY RIFT AND KATHERINE'S DEATH

Just as he began to understand that he could be a liability to the Duchess, telling her on one occasion that: 'I must not let the breath of scandal injure you!' He also became aware that the relationship had created a rift in his own family. He was a consistent correspondent with his wife, writing letters that continued to be tender and loving. In July 1918, he received the news that she had been taken seriously ill when in London. He dropped everything and caught the first train south. He arrived in time, for her illness was fatal, and had several days during which he was able to help nurse her. He continued to write to the Duchess giving a daily account of his wife's condition.

He wrote on 8 July:

One is living in a most agonising condition. As any second Death may come. This is the first day that I have been excluded from the sickroom and everyone else. She has been told the reason and simply acquiesces! Simple perfect silence is her hope of life![6]

Lady Fisher lingered for another ten days, heavily sedated by morphine. She died on 18 July. 'A most perfect, peaceful, blissful end at 2.30 am,' he wrote to the Duchess. 'I will tell you more when by and by we meet. A kindly providence gave a beautiful closed life. May your saintly end be the same!'

He found time to write:

And such was Katharine Delves Broughton, for fifty-two years the wife of Admiral of the Fleet Lord Fisher of Kilverstone, having married him as a young lieutenant without friends or money or prospects, and denied herself all her life long for the sake of her husband and her children – to them she was ever faithful and steadfast, and to such as condemned them she was a Dragon![7]

The war was drawing to an end, and on 11 November 1918, the armistice was declared and the fighting stopped. Fisher was hurt that he was not invited to the surrender ceremony for the German fleet at sea, and his feelings were even worse when King George V did not mention his name in the victory speech to Parliament on 19 November. He blamed the King for this, 'King George arranged my omission!'

He continued to write letters to newspaper editors and politicians, but now found time to write his memoirs, or at least dictate them. For a man who saw himself as an efficient and orderly administrator, these were a disconnected collection of memories with unlimited scope, with reminiscences, extracts from letters, brief appraisals of those whom he had known, and far from an orderly autobiography. Surprisingly, almost all of his recollections were kindly and charitable, except for those about Beresford, and even these were struck out when his old enemy died during drafting. All in all, the memoirs came to 200,000 words, and were cut in half, with *Memories* published on Trafalgar Day, 21 October 1919, and *Records* published on 8 December 1919, the fifth anniversary of the Battle of the Falklands. He used his publishers' advances to take the Duchess of Hamilton to Monte Carlo in February 1920, accompanied by one of her sons, convalescing from an illness. This was his first visit to Monte Carlo, and he loved it, writing: '*It's Paradise!!!* And fancy my not finding it till in my 80ᵗʰ year!!! If the Duchess dies (as is quite likely – she troubles about so many things!) – *I shall live here altogether!*'

HIS LAST ORDERS IGNORED

He was feeling well and his spirits had recovered. He was advised by the King's surgeon, Sir Frederick Treves, who was also visiting Monte Carlo, to remain and enjoy the heat. Nevertheless, on 5 March he suffered a sore throat and this was followed by rheumatic pains. He was ordered back to England as Treves diagnosed cancer and Fisher needed an immediate operation.

Back in London, Fisher had four major and painful operations with the first on 17 March and the last on 9 July. He showed his customary courage and resilience throughout. After the third operation, he seemed to be recovering and on 6 June he was taken by the Duchess to Ferne, near Salisbury. The weather was good and he was able to sit outside. His condition worsened and he was brought back to London for one last operation on 9 July at the Hamilton's London home in St James's Square. He did not recover full consciousness. Early in the morning of 10 July, it was clear that he was dying and the Duchess fulfilled a promise to offer a last prayer, whispering in his ear: 'O Lord, in Thee have I trusted, let me never be confounded.' He seemed to be comforted by this, and at 7.15 a.m., he died.

Fisher did not fear death. His faith was too strong for that. He had prepared instructions for his funeral in an envelope marked 'PRIVATE. To be opened when necessary.' Inside there was just a single sheet of paper, giving the name and address of his undertakers, followed by:

The nearest cemetery
No flowers
No one invited except relatives
No mourning

A line was drawn below which followed:

Words under tablet at Kilverstone Church
as arranged in memorandum in my writing case

It was not to be, to the very last his superiors had other ideas. He received a state funeral three days later in bright summer sunshine. His coffin, draped with a Union Jack, was carried on a gun carriage drawn by naval ratings along Pall Mall, the Mall, close to Buckingham Palace and then past the Admiralty and down Whitehall, past the shrouded Cenotaph and to the west door of Westminster Abbey. The funeral service was followed by a cremation and finally the ashes were taken to the parish church at Kilverstone and buried beside Kitty's grave. He had chosen the inscription for his stone:

> Seest thou a man diligent in his business?
> He shall stand before Kings,
> He shall not stand before mean men

While on the footstone followed:

> Fear God and Dread Nought

Meanwhile, *The Times*, which had so often helped him in his battles, reported on the funeral the morning afterwards, 14 July, under the headline, 'The People's Homage'.

Yesterday morning the mortal remains of Admiral of the Fleet Lord Fisher of Kilverstone, GCB, OM, GCVO, were borne in solemn state to Westminster Abbey, where, in the presence of a vast congregation representing all that is most eminent in our national life, an august ceremonial celebrated the passing of a great spirit from the earthly scene of its stupendous labours.

And yesterday morning the British public showed that it loved and mourned one 'Jacky Fisher'. There is no surer test of public feeling than the size and behaviour of the crowd in the streets. Till within the last weeks of his long and bellicose life, Lord Fisher was a stormy petrel, bringing the tempests he rejoiced in. Behind him he had, at first, no one; behind him, he had, in these later years, the whole solid affection and admiration of the people. And yesterday morning the people, in its silent, solid, reverent British way, wrote its affection and

admiration for 'Jacky Fisher' upon the social history of our time ...
With infinite slowness to music the procession moved up the length
of the Nave to the choir, the choristers, white surpluses over scarlet,
in front, then the canons and other dignitaries of the Abbey and the
Dean. Behind the Dean was the crimson cushion on which the dead
man's Orders and Decorations were displayed, a glittering mass of
stars and ribbon, and then the coffin ... crowned with the Admiral's
hat and sword, borne by eight bluejackets ...[8]

Notes

1 Kilverstone, Admiral of the Fleet Baron, *Memories*, London, 1919
2 Ibid
3 Ibid
4 Ibid
5 Ibid
6 Ibid
7 Ibid
8 *The Times*, 14 July 1920

17

A Life Remembered

What matters is that the spirit and power of Nelson live on this earth again.
C.P. Scott writing to the Duchess of Hamilton, 1916.

One can run through the life of an individual, recount his achievements and failures, strengths and weaknesses, but what matters is the impact he made on his chosen walk of life. Even here we have a problem. Did Fisher really want to join the Royal Navy in 1854, or was he pushed in that direction?

Was Fisher's choice of career pure chance, perhaps? There must be some pause for thought about this. After all, his godmother, who was so supportive of the young Fisher, knew not one but two admirals. For someone who was effectively acting as a guardian, looking for a career for a youngster, (for he was still just a teenager, not even a young man), without money and with few connections, cannot have been easy. Being nominated therefore by two senior officers and able to spend time as a cadet, must have given him the best start imaginable. Without money, he would have found it impossible to purchase a commission in the British Army. Without money, he would have been unable to go to university, or even complete his education, and so a career in the Indian Civil Service, as pursued by his son Cecil, would have been out of his reach.

There were other career opportunities open to him. He could have worked on the railways, not far short of completion at home and still expanding abroad, especially in the British colonies, but this lacked the status of, for example, the Indian Civil Service. The Merchant Navy was another option, but at the time it was a brutal life, and a harsh one, even worse than the Royal Navy. Once again, it lacked status, and someone of Lady Wilmot-Horton's standing would have been conscious of this. It is likely, therefore, that John Arbuthnot Fisher's choice of career was not entirely his own.

The fact that he suffered badly from sea sickness at first can be regarded as immaterial. Many professional seafarers suffered this at first. Even in later life, for a sailor, moving to a smaller ship or even a different stretch of water, could bring back the dreaded *mal de mare* to the seemingly hardened old sea dog.

What is clear is that Fisher joined at a time when the Royal Navy was undergoing radical change. Whether it wanted it or not, change was being forced upon it. It could not ignore technical progress, even if the conservative members of the service wanted to do so. It had to match foreign navies not just in size and what would today be described as 'global reach', but in technology. The ships were changing. Wood had given way to the ironclad, and then to iron hulls, and finally to steel. Propulsive systems were changing, not just with the steam engine and paddle wheel, but from reciprocating steam engine to steam turbine and from paddle wheel to screw, and then from coal to oil. Armaments were changing, from cannon to large turret guns, from muzzle-loading to breech-loading, from solid shot to explosive shells, from smooth bore to rifled barrels, and then there was the advent of the rapid firing lighter calibre gun. Amidst all of this, the mine and the torpedo made their appearance and meant great changes.

The frigate had disappeared and the destroyer, still very small, and the cruiser had appeared. Before the end of Fisher's life, the aircraft carrier was a reality, with the first two ships, HMS *Furious* and *Argus*, not only in commission, but the former had been used operationally in July 1918 with a raid on the airship sheds at Tondern. But, of course, in the meantime, the Royal Navy had once again lost control of its air element with the creation of the autonomous Royal Air Force on 1 April 1918.

THE INEVITABILITY OF CHANGE

That the Royal Navy was not completely dependent on Fisher for change is self-evident. In 1801, Nelson fought the first naval battle of Copenhagen using cannon and shot. In 1807, the Royal Navy was back at Copenhagen for another battle, but this time it used artillery rockets. Even before Fisher was born, the Royal Navy had started to introduce the first steam frigates.

On the other hand, after some unfortunate accidents with the early breech-loading guns, the Royal Navy reverted to muzzle loading, even though this was more time consuming, reduced the rate of fire considerably and, worst of all, meant that during reloading on the open deck of a turret or barbette gun, personnel were completely exposed to enemy fire. The Royal Navy was still building ironclad warships in Fisher's early career, even though simply bolting iron plates onto a wooden hull produced warships that were unbalanced and difficult to handle and, to put it bluntly, dangerous for those aboard.

The pace of change was uneven. For every officer who embraced change, there were others opposed to it. Fisher had to contend with men who regretted the passing of sail and hated steam. This was a serious problem. At first, many ships could sail almost as fast as a steam engine could propel them, and on long voyages, it was essential to make use of the wind as much as possible because the ships only had enough coal for eight to ten days under steam. Later, the improvement in the steam engine and the establishment of coaling stations throughout the British Empire meant that steam-powered ships could be where they were needed, when they were needed.

The attitude to gunnery was another problem that Fisher had to contend with. Apart from the reluctance to practise gunnery, as mentntioned earlier, on the extraordinary grounds that it made the ships dirty, guns were not used to their full potential. When Fisher joined the Mediterranean Fleet as its commander-in-chief, accuracy was poor and the ranges at which battles were fought were too short. This meant that a British warship risked being blown out of the water by the enemy before it even started firing. Worse still, as Beresford made clear when asked by the Admiralty how he would have tackled the Russian Second Pacific Squadron had it been necessary for the two countries to go to war, many senior officers would not have deployed all of their resources at their disposal unless forced to do so. Using four battleships instead of eight meant not only a reduced weight of fire, but also failed to force the enemy to have to divide his fire over eight ships. The four ships used would have been at greater risk of damage as a result.

Perhaps Fisher's most tangible achievement was the first modern battleship, HMS *Dreadnought*. Had conventional wisdom been allowed to hold sway, this ship would not have been the major step change in naval technology that she was. The big criticism of the old guard was that the ship incorporated too many changes at once, yet many feel it could have taken another decade to have produced a truly new generation of ships, had this step-by-step approach prevailed. Or would it? After all, the concept of the all-big gun battleship either originated in Italy or at least was shared by the Italians, so the Royal Navy might have been forced to adopt such designs within a couple of years. Nevertheless, under Fisher, change happened and it happened first in the Royal Navy.

UNDERSTANDING FISHER'S LEGACY

Fisher's legacy to the service was a combination of several things. The first of these was efficiency. He always expected in any new post to find inefficiency and waste, and he was never disappointed. He was impatient and saw productivity gains as vital, and it might have been a good thing for the British manufacturing industry had he been lured away by the generous offers, sometimes of more than five times his naval salary, as already British productivity was falling behind that of the leading European powers and the United States.

On the other hand, his idea of building warships in small numbers, while making technological innovation easier, reduced productivity and the number of ships the nation could get for the taxpayers' money. The dilemma was that taken to extremes, this could have meant a large number of Dreadnought-type battleships and battlecruisers during the First World War, but no super-Dreadnoughts. The evolution in warship design at the time and the growth in gun calibres was such that this would have been a fatal flaw.

The second major legacy was that of professionalism. Fisher paid attention to the training and career development naval officers and sought to broaden the pool of talent available by making promotion from the 'lower deck' (naval terminology for the 'ranks') far easier. This was an important step forward, not only because it gave the brighter and more able men who, for one reason or another, had joined the service as ordinary seamen, a way of achieving their full potential. It also gave the service the benefit of their practical experience. His original concept of selecting men for the various branches of the service almost at will was hardly practical and unlikely to have produced the best recruits, while he sometimes overlooked just how specialised training would be organised. These were understandable mistakes given his background and the speed at which the new technology was developing. Less forgivable was the way in which he treated those officers who ventured to suggest that specialised training needed longer – this was a case of Fisher ignoring the advice of those who knew better.

In contrast, he also did much for the Royal Navy's reserves, establishing the Royal Fleet Reserve, which consisted of regular naval personnel who had left the service or retired, but whose experience became available through the Royal Fleet Reserve in an emergency.

The third legacy was faith in technology. Fisher was an ardent enthusiast for technology and bold, perhaps also courageous, in his desire to see it implemented as fully as possible and as quickly as possible. While this was undoubtedly due at least in part to his fear that the Royal Navy would not be prepared for war, and his growing conviction that the conflict would be with Germany, it was also the case that he had no time for half-measures. Many felt that *Dreadnought* incorporated too many advances at once, but that saved time and enabled the Royal Navy to see how the different developments worked with each other. In any case, many developments were inter-related. The use of steam turbines reduced the height of the engine room, and that meant that heavier armour plating could be used above the engine room without affecting stability, and it also permitted heavier armament to be carried. That *Dreadnought* was far from perfect and that this led to practical difficulties, as mentioned earlier in Chapter 11, cannot be denied, but many of these problems could be easily resolved in later ships.

On the other hand, and there was often an 'other hand' with Fisher, his enthusiasm for change ran far beyond what was achievable *at the time*. He could have had a wonderful career as a rival to H.G. Wells in forecasting the shape of future warfare. His idea of diesel-engined battleships went beyond not just what was realistic in the First World War, but also what was achievable in the Second World War, during which the battleship became obsolete. His grasp of technology began to wear thin at this point as he also believed that a diesel-engined battleship would not need funnels or engineers.

Fisher's eagerness to embrace new forms of strategy and tactics were other elements in his legacy. While a proponent of the big gun battleship, he was quick to realise, indeed perhaps the first senior officer to recognise, that the day of the battleship would be limited by the submarine and the aeroplane. He was correct in stating that these would be the weapons of the future, and if at first he put his faith in the airship, it was simply because the airship was around first while the

Wright brothers were still fighting for recognition. The torpedo was something in which he firmly believed. Submarines and torpedo-boats meant that even small navies could wield immense power and pose a potent threat.

If there was a weakness in his planning of the fleet in the days before this massive weapon was needed, it was his espousal of the battlecruiser. To Fisher, the battlecruiser was far superior to the battleship, being faster, yet as heavily armed. Of course, this came at a price, and the price was that of armour protection. This was one reason why so many battle-cruisers were lost at Jutland, but there was another problem as well. No one had really considered just how a battlecruiser could, and should, be used. Fast scouts in the van of the fleet were obviously one role, but this left them vulnerable and in any case, at Jutland, Beatty failed to keep Jellicoe completely in the picture. His love of speed would have meant that only battlecruisers would have been built in the years immediately before the First World War, had not Fisher been blocked in this by his colleagues.

Nor were all of his ship design ideas practical. For his Baltic esca-pade, the invasion of Germany on the coast of Pomerania required so-called 'light battlecruisers' with a shallow draught. These ships were so light that one of them broke her back in a moderate swell. Two of them had 15-inch guns, while the third, HMS *Furious*, had 18-inch guns, which when fired sent rivets flying across the accommodation areas. Not for nothing did the cynics in the fleet called them the 'Outrageous-class'.

A sound sense of organisation was another Fisher attribute. He reduced bureaucracy to the essential minimum and also saw that the Royal Navy needed control of its own air power. While on the retired list, he encouraged Churchill to fight this battle before the outbreak of the First World War, but it had to be fought again between the wars. History repeated itself when the service regained control of the Fleet Air Arm on the eve of the Second World War, just as it had done with the Royal Naval Air Service in 1914. It was always important, and remains so, that naval aviators are not airmen who go to sea, but sailors who take to the air.

It is important to bear these things in mind, but as so often hap-pens with genius, there was a price to be paid. A man so brilliant in many ways had to have drawbacks in other senses. The most obvious of these was his complete lack of diplomacy, not when dealing with foreign potentates when he could be charming, but when dealing with those around him. He was not only undiplomatic; he was rude, hostile, and often aggressive. He even enjoyed much of this, revelling in his ferocious image. As he rose to senior rank, his sense of self-importance and omniscience reached unsustainable levels. His lack of discipline and restraint, and his battles with other officers and leaks to the press and politicians, began to bring the service, which he professed to love, into disrepute, and was certainly bad for morale. It was no coincidence that the man instrumental in his downfall at the end of his first period as First Sea Lord was someone who copied many of his own practices. Beresford may well have lacked Fisher's intellect and judgement, but he also felt free to write and lobby, and between them a sense of indiscipline and self-interest was fostered in the service.

Fisher liked to regard himself as the heir to Nelson. He deferred taking up the much-coveted post as First Sea Lord until Trafalgar Day, only then to slip in a day early. Later, he made important appointments and changes to coincide with Trafalgar Day. Unlike his hero, Fisher never commanded a fleet fighting a major battle at sea. None of his contemporaries had done this either. The one occasion when he could have made a difference was when the German High Seas Fleet ventured out as he was trying to leave the Admiralty, but the Germans returned to port, and even if the hoped-for naval battle had come about, he was refusing to have anything to do with it. Later, having left the Admiralty, he was markedly unsympathetic to Jellicoe after Jutland. What would Fisher have done in Jellicoe's shoes? He might well have jeopardised the Grand Fleet.

There were also major weaknesses in his plans for the Royal Navy in wartime. As mentioned earlier, he stopped work on Rosyth and that meant, until the new dockyard opened in 1916, the ships of the Grand Fleet had to be steamed all the way to the south of England when dockyard work was required. When at the Admiralty, Jellicoe had the foresight to position a floating dock at Invergordon on the Cromarty Firth, but this was of limited capacity. As it was, it was not until 17 March 1916 that the first ship entered the basin at Rosyth, the depot ship *Crescent*, converted from an old cruiser. On 28 March, the battleship *Zealandia*, originally commissioned as HMS *New Zealand*, was the first ship to use the dry docks.

While Jellicoe was right to base a floating dock at Invergordon, this base would not have been a good alternative to Rosyth as the entrance to the Cromarty Forth is in any case narrow, and ships passing in and out would be vulnerable to attack by waiting U-boats. If Fisher did not like Rosyth, and there were good reasons for this, he should have sought an alternative – perhaps at Aberdeen or Peterhead?

The other major flaw in the planning for war was the lack of a convoy system. The arguments against this were that the presence of so many merchant ships together would attract submarines, but unless submarines were attracted, there was little hope of hunting them down as even with ASDIC, which was not available, this was akin to seeking a needle in a haystack. The hydrophone system used at first suffered from interference from the ship's own noise. Using Q-ships as bait for submarines and then attacking them when they surfaced worked, but only nibbled at the edges of the problem, despite the undoubted bravery of the crews involved. The lack of a convoy system was a serious omission, all the more so since it had been used in earlier wars. It was not until 14 June 1917 that the Admiralty started to provide support for convoys, and only after political pressure had built up.

A LACK OF REALISM

Fisher was wise enough to appreciate that the soldiers would not want a sailor prying into the War Office and the British Army, but when asked to do so, did not hesitate. There can be little doubt that what he and his colleagues did on their small committee was beneficial to the War Office, but he did not end his involvement at this stage. As his plans for an invasion of Pomerania clearly showed, his strategic grasp could be flawed, a shortcoming made so much worse by his failure to create a small joint service planning team. This could have looked at the practicalities. Time was not on his side. Any such campaign would have stood a better chance of working had it been implemented during the first weeks of war.

Had Fisher not been embroiled in the scandal with Beresford, and had he not kept his war plans to himself, much planning for what could be done on the outbreak of a major war could have been put in hand. He could also have ensured that many other preparations were being progressed. The ships that were needed for an invasion could have been designed and even prototypes built and tested. At Gallipoli, the landings used barges towed by steam pinnaces and a landing ship crudely converted from a merchant vessel. When the plans for invasions were finally put in hand, the shipbuilding programme diverted resources from conventional warship construction and even from building merchant ships, and this during a war that nearly saw the population of the United Kingdom starve.

It was primarily his lack of realism in the role and use of the army that marked him down as a man who interfered without understanding. He objected to the dispatch of the British Expeditionary Force to France because he feared the effects of his country being involved in a continental war. Yet, what else could the politicians have done? Britain was a guarantor of the neutrality of Belgium, and so standing aside was really not possible. The country also had an 'understanding', the *Entente Cordiale*, with France. Fisher wanted the Royal Navy to project the army into battle, landing troops behind enemy lines to create new fronts, new diversions. This could have worked, but there was no way that the technology of the day and the resources available could have projected the numbers he imagined within such a short time as to ensure surprise and that enemy defences would be overwhelmed, and there was no way that the generals or the politicians would risk the lives of so many, at least, not at first – not until the disaster that was Gallipoli.

It was at Gallipoli, or from the naval viewpoint, the Dardanelles, that Fisher was at his worst. He was for it, and then against it. He kept quiet when his intervention might have saved the day. The impression is that he indulged himself in a massive sulk. True, it must have been difficult for him listening to men who knew nothing about the perils and pitfalls of such an undertaking grow increasingly enthusiastic. If he had employed the diplomacy that he had shown with foreign leaders, or the forbearance displayed when negotiating with the War Office for the Admiralty to regain control of its own armament and munitions, then he might have done his country one great service. Although without the shocking losses experienced on the shores of Gallipoli and on the waters of the Dardanelles, no one would ever have realised just what he had done.

Of course, with Fisher, diplomacy was selective. He was anything but diplomatic at the Hague Peace Conference in 1899. Perhaps he should have taken the same approach with the War Council in 1915. The problems were the same, men with no experience of war talking rubbish. Certainly, at The Hague, Fisher allowed no one to entertain any doubts about the true nature of warfare. 'War is Hell!' he barked.

Some of his rhetoric about the treatment of prisoners may have been intended to shock, but it also may have caused some to doubt his sanity.

He was absolutely right about the impact of a continental land war on the British economy. The loss of so much manpower from industry through conscription was one problem, and one of Fisher's victories during his second spell as First Sea Lord was to get conscripts returned from the Army into the shipyards. Conscription also affected the quality of munitions, with many shells used by the Army in France, and no doubt by the Navy at sea, proving to be duds. Despite the lessons of the Crimean War and despite Fisher's best efforts, all too often the wrong shells were in use at the wrong time on the Western Front, and on occasion the problem only became apparent when infantrymen advancing across no man's land to the enemy trenches found that barbed wire had not been blown up as expected.

Left to his own devices, Fisher would have played a waiting game and then thrown the cream of Britain's small professional army onto a European shore where he judged it to be most effective at diverting the Germans. His favoured spot was Pomerania, with strong Russian support. The British troops would have been used up in seizing Schleswig Holstein and the Kiel Canal, and then holding on to them. Meanwhile, the Germans would have been well on their way to Paris or even to the French coast. He also ignored the problems that social unrest were causing inside Russia, and especially in the armed services, which, combined with the country's poverty and inability fully to meet the armaments demands of her army and the navy, would have made Russia a doubtful partner in the Baltic adventure.

AN EMBARRASSMENT

If the row with Beresford that preceded Fisher's departure from the office of First Sea Lord for the first time was an embarrassment to the Royal Navy, then the manner of his departure the second time was even worse. He was not simply an embarrassment; he was a disgrace, leaving his post at a time when his country needed him. A lesser man might have been shot. It was no excuse that Fisher and Churchill were two completely incompatible personalities. Much has been said about their differences, but the root cause of the trouble was in fact their similarities. Both wanted to be what the Red Army would have described as a 'one man chief', combining operations and political affairs in a single individual. Both wanted ciphers as their supporting team. Churchill could do without the sea lords, although he needed the expertise of Fisher in particular, while Fisher could do without Churchill and would have been happier fighting his own battles in the Cabinet and in Parliament.

Both men favoured the grandiose and extravagant scheme. Churchill favoured the Dardanelles, Fisher Pomerania. Churchill was later to be as much a menace as a saviour of his country during the Second World War, with his many ideas often conceived late at night after a generous intake of cognac, and which were known to senior officers as his 'midnight follies'. That so few of these schemes survived the dawn ensured his position in history as Britain's Chief of Men.

Perhaps the truth was that neither was especially good at choosing people for senior appointments. There can be no doubt that many of those officers swimming in the Fishpond were extremely able, and Jellicoe was one of these. But Fisher's choice of his successor was a poor one, and his successor's successor no better.

Sometimes a creative friction can exist between two men who find it difficult to agree, but this is far rarer than many would like to believe. Certainly, the friction between Churchill and Fisher was anything but creative, it was destructive.

When Fisher left, his career was over, but he had already scaled the heights and made his reputation. Churchill left politics for a while and accepted a commission in the British Army. The real tragedy was that in the manner of his going, Fisher was once again an embarrassment to his many allies and supporters. What was it about him that led him to behave in this manner? Was it having so much power and believing that he was always right and that he was indispensable? That was certainly part of it. Was it old age? Possibly, but other great men have done their best work past the age of seventy years, and later Churchill was to be a case in point. Fisher was in good health for his age at the time he returned to the Admiralty. Perhaps the problem was that this was a boy who had never really grown up, and who throughout his life threw tantrums.

His language at The Hague Peace Conference may have been intended to shock, but one wonders. Was he really completely sane? Youngsters like to shock and horrify people, but a mature adult and a senior naval officer?

It also has to be accepted that the post of First Sea Lord was a poisoned chalice during the war. When Jellicoe succeeded Jackson in late November 1916, it soon became clear that this was a promotion too far. Fisher's suspicions of Jellicoe's abilities were in the end correct. He faced political pressure to introduce the convoy system and eventually did so in June 1917, and overall the relentless pressure of fighting a global naval war took its toll. Unlike Fisher, Jellicoe, who as Second Sea Lord had done much to repair the schisms in the Royal Navy created by Fisher and Beresford, had a Deputy First Sea Lord to help him, the competent and professional Vice-Admiral Sir Rosslyn Erskine Wemyss, described by many as able and likeable. On Christmas Eve, 1917, with Jellicoe depressed and broken down by the pressures of his job, a new First Lord, Sir Eric Geddes, simply demanded and received his resignation as First Sea Lord, promoting Wemyss to full Admiral as First Sea Lord in his place.

'Jellicoe was dismissed with a discourtesy without parallel in the dealing with Ministers with distinguished sailors and soldiers,' recalled Archibald Hurd, naval correspondent of the *Daily Telegraph*. He was not alone in this assessment, for King George V was 'greatly surprised'.

Beatty did rather better, holding his post as Jellicoe's successor as Commander-in-Chief of the Grand Fleet long enough to have the honour of taking the surrender of the German High Seas Fleet in 1918.

18

War Without Fisher

There seems to be something wrong with our bloody ships today.
Vice-Admiral Sir David Beatty to Captain Ernle Chatfield, May
1916.

Fisher's departure from the Admiralty came at a time when the war
was going badly for the Allies. In contrast to the Second World War in
which there was a marked turning of the tide in 1942, the impression
was that it was not until the last six or nine months of the First World
War that the pendulum seemed to swing in favour of the Allies. This
was not quite true. The German surface raiders were soon penned up
or sunk, even though this still left the U-boat menace. Annual totals
of merchant shipping tonnage in the North Sea and the Atlantic sunk
by U-boats rose from a meagre and sustainable 3,369 tons in 1914 to
700,782 tons in 1915, 508,745 tons in 1916, 2,895,983 tons in 1917 and
were still at 1,044,822 in 1918. To these could be added the 350,853
tons lost in the Mediterranean and the 44,520 lost to U-boats based at
Constantinople in 1915. Indeed, in 1916, losses in the Mediterranean
reached 1,045,058 tons, much higher than the Atlantic figures, while
in 1917, the Mediterranean figure was 1,514,501 tons, and it was still
slightly more than half this rate in 1918.

The First Lord seems to have been slow in finding a successor for
Fisher, possibly because Churchill hung on for far too long to the
notion that Fisher might change his mind. It was not until 28 May
that Admiral Sir Henry Jackson took over as First Sea Lord. During
the intervening period, Italy had joined the war on the side of the
Allies against Austria-Hungary. This must have been a relief as before
the war there had been fears of a Triple Alliance with Italy siding with
Austria-Hungary and Germany. It also meant that the Italians could
keep the Austria-Hungary Fleet bottled up in the Adriatic, although
the large barrage eventually created to do this consisted mainly of

converted British fishing vessels. Far less promising was the loss of two pre-Dreadnoughts on 25 and 27 May. In wartime, First Sea Lords do not have time to work themselves into their new position, and certainly don't enjoy a 'honeymoon period'. In little more than days after taking up his appointment, Jackson was faced with an extension of the U-boat campaign into the Mediterranean.

That the war was truly global had already been emphasised with the Battle of Coronel and then the Falklands, while there was also fighting in East Africa and in Mesopotamia. The Mediterranean was close enough for the actions in the Mediterranean and summer 1915 saw the Royal Navy active in Mesopotamia, helping to take Kut-el-Amara with the assistance of the Royal Indian Marine, the processor of the Indian Naval Service, while two monitors attacked and sank the commerce-raider *Konigsberg* in the Rufiji River. It was also the start of operations by the submarine *E11* in the Sea of Marmara, attacking Constantinople in August and taking the first periscope photograph of the city in December. Another E-class boat, *E21*, penetrated the Dardanelles and on 8 August sank the Turkish battleship *Hairedin Barbarossa*. Four days later, a Short 184 seaplane from the seaplane carrier *Ben-my-Chree* made the first successful aerial torpedo attack, sinking a Turkish cargo ship in the Dardanelles. The ship had already been damaged by a submarine. Later, on 18 December, the irrepressible naval aviator, Wing Commander (an RNAS rank originally) Charles Rumney Samson, dropped the first 500-lb bomb on Turkish positions.

Nevertheless, the British and the Australians were still bogged down in Gallipoli. On 6 August, the problems were compounded by further landings at Suvla Bay, a case of reinforcing failure. Once again, under different leadership and with better planning, these landings might have been a success, but they were not. Notwithstanding the achievements of the submariners and the aviators, the day after Samson dropped his bomb, 19 December, the withdrawal from Gallipoli began. The evacuation took until 9 January 1916, but this was the one aspect of the whole miserable campaign that actually worked well. Decisive intervention by the U-boats at this stage could have turned the evacuation into a bloodbath, but the withdrawal was a textbook example of what could be done, in contrast to the landings.

The end of the year saw continued involvement in East Africa, with the Royal Navy beginning operations on Lake Tanganyika, and two specially adapted lake steamers, *Mimi* and *Toutou*, captured the German

Kingani on 26 December, which was later renamed *Toutou* and replaced the older ship. On 9 February 1916, the 'new' *Toutou* and *Mimi* sank the *Hedwig von Wissman*, also on Lake Tanganyika.

NEW YEAR LOSSES AND JUTLAND

New Year 1916 had started badly, however, with the pre-Dreadnought *King Edward VII* striking a mine on 6 January, and sinking off Cape Wrath on the far north of Scotland. The Royal Navy could simply count itself lucky that it was not a Dreadnought, as the outcome would have been the same and the loss more serious. Even pre-Dreadnoughts could still be of value, albeit highly vulnerable if they encountered a Dreadnought. Perhaps appreciating the pressure, on 8 February, the British government formally sought naval assistance from its Far Eastern ally, Japan, which agreed to send two destroyer flotillas. These arrived in the Mediterranean during April. There was also a certain amount of rationalisation between the armed services. Churchill had offered the services of the Royal Navy in the air defence of the United Kingdom, in one of his typically extravagant gestures. This meant not only fighter cover, such as it was, by the RNAS, it also left the RN providing anti-aircraft gunnery protection, something that would logically have in the remit of the army. On 16 February, the War Office assumed control of the AA defences.

Looking at the monthly losses of merchant ships during the First World War shows fluctuations in the figures. This was due to the 'on-off' nature of the U-boat campaign. At first, operations were limited to attacking warships without notice, while merchant vessels had to be stopped and those aboard given a chance to take to the lifeboats before the ship was sunk. The U-boat commanders also stayed clear of neutral vessels. This was all very well, but as Fisher had stressed, it was completely impractical. A combination of factors, including losses of U-boats to the Q-ships, which the Germans thought to be treacherous, and the sheer need to make an impact on the steady stream of ships carrying cargo for the British war effort, meant that unrestricted U-boat attacks were soon authorised. This was stopped in the North Atlantic on 18 September 1915, when it provoked protests from the United States, but continued in the Mediterranean where the U-boats were less likely to find ships carrying US citizens. Nevertheless, unrestricted

U-boat attacks were authorised in British waters on 23 February 1916, although suspended again on 24 April following fresh American protests. Throughout this period, the Royal Navy attempted to keep the German fleet in its bases. On 7 March, the first British mine-laying submarine, E24, laid mines in the mouth of the River Elbe. By 1 May, the Germans not only returned to unrestricted U-boat warfare, they took the battle into the western Atlantic for the first time.

The U-boat was not the only example of new weaponry that appeared in the war. On 1 April 1916, towns on the East Coast of England were bombed by German Zeppelin airships, but further south, over the Thames Estuary, another Zeppelin, L-15 became the first to be brought down by AA fire and crash-landed in the Thames Estuary, where its crew surrendered to a passing warship. Towns on the East Coast also suffered shelling from German battlecruisers, which bombarded Lowestoft and Yarmouth on 23 April. It was not just over England that the Zeppelins were at risk, for on 4 May, L-7 was brought down south of the Horn Reefs on the eastern side of the North Sea by fire from the light cruisers *Galatea* and *Phaeton*. These large craft were difficult to destroy completely, unless the hydrogen gas caught fire, and so L-7 was able to ditch in the North Sea where she was destroyed by the submarine E31, which also rescued seven survivors.

The problem with the airship was that the fighter aircraft of the day lacked the rate of climb to intercept them successfully. It was a long and laborious business climbing up over a Zeppelin to then shoot into its envelope from above, while trying this exercise from below simply subjected the aircraft to a hail of defensive fire. It was bad enough with landplanes, almost impossible with seaplanes because of the extra weight and the drag of their floats. A Zeppelin carried water ballast, which if jettisoned gave it a far superior rate of climb to any aeroplane of the day. Even so, schemes were set in hand to see if the Zeppelin menace could be countered. It was clear that it was better to attack them over the sea rather than over land, especially heavily populated areas, and so the submarine E22 conducted 'float-off' trials using two Sopwith Schneider★ seaplanes. The diminutive aircraft was, nevertheless, still dragged down by its floats. Later in the war there were experiments using the Sopwith

★ The name given to the Sopwith Tabloid after its stunning victory at Monaco in 1914 in the Schneider Trophy.

Camel landplane fighter, flown off from a lighter towed at high speed behind a destroyer. The experiments were successful, but after its sortie the aircraft had to ditch in the sea. At this time there was no possibility of having fighter aircraft patrolling over the sea, just in case a Zeppelin put in an appearance – ranges were too short and endurance limited.

Quite what Fisher would have done had he still been First Sea Lord is difficult to say. The aeroplane really was very new to everyone, let alone Fisher who had left the Admiralty in 1910. It is perfectly possible that he could have looked at the airship in the same way he did the submarine, the torpedo and the mine, that it had to be accepted that it was virtually impossible to guarantee an effective defence against the threat. In fact, the Zeppelin was far less of a threat than the submarine, torpedo or mine. On 25 March, the seaplane carrier *Vindex* sent five aircraft on an unsuccessful attempt to bomb airship sheds at Hoyer, on the coast of Schleswig-Holstein, but three force-landed on enemy territories and their crews were made prisoner.

On 25 March, the cruiser *Cleopatra* rammed the German destroyer G-194, cutting the tiny vessel in half. Yet, the Royal Navy was also inflicting damage upon itself. The following month, when the Grand Fleet sallied forth towards the Skagerrak hoping to draw the German High Seas Fleet into battle, two of its battlecruisers collided in thick fog on 22 April, a battleship hit a merchantman, and that night, three destroyers collided. These were the days before radar, and collisions were much more a fact of nautical life than is the case today. The ships were also smaller, cheaper and, to be frank, expendable, unless they were a precious battleship or battlecruiser.

Losses there were during the Battle of Jutland. Beatty, in command of the battlecruisers, lost *Indefatigable, Invincible* – one of the victors of the Falklands – and *Queen Mary*, as well as three armoured cruisers and five smaller warships, while many other ships were damaged. The long-awaited battle saw 155,000 tons of British warships lost compared to 61,000 tons of German warships, while 6,090 British sailors and marines were lost compared with 2,550 Germans.

The truth was that for all of their speed, the battlecruisers were vulnerable. Perhaps the losses could have been lower had the Royal Navy learnt the lessons about the dangers of flashback from the turrets and into the magazines, already discovered the hard way by the Germans, but this is pure speculation. The German battlecruisers were better armoured. This must have been a massive disappointment for Fisher, but he was preoccupied with criticising Jellicoe for his timidity rather than analysing the weaknesses of his beloved battlecruisers. Had he still been at the Admiralty, doubtless the unfortunate Jellicoe would have been bombarded with wireless messages advising him what to do. Perhaps the only advantage Fisher would have conferred on his subordinate would have been that he would have ensured that accurate intelligence was conveyed. On the other hand, his undoubted 'gung-ho' personality would have forced Beatty to 'engage the enemy more closely' and no doubt losses amongst the battlecruisers and their escorts would have been even greater.

AFTER JUTLAND

Jutland was one of those seminal events in warfare. The world could never be quite the same again. Everyone in Great Britain had waited for this battle, impatiently, since the outbreak of war. Everyone assumed that the Royal Navy would be victorious. Everyone hoped that the victory would shorten the war, and perhaps even persuade the Germans to surrender or withdraw. None of these things happened, and even if there had been a British victory, it would not necessarily have been decisive. It might have persuaded the Germans not to hazard their fleet again, and in fact Jutland did at least succeed in that, but only after a further excursion into the open sea. On 18 and 19 August, when Scheer took the High Seas Fleet out into the North Sea again, he used a reconnaissance force of eight Zeppelins, and when the commander of one of the Zeppelins mistook light cruisers and destroyers from Harwich for the Grand Fleet, Scheer took his ships south hoping for a major naval engagement, but in so doing he took them away from Jellicoe and the Grand Fleet, who returned to base rather than risk his ships in the heavily mined southern waters of the North Sea. Both sides suffered losses, with the submarine *E23* torpedoing the German battleship *Westfalen* north of Terschelling, forcing her to return to base, while the British lost the light cruiser *Falmouth* to a U-boat's torpedo as she crossed the U-boat line. Not surprisingly, Commodore Tyrwhitt, taking his light cruisers and destroyers north, was unable to attack when he saw the High Seas Fleet. To have done so would have been suicidal and a waste of good men and useful ships.

War has always depended on intelligence, and in this the Zeppelins were to prove a weakness for the Germans. On at least two occasions, German signal books were recovered from the wreckage of a downed Zeppelin. The first was on 17 June 1916 when *L-48* was shot down, and then again on 24 September when *L-32* was shot down, and the new set of German naval codes fell into British hands.

U-boats apart, the High Seas Fleet spent most of the rest of the war on hit and run operations. In October, two of these were mounted. The first was a second bombardment from the sea of Lowestoft on 26 October, while that night, German destroyers were sent against Dover. The latter operation was probably not worth the effort, as most of the seven vessels sunk by the destroyers were British fishing vessels, small drifters, adapted to handle the barrage. This type of operation was to continue in early 1917, with German destroyers attacking Southwold in Suffolk on 25 January, then raiding Margate and Westgate in Kent on 25 February, while Dover was visited again by the destroyers on 17 March, sinking one ship and damaging another with a torpedo, while the following day, it was the turn of Ramsgate and Broadstairs in north Kent, with Ramsgate revisited on 27 April. The Germans did not always find themselves unopposed, and on the night of 23/24 January, the German 6th Destroyer Flotilla found itself facing the two Harwich destroyer flotillas off the Schouwen light vessel. In the frantic battle that ensued, both sides lost a destroyer.

GAINS AND LOSSES

The year 1917 started badly, just as had the previous year. The pre-Dreadnought HMS *Cornwallis* was torpedoed and sunk 62 miles off Malta by *U-32* on 9 January. Two days later, the seaplane carrier, *Ben-my-Chree*, a converted Isle of Man steam packet, was sunk off Kastelorizo by fire from Turkish shore batteries. English Channel and Irish Sea steam packets were popular for conversion to seaplane carriers, having a good turn of speed and the deck space suitable for building a hangar, but on this occasion, *Ben-my-Chree* was not fast enough.

If losses to enemy action were not bad enough, on 29 January, *K13*, a steam-powered fleet submarine, foundered during trials in the Gare Loch in the west of Scotland. Submarine strategy had still to evolve completely at this early date, and the Royal Navy persisted in the idea that submarines should be able to operate with the fleet, hence the use of steam power so that the vessels could keep up. *K*13 was recovered and re-commissioned as *K*22. It may have been the fault of the traditionalists, but keeping submarines with the fleet smacked of not trusting submarine commanders whilst away from the control of senior officers, but as operations in the Baltic and the Sea of Marmara showed, the right kind of submarine commander was highly motivated and imaginative. The irony was that, traditionally, the commanding officers of frigates and gunboats had been given considerable freedom of action, as in Nelson's day, when most of the day-to-day work of the Royal Navy was handled by these smaller ships. The Victorian Royal Navy had seen less of this freedom of action and more fleet manoeuvres. Fisher would certainly have approved of giving the younger and more radical officers their head, having enjoyed his own early experience of command in the Far East.

The loss of *K*13 was not to be the only instance of a ship being lost unnecessarily in the absence of enemy action that year. The battleship *Vanguard* was lost with the lives of 804 men on 9 July when one of her magazines exploded at Scapa Flow.

Nevertheless, there were successes with which to balance the defeats and failures. In Mesopotamia, the Navy manned river gunboats that assisted in the re-occupation of Kut-el-Amara on 24 February, a step towards the eventual occupation of Baghdad on 11 March.

Technical developments continued. On 16 March 1917, for the first time a moored mine was cut by a paravane drawn by the minesweeper *Cambria*. The first U-boat to be sunk by an aeroplane was *UB*-32, sunk in the English Channel by a Curtiss H12 Large America flying boat of the Royal Naval Air Service. The H12 was one of the fruits of the collaboration between the Royal Navy's Lieutenant-Commander Porte and the American Glenn Curtiss, although Porte was later to be accused of receiving bribes from Curtiss, but acquitted and honoured. Nine days later, another RNAS flying boat made the first air sea rescue.

Undoubtedly, the best news of all was that the United States finally declared war on Germany on 6 April 1917. Within a month, on 4 May, the first USN destroyers arrived at the Royal Navy's base at Queenstown, in southern Ireland, ready for convoy escort duties. This was to be the start of another fruitful Anglo-American collaboration, helped by the fact that Admiral William Sims, USN, appointed as naval attaché in London, established good working relationships with his British counterparts.

It was the USN as much as the politicians that worked hard to change opinions at the Admiralty over convoys.

On 10 May, an experimental convoy sailed from Gibraltar bound for the UK, and a transatlantic experimental convoy followed on 24 May from Newport News to the UK, with an escort that included an armoured cruiser, by which time additional American destroyers had joined those already at Queenstown. Admiralty approval for convoys was finally given on 17 June, and on 2 July, the first regular convoy of the war sailed for the UK from Hampton Roads. Before the end of the year, on 7 December, five American battleships arrived at Scapa Flow to join the Grand Fleet and become its 6th Battle Squadron.

Nevertheless, convoys were not always a guarantee of safety, as much depended on the balance of strength between the attackers and the defenders, and while hydrophones were being used to detect submarines and the first experiments with ASDIC were taking place, with the first trials at Harwich beginning on 6 June, submarine detection was still woefully primitive. It was not submarines but two German light cruisers, *Bremse* and *Brummer*, that found a British convoy between Bergen and Scotland and sank the two destroyer escorts and nine out of twelve merchant vessels. Two destroyers made an entirely unsatisfactory escort, but even if there had been twice the number, they would have been outgunned by the light cruisers.

The submarine remained the main menace. It was probably exactly what the Admiralty wanted when *UB-8* sank a dummy vessel designed to look like the battlecruiser HMS *Tiger* in the Aegean Sea. Not at all welcome news was the sinking of the armoured cruiser *Drake* by *U-79* in the North Channel off Rathlin Island, between Scotland and Ireland.

Improvements in dealing with the menace of the Zeppelin also continued. It was no small achievement when Flying Sub-Lieutenant Reginald Warneford shot down *LZ-37* near Ghent in Belgium, with the wreckage falling onto a convent and the sole survivor amongst the crew being the coxswain, who crashed through the roof to land on an empty bed. Warneford became the first member of the RNAS to be awarded the Victoria Cross. Another Zeppelin, *LZ-38*, was destroyed in her shed at Evere, also in Belgium, by RNAS aircraft. Nevertheless, while using landplanes meant that the Zeppelins could be tackled and sometimes shot down, the near impossibility of doing this with seaplanes remained. Even using landplanes from lighters was wasteful, so it was a step forward when, on 2 August 1917, Squadron Commander E.H. Dunning made the first deck landing on a ship underway when he put his Sopwith Pup down on the forward deck of HMS *Furious*. The battlecruiser had been completed with a flight deck in place of her 'A' turret, her only forward turret, and to land Dunning had to fly around the superstructure and the associated turbulence, and then slip to port to get above the flight deck, cutting his engine while crew members raced to pull his aircraft down onto the deck. This brave aviator was killed in a later attempt when his frail aircraft was blown over the side of the deck.

It soon became clear that a deck for landing aboard ships was necessary, and *Furious* was soon modified, losing her aft 18-inch gun. Meanwhile, another solution being tried in desperation was to fly aircraft off from crude platforms, and on 21 August, another Sopwith Pup flew off a cruiser to shoot down *L-23* off the Danish coast – the first time a shipborne aircraft had accounted for an airship. Another solution, with the advantage that it could be turned into the wind, was to launch aircraft from a platform mounted on top of a gun turret, and another Sopwith Pup did this for the first time from the battlecruiser *Repulse* on 1 October, flown by Squadron Commander Rutland. One of the early duties of naval aircraft was to provide reconnaissance and also plot and report the fall of shot in a naval engagement, but this needed a two-seat aircraft, and it was not until 4 April 1918 that a two-seat Sopwith 1½ -Strutter was successfully launched off a platform built over a forward turret on the battleship HMS *Australia*.

The naval aviators remained in action off Turkey despite the sinking of the *Ben-my-Chree* and the earlier withdrawal of Allied forces from Gallipoli. It was probably pure optimism that led the RNAS to bomb the former German battlecruiser *Sultan Selim* and the light cruiser *Midilli*, the other ex-German ship, at Constantinople. Even the light cruiser might have been a problem for the bombs of the day, but torpedoes might have been successful, if only the aircraft could have managed such a load over the range that the operation entailed.

The long-sought fleet engagement still eluded both sides. On 17 November 1917, German battleships and light cruisers had to put to sea to protect minesweeping forces which were being harassed by British light cruisers and destroyers. Instead of frightening the crews of light cruisers and destroyers, however, they suddenly found themselves facing three battlecruisers, *Courageous*, *Glorious* and *Repulse*, off Heligoland

Bight. The weather was worsening at the time and after an inconclusive initial exchange of fire, the Germans thought that they saw British battleships approaching and broke off the engagement. Fisher doubtless would have had the battlecruisers give chase, but the shallow draught *Courageous* and *Glorious* might have fared badly if the German shells had begun to strike home. *Courageous*, the first of her class, was known to the wits in the Fleet as 'Outrageous', while *Glorious* was 'Uproarious', and with *Furious* the three were sometimes also known as 'Helpless', 'Hopeless' and 'Useless'. On the night of 8/9 January 1917, in the undemanding conditions of sea state 4, barely choppy water, *Courageous* broke her back when her stem lifted by just three feet.

Again, on 20 January 1918, the German-manned battlecruiser *Sultan Selim* and light cruiser *Midilli*, ventured into the Aegean to attack British shipping. If a couple of British battleships had been present, a naval engagement might have ensued, but they found two British monitors, and in a one-sided engagement, both were sunk. Nevertheless, it was a pyrrhic victory, as on their return to Constantinople, *Midilli* struck a mine and sank, while *Sultan Selim* ran aground. Over the next five days, the disabled battlecruiser suffered repeated attacks by the RNAS, but she was finally refloated on 25 January and returned to base. This was a missed opportunity, but a ship lying aground can be a difficult target as she is unlikely to sink, and shallow water makes torpedo attack almost impossible.

On 15 February, German destroyers attacked the barrage between Folkestone and Cape Gris Nez, but to little effect, while a destroyer action on 21 March off Dunkirk saw eleven British destroyers and four French engage eighteen German, of which two were sunk by the Allies.

January had ended with a bad day for the British submariners. On 31 January, *E50* struck a mine and was lost with all hands in the North Sea. Further north, a major fleet exercise was taking place in the Firth of Forth that day, and once again the unwieldy large K-class submarines proved to be a disaster, with *K4* and *K17* in (separate) collisions off the Isle of May and sinking with the loss of 103 men.

THE NAVY LOSES ITS AVIATION

One development that would not have found favour with Fisher was the creation of the Royal Air Force on 1 April 1918, merging the RNAS with the rival Royal Flying Corps. The RNAS provided 2,500 aircraft and some 55,000 personnel, about a fifth of the number provided by the British Army. What had started as an 'air service' had been recommended by a committee headed by the South African statesman and soldier, Jan Smuts, as a result of concerns over overlap and wasteful duplication between the two air arms. If Fisher had still been at the Admiralty, which would have been unlikely since he would have been seventy-seven at the time, he would have fought this merger. He would have had an ally in the head of the RFC, Hugh Trenchard, who believed that the merger was right, but objected to it taking place while the services were fighting a major war. The two men might even have compromised, with carrier-borne aviation and maritime-reconnaissance staying with the Royal Navy, as was the case in France between the wars when the *Armee de l'Air* was established. This was an unpopular merger and during the 1930s pressure to bring naval aviation back under Admiralty control resulted in a decision to allow this in 1937, with the transfer finally taking place in spring 1939.

It was ironic that the RAF was formed just a little over two weeks after HMS *Furious* was recommissioned with the landing-on deck and the first aircraft lifts. So it happened that the first carrier-borne naval strike took place on 19 July 1918, when *Furious* sent seven aircraft to attack the airship sheds at Tondern, destroying *L-54* and *L-60*, with RAF personnel at the controls. Some eight weeks later, a second aircraft carrier, HMS *Argus*, the first flush-deck carrier and converted from a liner being built for Italy, was commissioned.

Of course, other changes had taken place. Fisher would probably have agreed with the creation of the Women's Royal Naval Service on 26 November 1917. He would have done so because each woman freed another man to go to sea, while he also appreciated and respected women who were intelligent and capable. It was a reflection of the demands of wartime that the Royal Navy had gone from a considerable surplus of men, between 20,000 and 30,000 in 1914, to a marked shortfall in 1917. In fact, the Royal Navy was slightly slow off the mark in deciding to recruit women, many of whom had been doing 'war work' for some time.

The world was changing in other ways. The Bolshevik Revolution was taking place in Russia, and the British submarines that had been moving their Baltic base in the face of advancing German forces now found that they had another opponent. On 3 April the decision was taken to evacuate the men, but the seven submarines based on Helsingfors (now Helsinki) in what was to become independent Finland but was then part of Russia, had to be destroyed so that they could not be captured.

Nevertheless, with a successful naval blockade of Germany established, there was sufficient confidence to move the Grand Fleet from its forward wartime base at Scapa Flow in Orkney to the new naval base and dockyard at Rosyth, on 12 April. There was also a partially successful and extraordinarily courageous amphibious operation to block the entrances to the German-held naval bases at Zeebrugge and Ostend, to close the entrances to U-boat and torpedo-boats using blockships while harbour installations were also destroyed. Fisher would most definitely have approved, and might even have demanded such action much earlier. (For the complete story of the first raid, see Paul Kendall's *The Zeebrugge Raid 1918: 'The Finest Feat of Arms'*.)

While the first offensive operation from an aircraft carrier against Tondern on 19 July marked a change in naval warfare, the situation was changing in other ways as well. On 8 August, the Royal Navy laid the first magnetic mines off the French coast at Dunkirk. This was a bold step, not least because at the time, and for many years afterwards, no one knew how to sweep magnetic mines. Even so, the more traditional ways of stopping shipping also remained, and it was on 1 October that the net barrage across the Straits of Otranto was completed.

As fuel supplies in Germany began to run low due to the blockade, the U-boats ceased commerce raiding on 21 October, the anniversary of Trafalgar, as Fisher would have been quick to point out. There was just one last blow for the U-boats left at sea looking for British warships, when on 9 November, the pre-Dreadnought *Britannia* was torpedoed and sunk off Cape Trafalgar by *U-50*. Fisher would most certainly not have approved. A few days earlier, on 5 November, the largest and fastest First World War seaplane carrier, the converted Cunard liner *Campania*, was sunk after being in collision with the battleship *Royal Oak* and the 'light' battlecruiser *Glorious* in the Firth of Forth on 5 November. Had she not been lost, perhaps *Campania* would also have been converted to an aircraft carrier.

Change also continued in the Royal Navy despite the war continuing. On 8 November, almost on the eve of the Armistice, paymasters, instructors and surgeons all acquired executive ranks, becoming, for example, surgeon lieutenant or paymaster commander. This was a logical step, the same status having been accorded engineer officers since early 1915.

The Armistice on 11 November was no doubt as welcome to the Royal Navy as to anyone else, and for Fisher it meant that he could resume his European travels. Most modern German warships and all of the surviving U-boats were ordered to Scapa Flow, and although a few also reached the United States, including the Dreadnought *Ostfriesland*, those at Scapa were all scuttled without warning on 21 June 1919.

While Fisher had done much to prepare the Royal Navy for the First World War, it is also true that the Great War introduced much that is more usually associated with the Second World War. The war, combined with the Russian Civil War that overlapped with it, not only defined the political geography of Europe for much of the twentieth century, it also defined warfare. There was nothing new about trench warfare, barbed wire, the machine-gun, or the exploding shell, all of which had been tried and tested during the American Civil War. The devastation caused by the submarine when used against merchant shipping was new, and so too was the aircraft carrier, while the minelayer was used in anger for the first time and was responsible for the mine sweeper and the paravane. While aerial warfare may have started during the Balkan Wars, the systematic use of aerial bombing, the mounting of fighter and anti-aircraft defences, even using hydro-aeroplanes for air-sea rescue, all originated in the First World War. ASDIC was being tested as the war drew to a close. The frail aircraft that flew off from *Furious* to bomb the airship sheds at Tondern that last July of the war, were the predecessors of those that flew off *Illustrious* to attack the Italian fleet at Taranto, and those that flew off the Japanese carriers to attack Pearl Harbor a little more than a year afterwards. While Fisher was right in saying that the submarine posed a threat to the battleship, an even bigger threat was the carrier-borne aircraft.

Glossary

AA – Anti-aircraft

ADC – Aide de Camp

Aeronautics – Embraces both lighter-than-air flight, or aerostation, and heavier-than-air flight, or aviation.

Aerostation – Lighter-than-air flight or ballooning.

Airship – A balloon that is streamlined and with a torpedo-like shape which can be powered and steered.

ASDIC – This is not actually a conventional acronym but a 'tag' for the experimental and top secret submarine sound detection apparatus developed by Canadian Robert William Boyle and the British physicist Albert Wood for the British Board of Invention and Research, using quartz pizoelectric crystals.

Aviation – Heavier-than-air flight, including gliding as well as powered aircraft.

Balloon – A lighter-than-air vehicle with an envelope that can be inflated either by hot air or by gas, originally usually hydrogen. It has no means of control other than ascent and descent, and is at the mercy of the prevailing wind.

Battlecruiser – The concept of the battlecruiser differed between Britain and Germany. For the RN, this was a category of ship that placed the emphasis on speed and armament at the expense of armour. These vessels were expected to keep out range and destroy inferior ships, and also to act as a scouting force. The German battlecruisers were intended to act as the vanguard in a fleet action, and consequently sacrificed speed for better armour protection.

C-in-C – Commander-in-Chief

Carried away – the loss of sails to the wind or seas in a storm.

Courageous Class – A light battlecruiser class (1916-17) intended to take the war to the Baltic with an invasion by British and Russian forces on the coast of Pomerania. Displacement 22,700 tons. The two 18-inch guns on *Furious* proved to be too heavy for such a light vessel, so they were both removed and she was converted to an 'aerodrome' ship.

Displacement – the tonnage of a warship measured by the volume of water displaced. Usually, the displacement is the standard figure, sometimes referred to as 'light', without fuel, munitions or supplies, which when taken aboard give the 'heavy' or 'full load' displacement.

Floatplane – The correct term for a seaplane, a name supposedly invented by Winston Churchill when First Lord of the Admiralty.

Flying boat – A hydro-aeroplane that has its hull sitting in the water.

Hydro-aeroplane – Any aircraft that can land on water, whether it is a seaplane, floatplane or flying boat.

KCB – Knight Commander of the Bath

MBE – Member of the British Empire

Minutes – Civil Service term for a memo or memorandum.

Monitor – A shallow draught coastal vessel designed specifically for coastal bombardment.

OBE – Officer of the British Empire.

Post-captain – officer holding the rank of captain and also captain of a major warship.

Queen Elizabeth Class – Battleships produced in 1915-16. Regarded as the finest battleships of their day, they introduced 15-inch guns, oil-fired propulsion and geared turbines for the first time. Displacement 31–33,000 tons, maximum speed 25 knots.

Seaplane – a hydro-aeroplane that has floats and the fuselage clear of the water.

SNL – Senior Naval Lord, equivalent to the contemporary First Sea Lord, or 1SL.

Super-Dreadnought – Not an official term, the Super-Dreadnoughts had five turrets, all superimposed, and guns of larger than 12-inch calibre. The classes were Orion (1912), King George V (1912-13), Iron Duke (1914), Erin (1914), Canada (1915), Queen Elizabeth (1915-16) and Royal Sovereign (1916-17).

U-boat – German submarine, from *Unterseeboot*.

Yards – cylindrical spars placed horizontally across mast to support sails.

Ranks – Royal Navy and British Army

ROYAL NAVY
Admiral of the Fleet★
Admiral
Vice-Admiral
Rear Admiral
Commodore 2nd Class
Captain
Commander
Lieutenant-Commander+
Lieutenant
Mate
no equivalent
Midshipman
no equivalent

ARMY
Field Marshal★
General
Lieutenant General
Major General
Brigadier-general★★
Colonel
Lieutenant-Colonel
Major
Captain
First Lieutenant
Second Lieutenant
no equivalent
Sergeant Major (RSM and CSM)

★ Rank discontinued in recent years to accord with absence of five star ranks in other NATO countries.

★★Rank re-titled as Brigadier after the First World War.

+ Rank introduced as lieutenant with 8 years seniority in late nineteenth century, then formally introduced to the Royal Navy in 1914 – it had been a USN rank for much longer.

RATINGS (RN) AND NON COMMISSIONED RANKS

ROYAL NAVY
Chief Petty Officer
Petty Officer
Leading Seaman
Able Seaman
Ordinary Seaman

ARMY
Colour Sergeant
Sergeant
Corporal
no equivalent
Private

Chronology

Major Naval Events during Fisher's Lifetime

The Victorian era was one of world peace and few naval engagements, but it was not completely without conflict, much of which centred around the quest for colonies, colonial uprisings or independence movements. It could even be said to be similar to the Cold War that followed the Second World War, with an absence of global conflict, but many smaller conflicts, which often proved extremely bloody.

The nature of these battles had a bearing on Fisher's lifetime, his career, and the decisions he made. He lived through a period when the main threat ceased to be France and became Germany, while Russia was at one time a threat and then an ally, and the opposite happened in the relationship with Turkey. Fisher was close to the Spanish–American War of 1898, but not involved, doubtless to his disappointment.

Looking through these events, the rise of the submarine, the torpedo and the mine can be seen, as can in later years the significance of the aeroplane and the airship. In the beginning, armour made its presence felt, and during the American Civil War, proved effective against the shells of the day. By the end of Fisher's life, armour was not always proof against shells, and more often, insufficient protection against the torpedo or the mine.

1841   John Arbuthnot Fisher was born at Rambodde, Ceylon, on 25 January.

1853   Start of Crimean War.
30 November – Action off Sinope. A Turkish squadron of at least thirteen ships at anchor is attacked by nine Russian ships, with only one small Turkish steamer escaping. The Russians use exploding shells, the Turks have mainly solid shot. The Turks lose 2,960 men, the Russians 37. Shortly afterwards, the Mediterranean Fleet, commanded by Vice-Admiral Sir James Dundas, was dispatched to the Black Sea.

1854   June – Fisher passes medical for service in the Royal Navy.
16 August – French forces capture Russian fortress of Bomarsund in the Baltic, but have to evacuate with the onset of winter.
14 September – An Anglo-French-Turkish expeditionary force of 60,000 men transported from Varna to Eupatoria, landing on 14 September.
17 October – Allied forces soon besiege Sevastapol, and to assist the armies ashore, the Royal Navy joined in a bombardment from the sea, with an Allied naval force consisting of 6 screw-driven ships and 21 of sail, with the latter towed into position by steamers.

1855   9–11 August – Anglo-French fleet bombards fortress of Sveaborg in the Baltic.
9 September – Sevastopol falls to the Allies, with the Russians scuttling their Black Sea fleet, which includes 14 ships of the line and 100 other vessels.
17 October – Bombardment of Fort Kinburn, controlling entrance to Nikolaev Harbour, with the French using armoured warships in action for the first time.

1856   Peace of Paris includes Declaration of Paris. Piracy is outlawed. Guiding principle is 'free ships and free merchandise'.

1861   American Civil War begins. This sees the Southern or Confederate states conduct commerce raiding campaign throughout the war, which lasts until 1865.
12 April – Hostilities start, and the North opens a blockade of southern ports to destroy the Confederate economy.

3 August – Union forces use a captive balloon from a ship, *Fanny*, moored in Hampton Roads, for artillery observation purposes.

1862   8–9 March – Naval engagement in Chesapeake Bay between armoured steam frigate *Virginia*, converted by the South, which attacks the Northern Blockade at Hampton Roads. *Virginia* destroys frigate *Congress* and corvette *Cumberland*, but is damaged just slightly. The following morning, a battle commences between *Virginia* and the North's new armoured ship, *Monitor*, which ends in stalemate as neither side has armament that can pierce the other's armour.

24 April – Storming of the Mississippi forts. The North sends a force of some twenty vessels under Commodore Farragut to attack Confederate Fort Jackson and Fort St Philip, while Confederate Commodore Mitchell commands the ram *Manassas*, an armoured ship and a number of armed steamers. After bombarding the forts for eight days, on 24 April Farragut forces a way past them, allowing New Orleans and most of the Mississippi to be taken by the North.

12 December – North loses gunboat *Cairo* to a Confederate mine in a Mississippi tributary – the first ship to be lost to a mine.

1863   4 July – North captures Vicksburg and cuts Confederate forces in two.

1864   17 February – Using primitive 'spear' torpedoes, the Southern submersible *H L Hunley* sinks blockade ship *Housatonic* in Charleston Harbour, another naval first.

9 May – In European waters, Denmark fights Prussia and Austria for Schleswig-Holstein, with a Danish squadron blockading and engaging in indecisive combat with two Austrian frigates.

5 August – Battle of Mobile Bay. Mobile remains the only port open to the Confederates, and Commodore Farragut attempts to close it. The harbour is covered by Fort Morgan with a mine barrier in the entrance to the bay, behind which Rear Admiral Buchanan has a small force that includes the

ram *Tennessee*. Farragut has four monitors, nine screw frigates and corvettes and ten gunboats. In the morning Farragut attacks in two lines with the monitors closest to Fort Morgan, which fires weakly, but the leading monitor, *Tecumseh*, strikes a mine and is lost with heavy casualties. Farragut takes the lead in a steam frigate and the force charges through the minefield without further loss, while *Tennessee*'s ram fails to stop the Northern fleet, and after suffering heavy fire, she surrenders.

1866   War breaks out between Austria and Italy, also known as the 'Seven Weeks War'. The Italian Army is defeated at Custozza, and the Italian Navy takes the leading role in the conflict.
18 July – Italian fleet attacks Lissa, but fails to suppress fire from Austrian coastal defences on the island.
19 July – Two Italian armoured ships enter the harbour at St Giorgio, but have to withdraw under heavy fire.
20 July – Battle of Lissa. Austrian and Italian fleets clash, with the former having eight armoured ships against the latter's eleven, and both fleets divide their armoured ships from their unarmoured. Austrians arrive to find Italians engaged in landings, but the Italians break off to engage the Austrian fleet. The Italians leave their unarmoured ships out of the battle, but the Austrians put their entire force into combat. The Austrian spear-headed formation breaks through the Italian line, with the Italians soon losing two ships, before breaking off. This was the first sea battle between armoured ships and the first in the open sea since Trafalgar.

1869   Suez Canal opens, linking the Mediterranean and Red Seas, cutting the length of the passage between Europe and India and Australia considerably. The Mediterranean becomes an important thoroughfare again.

1870–71   Franco-Prussian War sees the French attempt blockade off Germany's North Sea coast, but this is abandoned as Prussian forces besiege Paris, and the crews of the ships are sent ashore to defend the city.

1876–1880   In Italy, Benedetto Brin builds the first ship with heavy turrets, the battleship *Duillo*.

1878   John Holland builds his first submarine.
            26 January – Russian torpedo-boats use Whitehead torpedoes successfully for the first time, sinking the Turkish gunboat *Intibah* off Batum.

1879   Chile and Peru are at war. Peruvian turret-ram *Huascar* attacks commerce off Chilean coast until Chilean armoured ships *Almirante Cochrane* and *Blanco Encalada* force her to surrender after a gun battle off Angamos that lasts 90 minutes.

1880–1890   Steam-power is now reliable and gradually the major fleets abandon sail rigging, leaving just signal and combat masts, although some retain sail for training vessels.

1882   11 July – British Mediterranean Fleet sends eight armoured ships and supporting vessels to bombard forts at Alexandria after anti-foreign riots start. Later, Fisher and Wilson lead landing parties and also create one of the first armoured trains.

1883–1885   Sino-French War fought as the French press for recognition of their sovereignty over Indo-China.

1884   23 August – Rear Admiral Courbet attacks Chinese fleet lying in the Pagoda Roads at Foochow. French have five cruisers, three gunboats and two torpedo-boats, while Chinese Admiral Ting has six cruisers and a number of smaller vessels including nine armed junks. Opening fire at 14.00, Courbet sends a torpedo-boat with a towed torpedo which sinks the Chinese flagship, and it takes just 30 minutes to destroy the Chinese fleet. The French then destroy the coastal batteries, and the following day they bombard the arsenal.
            25–29 August – Courbet takes his ships to bombard and destroy the forts at the mouth of the River Min.
            29–31 August – Courbet captures Mekong.

1885	Trials begin in Sweden of George Garrett's *Nordenfelt I*, the first submarine with a surface armament, while a Whitehead torpedo is carried in an external casing over the bow. 9 June – Peace of Tientsin between France and China.
1888	First electrically-powered submarine, *Gymnote*, completed in France.
1891	April – Chilean Revolutionary War sees the first sinking of an armoured warship by a self-propelled torpedo when the *Blanco Encalada* is sunk by a torpedo-boat.
1894–95	Sino-Japanese War breaks out over possession of Korea. Without first declaring war, 4 Japanese cruisers attack Chinese troop convoy, sinking a transport and damaging a cruiser.
1894	April – During Brazilian Civil War, a torpedo-boat sinks the turret-ship *Aquidaban*. 1 August – War officially declared between Japan and China. Both sides use convoys to supply their forces in Korea. September – Chinese escort a convoy to Korea, and the Japanese attempt to intercept, but only find the convoy on its return voyage. 17 September – Battle of the Yalu River. Chinese Admiral Ting has two battleships, *Ting-Yuen* and *Chen-Yuen*, eight armoured cruisers and three torpedo-boats; Japanese Admiral Ito has eight armoured cruisers, *Fuso*, an old armoured ship, a gunboat, an old armoured steamer and an armed transport. Ito divides his fleet into a fast squadron of four cruisers and the main body. The Chinese steam in an arrow head formation with the battleships in the centre. Ito's fast squadron outflanks the starboard wing and bombards the two nearest Chinese ships, then turns to port, repels attack by torpedo-boats and concentrates on Chinese cruisers before circling the Chinese fleet, during which the slowest Japanese ships come under Chinese fire. Ito is forced to transfer from flagship *Matsushima* to *Hashidate*, but Chinese lose three cruisers and another catches fire, and the following day two more that ran aground are also destroyed. Engagement

broken off after five hours as both fleets run out of ammunition, while the two Chinese battleships are only slightly damaged.

October – Japanese land near Port Arthur and Chinese move fleet to Weiheiwei.

22 November – Port Arthur falls to Japanese.

1895   19 January – Japanese troops land on the Shantung Peninsula, isolating Weiheiwei.

29 January – Weiheiwei besieged, trapping fleet, although Chinese battleships inflict damage on Japanese ships blockading port.

4/5, 5/6 February – Night attacks by Japanese torpedo-boats, and on first night for the loss of two torpedo-boats, the *Ting-Yuen* is sunk. Two more Chinese ships sunk the second night.

7 February – Ten Chinese torpedo-boats attempt to escape, but only two succeed.

12 February – Weiheiwei surrendered, but Japan forced to return Port Arthur to China by the Great Powers.

1897   John Holland launches his submarine *Holland* for the United States Navy.

1898   Spanish-American War.

February – USS *Maine* explodes in Havana harbour, now believed to have been caused by unstable explosives, but the US accuses Spain of sabotage.

April – USA declares war on Spain. Alone amongst the colonial powers, the UK supports the US against Spain. At the time, the USN consisted of five battleships, two armoured cruisers, sixteen cruisers, and monitors, torpedo-boats and gunboats, while Spain had one ship of the line, six armoured cruisers, eleven cruisers, and large numbers of torpedo-boats and gunboats.

1 May – Action in Manila Bay. Commodore Dewey has four cruisers and two gunboats, while his Spanish opponent Rear Admiral Montojo has just two old cruisers and five gunboats. As Dewey's force enters Manila Bay, unprepared for battle, Montojo withdraws under the protection of shore batteries.

Entering at dawn and repeatedly steaming in line past the Spanish ships at 5,000 feet, after two hours all of the Spanish ships were sunk.

12 May – Bombardment of San Juan de Puerto Rico starts US offensive in the Caribbean.

19 May – Admiral Cervera arrives from Spain and enters the harbour at Santiago in Cuba, where he is blockaded by Admiral Sampson.

31 May – Attempt to block the harbour with a blockship fails.

22 June – US troops land near Santiago, causing Cervera to plan a break out.

3 July – Battle of Santiago. Blockading vessels under Commodore Schley, aboard the armoured cruiser *Brooklyn*, include four battleships. The Spanish steam out at 09.30, and at 09.40 the *Brooklyn* and two battleships open fire. By noon, two Spanish armoured cruisers are run aground and both tor-pedo-boats sunk. The new armoured cruiser *Cristobal Colon* is chased for 50 miles by *Brooklyn* and the battleship *Oregon*, and badly damaged, is run aground. By this time all the Spanish ships have been destroyed. Sampson arrives aboard armoured cruiser *New York* and reaches battle towards its end.

12 August – Armistice between USA and Spain. Peace treaty that follows allows Cuba to become independent and cedes Philippines, Guam and Puerto Rico to the USA.

1899   In France, Laubeuf designs the forerunner of the modern submarine, *Narval*.

1901   Royal Fleet Reserve established.

1903   Royal Naval Volunteer Reserve established.

1904–05   Russo-Japanese War. Russia and Japan are both expanding, with the former into eastern Asia and the latter onto the mainland of Korea and China. Russia starts a naval build-up in the Far East, and leases Port Arthur from China. With ambitions in Manchuria as well as Korea, Japan needs control of the Yellow Sea. At the time, Russia had seven battleships, four cruisers, six light cruisers and 27 destroyers, while Japan had six battleships, six cruisers, four elderly armoured ships, twelve light cruisers and nineteen destroyers. Japan was also waiting on two new cruisers, while Russia had new battleships fitting out at Baltic ports as well as some armoured ships and cruisers.

1904   6 February – Japan breaks off diplomatic relations with Russia.

8/9 February – Without a declaration of war, Japan mounts night attack on Russian ships at Port Arthur, with ten destroyers putting two battleships and a cruiser out of action for several months.

9 February – Admiral Togo takes Japanese fleet into action against Russian ships lying off Port Arthur, but little damage caused. At the same time, Japanese convoy is escorted to Inchon, the harbour for Seoul, and in fighting, a Russian cruiser and gunboat are so badly damaged that they are scuttled.

10 February – Japan declares war on Russia.

13/14 February – Japanese fail to block entrance to Port Arthur with blockship.

March – Vice-Admiral Makarov takes command of First Russian Pacific Squadron. Both fleets begin minelaying.

April – Japanese set up naval base on Elliot Island to cover landing of an army on Kwantung Peninsula to besiege Port Arthur.

12 April – Two Russian battleships run into minefield and sink, with Makarov going down with his ship.

3/4 May – Further attempt to sink blockship at Port Arthur fails.

15 May – Japanese lose two battleships in minefield.

23 June – Breakout attempt by Russians, now under Admiral Vitgeft, fails. By this time, harbour is within reach of Japanese artillery and at the end of the month, Vitgeft attempts further breakout.

10 August – Battle of the Yellow Sea. The Russians leave Port Arthur with six battleships, four cruisers and fourteen destroyers, while the Japanese have four battleships, two armoured cruisers, eight cruisers, eighteen destroyers and thirty torpedo-boats. At noon, their way is blocked off the

Shantung Peninsula and at 13.00 fighting begins, lasting just one hour before the Russians break out. Admiral Togo gives chase and at 16.00 fighting resumes at ranges of up to 10,000 yards. Vitgeft is killed by a shell splinter at 18.00, and at 18.12 the commanding officer of his flagship is killed and the Russian line breaks up. As darkness falls, Togo withdraws his larger ships and sends his destroyers in on a series of night attacks. Although the Russians break up many of these attacks, their fleet is scattered, with five battleships, a cruiser and nine destroyers returning to Port Arthur, but other ships flee to Tsingtao, Shanghai and Saigon, where they are interned. The cruiser *Novik* attempts to reach Vladivostok, but is driven aground at Sakhalin by Japanese cruisers. The three armoured cruisers and a cruiser based at Vladivostok become commerce raiders in the Sea of Japan.

14 August – Battle of the Japanese Sea (also known as Battle of Ulsan). Rear Admiral Yessen takes the three armoured cruisers to support another break out by the Russian First Pacific Squadron. At dawn they are confronted by Vice-Admiral Kamimura with four armoured cruisers and two cruisers. A four-hour battle ensues with the Russians losing one armoured cruiser, after which they return to Vladivostok and commerce raiding ceases.

October – Russian Second Pacific Squadron leaves for Far East with four new battleships and four new cruisers. Meanwhile, at Port Arthur, the crews of the Russian ships join the land battle while their guns give covering fire.

20 October – Admiral Sir John Fisher becomes First Sea Lord.

6 December – 203 Metre Hill falls to Japanese and is used for artillery direction, sinking two Russian battleships that day, while another is scuttled and one has already been run aground. The remaining ship fends off torpedo-boat attacks outside the harbour before being scuttled.

1905   2 January – Port Arthur surrendered.

March – Vice-Admiral Rozhdestvensky in command of Second Pacific Squadron waits off Indo-China for a squadron of older armoured ships that has used the Suez Canal to catch up with him.

May – Towards the end of the month the combined Russian fleet approaches Korea, while Togo is waiting, well aware of their approach.

27–28 May – Battle of Tsushima. The Russians have eight battleships, three armoured cruisers and three armoured coast defence ships, six cruisers and an auxiliary cruiser, nine destroyers and many auxiliaries, while the Japanese have four battleships, eleven armoured cruisers, fourteen cruisers, 21 destroyers and a large number of gunboats and torpedo-boats. The battle commences at 14.10, and by 16.00 the Russians have lost two battleships before the fleets lost sight of each other in fog and smoke, while Rozhdestvensky is badly wounded and is taken off his ship. Command passes to Rear Admiral Nebogatov. Meanwhile, the opposing cruiser squadrons are engaged. The battle squadrons re-engage at 18.20, and by 19.30, two more Russian battleships have been lost. Overnight, three more follow.

28 May – With two battleships, two armoured ships and a cruiser, when sighted at 10.30, Nebogatov surrenders, and while the cruiser escapes, she is soon run aground. At 18.00, the old armoured ship *Admiral Ushakov* goes down fighting, while the armoured cruiser *Dimitry Donskoi* is attacked repeatedly and is scuttled at 07.00 on 29 May.

The Russians have lost six battleships sunk and two captured, one armoured cruiser sunk and two captured, three armoured cruisers sunk, two cruisers sunk and three interned, seven destroyers sunk, one captured, one interned, four transports while another four escaped, with 5,000 men killed, 500 wounded and 6,000 taken prisoner, against 600 Japanese killed and wounded, three torpedo-boats sunk and two cruisers badly damaged.

June – Mutiny aboard Russian battleship *Potemkin*.

September – Treaty of Portsmouth. South Sakhalin and Port Arthur ceded to Japan.

1906   HMS *Dreadnought* launched.

1910   14 November – Lt Eugene Ely, USN, makes first take-off in a wheeled aircraft from a warship.

1911   18 January – Ely makes first landing on a warship in a wheeled aircraft.

1912–1913   First Balkan War with Greece, Serbia, Bulgaria and Montenegro pushing Turkey out of her territories in the Balkans.

1912   16 December – Action off Dardanelles as Turks attempt to force two battleships, two cruisers and a number of torpedo-boats into the Aegean, but are pushed back by a Greek armoured cruiser and three coastal armoured vessels.

1913   18 January – Turks attempt repeat of December action, with same result.
January-May – Turkish cruiser *Hamidije* raids commerce in the Mediterranean and the Red Sea.
6 February – Greek hydro-aeroplane on reconnaissance over Dardanelles, a first.

1914   The Panama Canal is opened, dramatically cutting the voyage time between the Atlantic and the Pacific, and also making it easy for USN ships to be transferred between the East and West Coast.
The Kiel Canal widening is completed, allowing the German High Seas Fleet to move its Dreadnoughts and Super-Dreadnoughts between the Baltic and the North Sea with ease.
1 July – RNAS formed from the Naval Wing, Royal Flying Corps.
4 August – At 08.30, Admiral Sir John Jellicoe relieves Admiral Sir George Callaghan as commander-in-chief of the Grand Fleet at Scapa Flow. At 23.00, British ultimatum expires and the United Kingdom and Germany are at war.
4–10 August – The German battlecruiser *Goeben* and light cruiser *Breslau* bombard the harbours of Bone and Philippville in the French colony of Algeria, before evading the British

Mediterranean Fleet and entering the Dardanelles, later transferring to the Turkish Navy. On 5 August, light cruiser *Gloucester* is the first to use wireless interception to detect *Goeben* in Messina.

25 August – Royal Marines land at Ostend, but have to be withdrawn on 31 August.

27 August – First RNAS squadron arrives at Ostend.

28 August – Battle of the Heligoland Bight. Rear Admiral Beatty takes his squadron of five battlecruisers, supported by light cruisers and a number of destroyers, encounters a German light cruiser squadron, and despite heavy damage to one British cruiser, *Arethusa*, sinks three German light cruisers before the German battlecruisers can intervene.

30 August – Occupation of German colony of Samoa by Australian, New Zealand and French warships.

4 September – With naval support, British forces take Dar-es-Salaam.

5 September – U-21 makes the first successful submarine attack, sinking the light cruiser *Pathfinder* off St Abb's Head.

19 September – Royal Marines land at Dunkirk.

20 September – German cruiser *Konigsberg* sinks seaplane carrier HMS *Pegasus* in the harbour at Zanzibar.

22 September – U-9 sinks the British armoured cruisers *Aboukir*, *Cressy* and *Hogue* off the Belgian coast in less than one hour.

27 September – Capture of Duala, Cameroons, supported by five naval vessels.

3 October – First units of the Royal Naval Division arrive at Antwerp.

8 October – RNAS Sopwith Tabloid succeeds in the first destruction of a Zeppelin, *LZ-25*, in her shed at Dusseldorf.

9 October – RNVR AA Corps established to provide air defence, initially of London.

27 October – Dreadnought HMS *Audacious* strikes a mine off Londonderry and sinks, many of her crew are taken off by lifeboats from the liner *Olympic*.

30 October – Admiral of the Fleet Lord Fisher of Kilverstone, First Sea Lord 1906–1910, recalled to the Admiralty by the First Lord, Winston Churchill.

1 November – Battle of Coronel in which two elderly British armoured cruisers, *Good Hope* and *Monmouth*, are sunk by two modern German armoured cruisers, *Scharnhorst* and *Gneisenau.*

3 November – First naval bombardment of the Dardanelles by the British and French fleets.

German battlecruisers bombard Great Yarmouth and Gorleston.

9 November – HMAS *Sydney* finds the commerce raider *Emden* in the Cocos Islands and sinks her.

21 November – Three RNAS Avro 504s attack Zeppelin sheds at Friedrichshafen.

24 November – British forces take Basra, supported by British and Indian warships.

26 November – Pre-Dreadnought *Bulwark* destroyed by ammunition explosion at Sheerness, killing 746 men from her ship's company of 758.

8 December – Battle of the Falkland Islands. Expecting to find the islands undefended, *Scharnhorst* and *Gneisenau* attack, but the naval force has been reinforced by two battlecruisers, *Invincible* and *Inflexible*, which give chase and sink both German armoured cruisers and two out of the three light cruisers.

9 December – Seaplane carrier *Ark Royal*, a converted collier, commissioned.

16 December – Hartlepool, Scarborough and Whitby bombarded by German battlecruisers.

21 December – First night bombing raid on Ostend by Wing Commander Charles Rumney Samson.

25 December – Seven seaplanes flown off from the seaplane carriers *Engadine*, *Riviera* and *Express* to attack the German airship sheds at Cuxhaven in the first bombing raids by ship-borne aircraft.

1915   1 January – U-24 sinks the pre-Dreadnought HMS *Formidable* in the English Channel. Engineer officers allowed to wear the executive curl, but retain purple cloth.

2 January – Bombardment of Dar-es-Salaam by pre-Dreadnought battleship *Goliath* and cruiser *Fox*.

4 January – Start of relief operation for Kut-al'Amara in Mesopotamia.

12 January – Capture of Mafia Island, German East Africa.

14 January – German destroyers raid Great Yarmouth.

15 January – RNAS aircraft attack U-boat alongside the mole at Zeebrugge.

23 January – Royal Marines occupy Greek island of Lemnos.

24 January – Battle of Dogger Bank between opposing battlecruiser forces when Beatty is able to surprise a German raid against trawlers. As Germans try to escape, the British manage to sink the German armoured cruiser *Blucher* and seriously damage the battlecruiser *Seydlitz*, but allow the remaining German ships to escape after the flagship *Lion* is badly damaged and the chain of command falters.

3 February – British, French and an Indian ship repulse a Turkish attack on the Suez Canal.

4 February – Drifter *Tarlair* fitted with prototype anti-submarine hydrophones.

16 February – Sloop *Cadmus*, lands naval shore party to help contain Indian Army mutiny.

18 February – Germany declares British territorial waters to be an unrestricted war zone. U-boat campaign starts.

19 February – Anglo-French bombardment of the outer forts of the Dardanelles begins.

25 February – Bombardment of Dardanelles forts resumes.

5 March – Bombardment of the Smyrna forts starts with three warships, the French seaplane tender *Anne Rickmers* and five minesweepers, one of which was sunk.

7 March – *Winifred* and *Kavirondo* force the German *Mwanza* ashore at the southern end of Lake Victoria.

14 March – *Dresden*, the only German survivor of the Battle of the Falkland Islands, is attacked by the armoured cruiser HMS *Cornwall* and light cruiser *Glasgow* off Chile, and sunk.

15 March – German aircraft attack merchantman *Blonde*, the first to be attacked from the air.

18 March – British and French naval forces enter the Dardanelles after heavy bombardment of the lower forts. One French ship hits a mine and explodes, while HMS *Inflexible* is

badly damaged by a mine before two pre-Dreadnought battleships *Irresistible* and *Ocean* are sunk by mines, after which the operation is abandoned. First time two British battleships lost on the same day.

6 April – False bow waves to be painted on all ships.

9 April – First American-built minelayers ordered.

25 April – Royal Navy provides support for landings by British and Australian troops on the Gallipoli peninsula.

13 May – Pre-Dreadnought HMS *Goliath* sunk by Turkish torpedo-boat.

17 May – First Sea Lord Admiral of the Fleet Lord Kilverstone ('Jacky' Fisher) walks out of Admiralty, aged 74.

24 May – Italy joins the war on the side of the Allies against Austria-Hungary.

25 May – *U-21* sinks the pre-Dreadnought *Triumph* off Gallipoli.

27 May – *U-21* sinks the pre-Dreadnought *Majestic*.

28 May – Admiral Sir Henry Jackson succeeds Fisher as First Sea Lord.

June – U-boat campaign spreads to Mediterranean using bases in the Adriatic.

4 June – British forces take Kut-Al' Amara in Mesopotamia, aided by thirteen RN and Royal Indian Marine vessels.

23 June – Submarine *C24* being towed submerged by trawler *Taranaki* sinks *U-40*, the first U-boat to be sunk by a decoy ship.

11 July – Two British monitors *Severn* and *Mersey* attack and sink *Konigsberg* in the Rufiji River.

1 August – British submarine *E11* raids Constantinople harbour.

6 August – Start of landings at Suvla Bay.

8 August – *E21* penetrates the Dardanelles and sinks the Turkish battleship *Hairreddin Barbarousse*.

12 August – Short 184 seaplane from the seaplane carrier *Ben-My-Chree* makes the first successful aerial torpedo attack against a Turkish cargo ship, previously damaged by a submarine, and sinks her in the Dardanelles.

18 September – U-boat campaign in Atlantic suspended following protests by the United States over the sinking of

British ships carrying US nationals, but campaign in the Mediterranean continues.

13 December – First periscope photograph, of Constantinople, from *E11*.

18 December – Wing Commander Charles Rumney Samson drops first 500-lb bomb on Turkish forces.

19 December – Start of evacuation from Gallipoli.

23 December – Naval operations start on Lake Tanganyika.

26 December – *Mimi* and *Toutou* capture German *Kingani* on Lake Tanganyika.

1916   6 January – pre-Dreadnought battleship *King Edward VII* strikes a mine and sinks west of Cape Wrath.

9 January – British withdrawal from Gallipoli completed.

8 February – British government seeks naval assistance from Japan, resulting in two Japanese destroyer flotillas arriving in the Mediterranean in April.

9 February – Lake steamers *Mimi* and *Toutou* (formerly German *Kingani*) sink German *Hedwig von Wissman* on Lake Tanganyika.

16 February – War Office takes over control of anti-aircraft defences from the Admiralty.

18 February – Conquest of the Cameroons completed.

23 February – Resumption of unlimited U-boat campaign in British waters.

7 March – Second attempt to relieve Kut-al' Amara in Mesopotamia. *E24*, the first British minelaying submarine, lays her first mines in the mouth of the River Elbe.

17 March – Depot ship (ex-cruiser) *Crescent* becomes the first ship to enter the basin at Rosyth.

25 March – Five seaplanes sent from seaplane carrier *Vindex* in unsuccessful attempt to bomb airship shed at Hoyer on the coast of Schleswig Holstein, but three come down in German territory and their crews are captured. HMS *Cleopatra* rams German destroyer G-194, cutting her in half.

28 March – Battleship *Zealandia* (formerly *New Zealand*) is first ship to enter dry dock at Rosyth.

1 April – East coast towns attacked by German Zeppelin airships, while *L-15* becomes the first Zeppelin to be brought

down by AA fire, landing in the Thames Estuary and surrendering to a British warship.

5 April – Further attempt to relieve Kut-Al' Mara, using seven river gunboats, ends in failure.

22 April – Grand Fleet makes thrust towards Skagerrak in an attempt to bring High Seas Fleet to battle, but two battlecruisers collide in fog, a battleship collides with a merchantman and after dark, three destroyers collide.

23 April – German battlecruisers bombard Lowestoft and Yarmouth.

24 April – U-boat campaign again suspended following further US protests. *E22* conducts 'float-off' trials with two Sopwith Schneider seaplanes to see if these can intercept Zeppelins over the North Sea before they can reach the East Coast.

24/25 April – German battlecruisers bombard Lowestoft and Great Yarmouth while the High Seas Fleet is at sea to intervene if British battlecruisers appear.

27 April – Pre-Dreadnought battleship HMS *Russell* hits a mine off Malta and sinks.

29 April – Surrender from starvation of British troops at Kut-Al' Amara, allowing the armed tug *Samana* also to be captured.

1 May – U-boat campaign extended to western Atlantic. *E14* sinks Turkish *Nur-ul-Bahir* in Sea of Marmara.

4 May – Zeppelin *L-7* brought down by light cruisers *Galatea* and *Phaeton* south of the Horns Reef. *E31* rescues seven survivors and destroys *L-7*.

31 May – Battle of Jutland, with the first use of aerial reconnaissance by a seaplane flown off the seaplane carrier *Engadine*. British force heavily outnumbers and outguns the Germans, but battle is plagued by poor visibility and poor communications between British scouting forces and the Grand Fleet, while the Admiralty does not pass on information from intercepted signals traffic. In a fast moving battle, Beatty loses the battlecruisers *Indefatigable*, *Queen Mary* and *Invincible*, and the armoured cruisers *Defence*, *Warrior* and *Black Prince*, plus another five smaller warships, losing a total tonnage of 155,000 tons, and other warships are damaged, while

the Germans lose eleven warships, with a total tonnage of 61,000 tons, before managing to regain the safety of their harbours. The Royal Navy lost 6,090 men against 2,550 for the Germans.

5 June – Armoured cruiser *Hampshire* sunk by mine off Orkney, with 643 men lost, including the Secretary of State for War, Lord Kitchener.

17 June – Zeppelin *L-48* shot down and German naval signal book found in wreckage.

26 July – Turkish destroyer *Yadighiar-i-Milet* damaged by bombing by RNAS aircraft in Eastern Mediterranean.

9 August – Submarine *B10* sunk by Austrian aircraft while being repaired at Venice – the first submarine sunk by enemy aircraft.

18/19 August – Scheer takes the High Seas Fleet to sea again preceded by a reconnaissance force of eight Zeppelins. Submarine *E23* torpedoes the German battleship *Westfalen* sixty miles north of Terschelling, forcing her to return to port. Confusion caused by Zeppelin commander mistaking Harwich light cruisers and destroyers for the Grand Fleet leads Scheer south, away from Jellicoe, who returns to base, losing the light cruiser *Falmouth* as the Grand Fleet crosses the German U-boat line. Tyrwhitt heading the Harwich flotilla sees the High Seas Fleet but is unable to attack.

24 September – Zeppelin *L-32* shot down and new German naval signal book salvaged from the wreckage.

26/27 October – German destroyer raid in Straits of Dover, with seven vessels sunk, mainly drifters handling the barrage.

26 October – Second German raid on Lowestoft.

29 November – Jellicoe becomes First Sea Lord, replacing Admiral Sir Henry Jackson, while Beatty becomes Commander-in-Chief of the Grand Fleet.

1917   9 January – *U-32* sinks the pre-Dreadnought HMS *Cornwallis* 62 miles off Malta.

11 January – Seaplane carrier *Ben-my-Chree*, sunk off Kastelorizo by fire from Turkish batteries.

23/24 January – Ships of the Harwich destroyer flotillas engaged with German 6th Destroyer Flotilla off the Schouwen light vessel. Each side loses one ship.

25 January – German destroyers attack Southwold in Suffolk.

29 January – *K*13 steam-powered submarine founders during trials in the Gare Loch.

24 February – Reoccupation of Kut-al'Amara, aided by river gunboats.

25 February – German destroyers raid Margate and Westgate.

11 March – British forces reach Baghdad.

16 March – First cutting of a moored mine using a paravane by the minesweeper *Cambria*.

17 March – German destroyers raid Dover Straits, torpedoing one British ship and sinking another.

18 March – German destroyer raid on Ramsgate and Broadstairs.

6 April – United States declares war on Germany.

27 April – German destroyers raid Ramsgate.

4 May – First USN destroyers arrive at Queenstown, Ireland, for convoy escort duties.

10 May – Experimental convoy sails from Gibraltar to the UK.

15 May – Action in the Straits of Otranto when an Allied blockading force is attacked by an Austrian squadron with three light cruisers and two destroyers, which sinks fourteen armed trawlers, a destroyer and two merchantmen before turning back.

17 May – Additional US destroyers arrive at Queenstown.

20 May – *UB*-32 sunk by RNAS Curtiss H12 Large America flying boat in English Channel close to Sunk Light vessel, the first U-boat to be sunk by an aeroplane.

24 May – Experimental convoy sails from Newport News to the UK with an armoured cruiser as an escort.

29 May – First air-sea rescue by RNAS flying boat.

30 May – Dummy of HMS *Tiger* sunk by *UB*-8 in Aegean.

6 June – First experiments with ASDIC at Harwich. Sheerness and nearby naval establishments attacked by German aircraft.

7 June – Flight Sub-Lieutenant Reginald Warneford wins the first RNAS VC for shooting down a Zeppelin, *LZ*-37, near

Ghent. RNAS aircraft destroy *LZ-38* in her shed at Evere, Belgium.

14 June – Convoys receive Admiralty approval and support.

22 June – RNAS observer officers to wear wings instead of eagle on their sleeves.

2 July – First regular convoy sails from Hampton Roads for UK.

9 July – RNAS aircraft from Mudros bombed *Sultan Selim* and *Midilli* in Constantinople. Battleship *Vanguard* suffers a magazine explosion at Scapa Flow and sinks, taking the lives of 804 men.

2 August – Squadron Commander E.H. Dunning makes the first deck-landing on a ship underway, landing aboard *Furious* in a Sopwith Pup. He was drowned in a later attempt when his aircraft went over the side.

21 August – Sopwith Pup landplane flies off cruiser to destroy Zeppelin *L-23* off the Danish coast – the first time this has been achieved.

1 October – Squadron Commander Rutland makes the first flight from a platform on top of a gun turret in a Sopwith Pup using B turret aboard the battlecruiser *Repulse*.

2 October – Armoured cruiser *Drake* torpedoed by *U-79* in the North Channel between Ireland and Scotland and later sinks off Rathlin Island.

17 October – German light cruisers *Brummer* and *Bremse* attack a British convoy running from Bergen, sinking both escorting destroyers and nine out of the twelve merchant-men.

17 November – Action off Heligoland Bight follows German battleships and light cruisers being deployed to safeguard minesweeping forces, but surprised by British battlecruisers *Courageous*, *Glorious* and *Repulse*. In bad weather, the initial exchange of fire between the British battlescruisers and three German light cruisers is inconclusive and the German ships escape in poor visibility as two battleships appear to provide cover.

23 November – Dame Katherine Furse appointed first Director of the WRNS.

26 November – WRNS officially formed.

7 December – Five US battleships arrive at Scapa Flow to form 6th Battle Squadron, Grand Fleet.

24 December – First Lord Sir Eric Geddes demands, and receives, resignation of First Sea Lord, Admiral Sir John Jellicoe. Admiral Sir Rosslyn Wemyss takes over.

1918

20 January – Turkish battlecruiser *Yavuz Sultan Selim* (ex-*Goeben*) and light cruiser *Midilli* (ex-*Breslau*) enter the Aegean and sink two British monitors, but on their return the *Midilli* strikes a mine and sinks, while the *Yavuz Sultan Selim* runs aground, but despite repeated British aerial attacks is refloated on 25 January and returns safely to base.

31 January – Three submarines lost on one day. *E50* mined and lost in the North Sea. *K4* and *K17* both lost in a major fleet exercise off the Isle of May in the Firth of Forth with the loss of 103 lives.

15 February – German destroyers raid the Folkestone-Griz Nez Barrage.

15 January – *Furious* recommissioned with landing on deck and the first aircraft lifts.

21 January – Destroyer action off Dunkirk, with eleven British ships and four French fighting eighteen German, of which two are sunk.

1 April – Royal Air Force founded, absorbing 55,000 RNAS personnel and 2,500 aircraft. World's first autonomous air force.

3 April – Seven British submarines destroyed at Helsingfors (now Helsinki) to avoid capture.

4 April – First successful launch of a two-seat reconnaissance aircraft from a ship when a Sopwith 1 ½-Strutter flies off a platform on a forward gun turret of HMAS *Australia*.

12 April – Grand Fleet moved from Scapa Flow to Rosyth.

23 April – Attacks on Zeebrugge and Ostende to close entrances to U-boat and torpedo-boat bases using blockships enjoy partial success, but the entrances are soon re-opened.

19 July – Aerial attack on the airship sheds at Tondern with seven aircraft flying from the aircraft carrier *Furious,* which

succeed in destroying *L54* and *L60*. This is the first successful attack by landplanes flying from an aircraft carrier.

8 August – First magnetic mines laid by the Royal Navy off Dunkirk.

14 September – First flush-deck carrier *Argus* commissioned.

1 October – Allied net barrage across Otranto Strait is completed.

21 October – U-boats cease commerce raiding.

5 November – Seaplane carrier *Campania* sinks after collision with *Royal Oak* and battlecruiser *Glorious* in Firth of Forth.

8 November – Executive ranks for paymasters, instructors and surgeons, preceded by branch, as in Surgeon Lieutenant.

9 November – *U-50* sinks pre-Dreadnought *Britannia* off Cape Trafalgar.

11 November – Armistice ends First World War. Most modern German warships and all U-boats ordered to Scapa Flow.

1919   Treaty of Versailles limits the German Navy to six coastal battleships with 11-inch guns and maximum displacement of 10,000 tons; 6 6-inch light cruisers, maximum displacement 6,000 tons; 12 torpedo-boats of 800 tons maximum displacement. Aircraft, aircraft carriers and submarines are banned.

21 June, Surrendered German warships scuttled at Scapa Flow.

18 August – Red Fleet attacked in Kronstadt harbour by British coastal motorboats, sinking the battleships *Andrei Pervozvanni* and *Petropavlovsk* in shallow water, while aircraft from the seaplane carrier *Vindictive* bomb harbour installations.

1920   10 July – Admiral of the Fleet Lord Kilverstone dies in London.

Bibliography

Bacon, Admiral Sir R.H., *The Life of Lord Fisher of Kilverstone*, Hodder & Stoughton, London, 1929

Bayly, Admiral Sir Lewis, RN, *Pull Together*, Harrap, London, 1939

Brett, Maurice V., and Esher, Viscount Oliver, *Journal and Letters of Reginald, Viscount Esher*, Nicholson & Watson, London, 1934–1938 (3 volumes)

Chalmers, Rear Admiral W.S., *The Life and Letters of David, Earl Beatty*, Hodder & Stoughton, London, 1951

Chatfield, Admiral of the Fleet Lord, *The Navy and Defence*, Heinemann, London, 1942–47 (2 volumes)

Hough, Richard, *First Sea Lord, An Authorised Biography of Admiral Lord Fisher*, Unwin Brothers, London, 1969

Hurd, Sir Archibald, *Who Goes There?* Hutchinson, London, 1942

Kemp, Lieutenant-Commander P.K., *The Papers of Admiral Lord Fisher*, Naval Records Society, London, 1960–1964 (2 volumes)

Kendall, Paul, *The Zeebrugge Raid 1918: 'The Finest Feat of Arms'*, The History Press, Stroud, 2008

Kilverstone, Admiral of the Fleet Baron, *Memories*, Hodder & Stoughton, London, 1919

Kilverstone, Admiral of the Fleet Baron, *Records*, Hodder & Stoughton, London, 1919

King-Hall, Admiral Sir George, *Sea Saga*, Faber, London, 1935

Lawson, Lionel, *Gone for a Sailor*, London, 1936

Mackay, Ruddock F., *Fisher of Kilverstone*, Clarendon Press, Oxford, 1973

Marder, Arthur J., *The Anatomy of Sea Power: British Naval Policy 1880–1905*, Putnam, London, 1941

Marder, Arthur J., *Fear God and Dread Nought: The Correspondence of Admiral of the Fleet Lord Fisher of Kilverstone*, Cape, London, 1952–1959 (3 volumes)

Morris, Jan, *Fisher's Face*, Viking, London, 1995

Penn, Geoffrey, *Infighting Admirals – Fisher's Feud with Beresford and the Reactionaries*, Leo Copper, Barnsley, 2000

Ramsay, David, *'Blinker' Hall: Spymaster*, The History Press, Stroud, 2008

Wragg, David, *The Royal Navy Handbook 1914–1918*, Sutton, Stroud, 2006

Wragg, David, *Snatching Defeat from the Jaws of Victory*, Sutton, Stroud, 2000

Index